MW00774754

The Artificial Paradise

Titles in the series

The Artificial Paradise

Science Fiction and American Reality

Sharona Ben-Tov

Ann Arbor

The University
of Michigan Press

Published in the United States of
America by The University of
Michigan Press

Manufactured in the United States
of America

♾ Printed on acid-free paper

1998 1997 1996 1995   4 3 2 1

*A CIP catalogue record for this book
is available from the British Library.*

Library of Congress Cataloging-in-Publication Data

Ben-Tov, S. (Sharona)
     The artificial paradise : science fiction and American reality /
Sharona Ben-Tov.
          p.   cm. — (Studies in literature and science)
     Includes bibliographical references (p.   ) and index.
     ISBN 0-472-10580-9 (acid-free paper)
     1. Science fiction, American—History and criticism.
     2. Literature and technology—United States—History—20th century.
     3. Literature and history—United States—History—20th century.
     4. National characteristics, American, in literature. 5. United
     States—In literature. 6. Paradise in literature. I. Title.
     II. Series.
     PS374.S35B38   1995
     813'.0876209—dc20   95-1033
                                                              CIP

To my mother, Marilyn,
and to the memory of my father, Itzhak,
this book is affectionately dedicated

Contents

Introduction

In her recent book about the Chernobyl disaster, German writer Christa Wolf describes seeing *The Return of the Jedi*[1] in a crowded movie theater in Berkeley, California. Embarrassed by the fanatic yells of the audience, she watched colorful bombs exploding on the screen and suddenly realized that those were nuclear weapons. Perhaps, she conjectured, the movie's director had consulted with Strategic Defense Initiative (SDI) experts at the nearby Livermore National Laboratory or the "star warriors" of SDI with the film people—and both "with the politicians," the facilitators of technical and cultural arsenals. Being German and leftist, Wolf naturally thinks of the scientists at Livermore as so many Drs. Faustus and sees the "Star Wars" phenomenon as proof that America's brains are preoccupied with the machinery of death, "the fabrication of the void," or even addicted to death. What immense, compelling fear, she asks, insulates technology's star warriors against life?

When *Jedi* came to my neighborhood, in MIT's backyard, I was writing a study of science fiction (SF) that I hoped did something new. Rather than adopting a pure standpoint of literary studies, I worked from a strong, Wolfish hunch that the meaning of science fiction went beyond its popular culture manifestations and that the lavish displays of science fiction at the MIT campus bookstore supplied more than entertainment to people closely involved in the production of modern technology. At first the hunch came from having discovered in science fiction regular variations of some very old myths, notably the myth of the Earthly Paradise, spelling out patterns too consistent and basic to be explained only as conventional literary devices. Since all the myths had to do with nature, gender, and technological power, perhaps science fiction told a story that was not articulated elsewhere, connecting these topics and meeting a serious need. Then, after watching two sequels to *Star Wars,* I began to pursue the idea that science fiction constituted a national mode of thinking in the United States and was a major part of the apparatus determining what "American" means, as a cultural identity and as a system of production. By the 1980s, in contrast to George Lucas's "space westerns," feminist science fiction was well established and thriving; and I wanted to investigate whether science fiction could be, simultaneously, part of one mode of thinking and a force against that same mode's inherent reactionary values. Feminist criticism, lately the most interesting approach to science fiction, usually analyzes plots, characters, and narrative styles. It asks whether the stories offer alternative social models, in which people enjoy equality, ethnic diversity, and respect for the natural environment; and whether aspects of feminist theory are illustrated.[2] I begin from a different kind of question. It is a question less about a literary/popular culture genre than about the relationship between our culture and its technological system: What immense fear insulates the star warriors against life? What are the shapes of the imaginative, psychocultural forces that underlie our science and technology? Such is the general inquiry that this book addresses (of course, very partially), rather than careers of particular authors, theories of genre, or tales of oppression and liberation taken at face value.

This book shows how science fiction expresses and reinforces certain cultural anxieties that arose during the Scientific Revolution and that continue to have a profound effect on modern life. These anxieties appear—packaged, if you like—in literary figures, metaphors, and images. My approach traces the cargo of old fears by looking at the history and patterns of these literary elements in science fiction. Broadly speaking, this is a literary study that expands into mythography and cultural criticism, in order to map the myths and imaginative trends that have nurtured the rise of science and technology. If popular literature is what Henry Nash Smith called it, in his landmark study of dime westerns, "an objectified mass dream,"[3] then science fiction is a dream about nature and the control of nature. It is a peculiarly American dream, because of the nation's special relation both to technology and to the myth of the Earthly Paradise in the New World.[4] What makes science fiction important in U.S. culture, however, is not only that its tropes contain complex ideological and mythical views of nature. Science fiction is a mass dream with an imperative: a dream upon which, as a nation, we act.

The Dream and Its Imperative

Even in the post–cold war era the genesis of SDI remains a good example of how science fiction enters our waking life, producing strange results. It is worth a brief look, along with the later appearance of "Nintendo war," before turning to less realized fantasies. In a film of the 1940s a United States secret agent is assigned to keep a new weapon out of the clutches of a Soviet spy ring. The so-called Inertia Projector can disrupt electric current from a distance, by remote control. Applying, with ominous anachronism, the familiar logic of deterrence, the top brass state their opinion that the device "not only makes the United States invincible in war, but in doing so, promises to become the greatest force for world peace ever discovered."[5] The spies manage to steal the weapon plans and are making their escape by air when the Projector goes into action. Our capable agent turns the deadly Inertia rays against the fleeing plane, sending it down in flames. He is played by Ronald Reagan.

While no one source inspired SDI, many scholars consider *Murder in the Air* an important factor. Michael Rogin, a political scientist at the University of California at Berkeley, claims that the film "helped inspire not only the President's antimissile plan, but his general presidential outlook." *Murder in the Air* was not the last science fiction movie to influence the former president. "The Force is with us," Reagan remarked, in a speech defending SDI and alluding, of course, to *Star Wars*. *Star Wars* also named the Gedi, an experimental, SDI-funded railgun at the University of Texas (the spelling *Jedi,* as used in the movie, is protected by copyright).[6] Reagan's confidence in SDI, despite the scientific community's doubts, seems to have drawn on science fiction's reputation as the oracle of technological feasibility. In *Star Wars,* images of futuristic weapons and technology sent the audience into raptures and made SDI's most ambitious aims seem within reach. You might say that the realism of *Star Wars* becomes the realizability of SDI.

Not only to the layperson: technical and scientific professionals are also affected by science fiction's power as a mass dream and take its images for a preview of the future. Peter Hagelstein, who invented the nuclear X-ray laser at Livermore, consulted science fiction to determine whether all the future applications of his work would be military. He cited three science fiction novels in his doctoral thesis, for the following reason:

> Writers of science fiction are supposed to look into the future.... So I started looking to see what they had in mind for X-ray lasers... all the science fiction references are to blowing things up. It's fairly discouraging.[7]

Perhaps similar thoughts occur to the young scientists of Livermore, who relax from all-night bouts of secret research with bouts of science fiction reading.[8] Since the 1950s American science fiction has become the favorite recreational reading of educated high-technology workers, so much so that the engineer or computer hacker who reads only science fiction is a cultural type—not infrequently, he or she is also the novel's protagonist.[9] What do we make of the connection between a trade paperback genre and the creation of monumental technological, and social, realities?

Umberto Eco writes in his satirical vein that "the American imagination demands the real thing, and, to attain it, must fabricate the absolute fake." When we tour the mechanical jungles of Disneyland, he adds, "Disneyland tells us that technology can give us more reality than nature can."[10] Eco's epigrams sum up a national mode of thinking, in which technology constitutes a "more real" world. A typical American attitude is that scientific knowledge and technological power do not merely influence reality but, in fact, *define* reality. James William Gibson, a historian of the Vietnam War, observes that science and technology are seen to give the United States "a highly privileged position of *knowledge*," a kind of epistemological monopoly. In the eyes of its military and governmental elite, "the United States knows more about 'reality' itself, reality being defined in terms of physical science."[11] Aspects of the Vietnam War that could not be measured in terms of technological sophistication, such as makeshift but effective guerrilla tactics or relationships within Vietnamese culture, were persistently discounted and overlooked—literally un-real-ized. When employing technology means possessing reality, a helicopter represents "more reality" than a hand-dug tunnel, or a poem.

More recently, a study of the Persian Gulf conflict reveals how war has come to be regarded as experimental science. A general of the U.S. Air Force has called Operation Desert Shield the "greatest laboratory experiment for force structure that we've ever had."[12] This statement means that war is literally part of standard experimental procedure. Experience gained in wartime flows back into the ongoing research programs of defense contractors, such as McDonnell Douglas and General Dynamics, verifying hypotheses about their weapons' performance and giving rise to follow-up projects. Real violence and devastation can be made invisible simply by redefining war in terms of scientific method: "The function of experimental verification is above all 'to keep the program going.'"[13]

Televised images of weaponry and bombings bore much the same relation to the Gulf war as *Star Wars* to SDI's cold war project. But Nintendo war goes one step further. The most realistic movie still takes place in a cinema and assumes a passive audience. Futuristic video games, however, require active participation and can be played on the same TV set that broadcasts the bombing of Baghdad. They blur the line between computer simulations that civilians use for fun and those that soldiers use for training, between simulated death and real death, peace and war, machinery and life. These distinctions are simply swallowed up in the drive to "keep the program (or the game) going." In the public mind, and in the scientific development and deployment of machines, the American national mode of thinking replaces the real world with the "greater reality" of cutting-edge technology.

Science fiction's power as a mass dream derives from this mode of thinking and supports it. The genre is not just a source of images that gratify national pride in U.S. technology; it also *reproduces* the ideologies that formed modern technology, and science fiction's very structure engages the reader in *reenacting* those ideologies. (The moment of suspended disbelief when a reader accepts the images of interstellar travel is also a moment of implicit, conspiratorial belief in the ideology of progress and a host of accompanying assumptions, as we will see.) Attitudes toward nature and technology that underlie U.S. industrialization continue to receive reinforcement from science fiction—even when the text is deliberately written to oppose such attitudes.

What This Book Is Not

This book is *not* a condemnation of science fiction. Science fiction is necessary and beneficial: in an age of accelerating technological development and information overload, our imaginations sorely need the means to integrate our feelings and dreams with the systems that shape our daily lives. What I investigate and sometimes criticize are cultural attitudes: their origins, forms of perpetuation, and implications.

The reason that I use science fiction to look at these attitudes is the genre's position at a unique intersection of science and technology, mass media popular culture, literature, and secular ritual. In what source other than science fiction's rich, synthetic language of metaphor and myth can we trace the hidden, vital connections between such diverse elements as major scientific projects (spaceflight, nuclear weaponry, robotics, gene mapping), the philosophical roots of Western science and technology, American cultural ideals, and magical practices as ancient as shamanism and alchemy?

It stands to reason that if science fiction springs from the need to understand the technological world system that we live in not just as passive consumers but as active participants, then the genre should be studied in its broadest context. Not, that is, purely for itself, as a popular culture or literary artifact, but for what the genre tells us about the philosophies, psychologies, social realities, and myths out of which we create our technological system and which, in turn, affect how the system shapes our lives.

This book is also *not* a genre survey. I am not trying to prove that all science fiction is alike nor to define a formula for all science fiction—a pointless task and an impossible one. The stories and novels discussed here represent basic types of American science fiction: 1950s "hard" SF (e.g., Isaac Asimov); modern mainstream SF (e.g., Robert Silverberg); space fiction (e.g., C. J. Cherryh); women's SF (e.g., Vonda McIntyre); cyberpunk (e.g., William Gibson)—with others. By no means do these authors and their works represent the entire gamut of science fiction, in its diversity and proliferating possibilities. But they do represent standard themes, images, and metaphors that we recognize as science fiction, and they share in our common imaginative universe. I have had to relinquish many wonderful stories, such as John Varley's charming tales and Octavia Butler's searching novels, simply because the value of particular science fiction authors is not the subject of this book.

Also, I have exempted from discussion science fiction tales that fall more into the category of utopia or dystopia (apart from technological utopias, which are a separate issue). The utopia asks us to think about our social existence and perhaps about science's and technology's roles in it. The kind of science fiction novel that I am investigating, the bulk of the genre, elaborates myths of nature and of the control of nature—that is, of science and technology. That is its raison d'être, which may or may not also involve social commentary. While a utopia is structured around an analysis of social meanings and values, the typical science fiction novel embodies a world in which the technological system *defines* meanings and values. In Marge Piercy's novel *Woman on the Edge of Time* science and technology present both utopian and dystopian possibilities: for example, her utopian communities blur gender lines by using reproductive technologies that free women from traditional motherhood. The point is to engage the reader in thinking about how certain kinds of oppression can be abolished or circumvented: we assume that even if its baby brooder broke down irreparably, Piercy's utopian community would find some other method of propagating its values. Social relationships are the key to the tale; technology is a vehicle. Similarly, in Ursula K. Le Guin's *The Dispossessed* other planets, space travel, and faster-than-light communication are suggestive elements in a tale whose purpose is to develop ideas about utopian anarchism; they do not constitute the mythic fabric of the tale itself. By contrast, the reproductive technologies in tales by C. J. Cherryh or John Varley may or may not be realizable, but they define the meanings of "nature," of "human being," of "power." The tale's ideological commitments are not only supported by but also embodied in its technological imagery. Loosely speaking, utopia is Sancho Panza to science fiction's Don Quixote: Sancho lives with chivalric romance; Don Quixote lives the romance. These distinctions, and their history, are explained more fully in the first two chapters.

By excluding the novels by Piercy and Le Guin, and similar tales, I am *not* claiming that such works should be called something other than science fiction, or that science fiction, as a genre, should be defined to exclude them. Rather, I am limiting this discussion to works that have a fundamentally different orientation toward the broad context with which I am ultimately concerned.

Finally, this is *not* a book about science fiction outside the United States. Although many of the cultural attitudes that I discuss originate in Western European traditions and are common to Western cultures, this book is about the United States. And because of the recent demographics of science fiction and the scientific-technological establishment, it is mostly about a white, masculine United States. But it is also about *why* such racist and sexist demographics exist at all and the possibilities for change.

Interpreting the Dream of Nature

Science fiction's dream, or dreams, of nature come from several mythic sources and reflect the great historical shift in the Western view of nature. They range from shamanic initiation rites to the alchemist's elixir of immortality. The most important is the myth of the Earthly Paradise, which made a long and strange journey to enter science fiction and be transformed by it—all the way from the garden of Eden to little green men. While the Earthly Paradise myth is an intriguing topic in itself, I am studying it to establish two facts about science fiction. First, that the ideologies of early modern science are "built into" the science fiction text through its use of the Earthly Paradise myth. At its built-in level the genre does not change. And so, science fiction continually adapts contemporary themes, whether they are feminist beliefs or speculations on gene research, to an older, invariant ideological structure, in which nature's "death" and the Cartesian re-definition of self are the central drama. Second, as I have mentioned, science fiction actively reinforces American ideologies, or, in Marxist phraseology, it is part of the reproduction of the mode of production. Both facts can be discovered by following science fiction's various myths through the narrative development of their meanings. One of my tasks is to show how the Earthly Paradise, the Rock and the Abyss of alchemy, and other myths endow science fiction with a structure that invariably reproduces certain ideological meanings.

This book is not an "anatomy" of science fiction, because I am concerned with elements in fluid patterns of relationships. The point is to assign not a single significance to each image but, rather, a field of significance to all of them. Nor, by referring to myths of nature, am I claiming that a myth has an independent life of its own and happens to appear in science fiction (the archetypal approach). The Earthly Paradise, to take my main example, is only the textual form of a myth. Following its transformations yields a grammar of science fiction's images as they respond to ideological pressures.

Science Fiction's Contexts

An old saw about science fiction complains that it is neither science nor fiction. Put another way, what does the genre have to do with science and with fiction? An interesting question lurks behind this one: Does the genre suggest that science and fiction have something to do with each other? To look at the literary and scientific contexts, I have combined two areas: one is American literary and cultural criticism, and the other, feminist philosophy and history of science.

Science fiction belongs in the American context that Leo Marx has defined: the conflict between pastoralism, the ideal of America as a vast garden, and the rhetoric of the technological sublime, which justifies industrialism and technological expansion. Marx's classic study, *The Machine in the Garden*, shows that even as Americans chose industrialization over the agrarian ideal, we never gave up the fantasy of returning to the garden, despite its historical impossibility. American attachment to the myth of the garden has made hopefulness a national characteristic, expressed and sometimes deflated in our literature. Unlike the texts that Marx surveys, however, science fiction does not try to temper hopefulness with history. Instead, it tries to create immunity from history. It reveals a curious dynamic: the greater our yearning for a return to the garden, the more we invest in technology as the purveyor of the unconstrained existence that we associate with the garden. Science fiction's national mode of thinking boils down to a paradox: the American imagination seeks to replace nature with a technological, man-made world *in order to return to the garden of American nature*. (Kurt Vonnegut's *Slaughterhouse-Five* beautifully illustrates this paradox.)

A related context for science fiction is the technological utopia. I have drawn on Howard Segal's admirable book, *Technological Utopianism in American Culture*, which places the technological utopia in the tradition of American thinking about the Machine. Not surprisingly, science fiction and the technological utopia have much in common, beginning with the fact that both are literary productions offering American visions of the machine, outside the canon of American literature. They both reflect the ideology of progress. They share similar assumptions about scientific rationality and technological expansion and much similar imagery. Marx's framework and the technological utopia provide science fiction's literary context in American culture.

Finally, science fiction has to be understood in the context of the mythology of the American frontier. Interpreting two major novels by way of the work of Richard Slotkin, Annette Kolodny, and Myra Jehlen, I have gone farther than is customary in articulating the relationships between nature, technology, and the frontier in science fiction. It is not enough to say that science fiction is like the western or is unlike it or is influenced by it. Science fiction combines frontier mythology with myths about collective technological power. It does so in an effort to define an American (white) identity, using the frontier myths to connect two aspects of American experience: the natural wilderness and the technological system. What is the connection between the frontiersman (I use the gendered term advisedly) and the scientist? How can we "civilize" the solitary frontiersman's violence into collective technological power over nature? How can we "naturalize" the technological system so that it becomes a second nature for Americans? These are the questions that place science fiction in the context of popular frontier mythology. Science fiction also reveals, in surprisingly vivid detail, that such mythic technological projects as spaceflight, immortality, and artificial reproduction are authentic American dreams.

Feminist theory is essential for understanding the dream of nature in science fiction—what it is and what it has to do with science. Feminist historians and philosophers of science explore how the Scientific Revolution changed the Western perception of nature from that of an animate, semidivine mother to inert, dead matter. Carolyn Merchant discusses how Francis Bacon, the earliest technological utopian, celebrates man's ability to appropriate nature's creative power. Expanding on the notion of appropriation, I show that utopia and science fiction appropriate the qualities of the nature myth, enacting at the literary level what science and industry were effecting in actuality. Evelyn Fox Keller's work, dealing with values that were accepted and rejected during the formation of the scientific method, provides an explanatory background for the hostile attitude toward nature that pervades science fiction's mythology.

Feminist analysis shows that scientific writing, from its earliest beginnings, relies on a strong metaphoric use of woman and sexual power relations. By examining metaphors of femininity and masculinity, feminist philosophers criticize the gender politics of the relationship between science and nature. I use this critique to interpret science fiction's metaphors, especially to show science fiction's construction of *alienated nature*—nature that is inevitably both female and monstrous. Finally, departing from the consensus of feminist writers on science fiction, I argue that feminist science fiction really cannot change science fiction's ideological structure or its construction of an alienated feminine nature. What feminist science fiction does, if read carefully, is to display key differences in the way that the feminine gendered subject, "Mother Nature's daughter," fits into the ideological framework designed by and for "Mother Nature's sons." The question at the heart of feminist science fiction seems to be something like: "If nature is feminine and human is technologically capable masculine, then how do I qualify to run this spaceship?" Without intending to, feminist science fiction tells a story about women's relationship to nature and to technology. The feminist version of alienated nature shows women's struggle with the cultural identification of woman-as-nature and the painful psychological effort to create a sense of female selfhood compatible with women's use of technological power.

It is my view that the cultural fears and anxieties present in science fiction's mass dream could be assuaged and resolved if a feminist science—such as Sandra Harding, Evelyn Fox Keller, and Donna Haraway envisage—were to become established. At many points throughout this book, at which science fiction seems to indicate problems in Western cultural psychology and the manifestations of those problems in our science and technology, I have suggested how feminist science may offer solutions.

Briefly about Definitions

It is the usual thing for a book about science fiction to begin with a definition of the genre, dating it back to Mary Shelley's *Frankenstein,* to Ludovico Ariosto's *Orlando Furioso,* or to earlier or later works, as the author fancies. Typically, science fiction is described as a hybrid genre, with elements of satire, romance, utopia, travel literature, and the Gothic. I do not propose a definition of science fiction but rely on the two working assumptions about it that seem the most useful. One is the standard observation that science fiction derives from the romance. Northrop Frye regards it as a mode of romance with a strong inherent tendency to myth, and science fiction's Earthly Paradise clearly comes from the Renaissance romance. The second assumption is that science fiction inherits the structure of utopia. I don't mean chronologically. Utopia alone, among all the influences, gives science fiction its definitive poetic structure. I would concur with the opinion of Eric Rabkin, who has written extensively on science fiction and offers the following definition of the genre:

> A work belongs in the genre of science fiction if its narrative world is at least somewhat different from our own, *and if that difference is apparent against the background of an organized body of knowledge.*[14]

In science fiction, myth or fantasy become rationalized, and phenomena point to a body of scientific knowledge that gives them meaning by explaining them. Darko Suvin, in *Metamorphoses of Science Fiction*, says succinctly that, while "naturalistic fiction does not require scientific explanation, [and] fantasy does not allow it, ... SF [*sic*] both requires and allows it."[15] Of all the generic strains in science fiction only utopia has this remarkable poetic structure, which creates an autonomous, rationalized world. Utopia is also the only literary genre, besides science fiction, that owes its existence to the ideologies of the Scientific Revolution.

One slightly problematical phrase that I use is "modern science," as in "our modern scientific-technological society," and so on. The models of reality produced by the Scientific Revolution, such as Newton's clockwork cosmos, have been more or less jettisoned by twentieth-century science. Yet I continue to call "modern" the notion of science based on the division between a rational, detached observer and a world of dead, passive matter, even though contemporary physics completely denies the possibility of such a division and questions the idea of matter being inanimate. I have chosen to do this, despite the changes in scientific models of reality during this century, for two reasons. First, the philosophical foundation of modern science has not changed in tandem with scientific theories; as many critics have pointed out, there is an enormous gap between what scientists do and what they think they do. And it is the latter, far more than the former, that affects our mass dreams of science and technology. The concept of objectivity, for example, is still basic to what scientists think they do as well as to the popular understanding of our relationship with nature. The image of the cool, detached expert exercizing uncanny control over the inanimate world has much more dream currency, so to say, than does Schrödinger's cat. Second, the Scientific Revolution's ideologies continue to pervade our attitudes toward technology. We build machines to fulfill our dreams of power. The kinds of power that we dream of possessing seem to be connected, historically and psychologically, to the death of nature. Whether this is inevitably true of modern technology, or whether the dreams of the machine might change if the social and cultural framework of technological production were to change, I leave to the reader to decide.

Wonder, the sense of wonder, is an important theme in the major critiques of technological Western society. In the sense that I use it, wonder is a specific, culturally mediated experience of nature. Wonder is what we feel in the presence of the nature myth: the response to our perception of the animate, numinous, feminine nature predating the Scientific Revolution. Yet the sense of wonder in the presence of nature need not, of course, be confined to the prescientific version of the nature myth. I would tend to agree with James Lovelock, inventor of the Gaia hypothesis, that we interact with nature "through a sense of wonder about the natural world and through feeling a part of it."[16] I pin down wonder to a specific, very old and deeply embedded response to the nature myth because it is the same "sense of wonder" that science fiction unwittingly tries to evoke. The dearth of wonder, magic, the truly strange and different, is the constant preoccupation of science fiction, which tries to compensate with its own fabrications, or with what I have called "man-made wonder." Here fiction and science are related, but they are at cross-purposes. Science fiction remains faithful to scientific rationality while trying, at the same time, to imagine the wondrous. "Magic and science," says Ioan Couliano, "in the last analysis, represent needs of the imagination, and the transition from a society dominated by magic to a predominantly scientific society is explicable primarily by a *change in the imaginary*."[17] That change haunts science fiction with the loss of a world and the wish for, as well as the terror of, its recovery.

In the narrower sense the traditions of magic and alchemy contribute substantially to science fiction: all space travel novels draw on their elements. Chapter 3, on C. J. Cherryh's *The Faded Sun* trilogy and Frank Herbert's *Dune,* interprets the myths of space-faring. The obvious stuff of space fiction, its much criticized racism and xenophobia, its campy version of manifest destiny, acquires depth against the complex background of ancient, Renaissance, and American mythology. In my opinion, that unexpected depth is the great reward of treating science fiction seriously, as more than a pop culture lunchbox stuffed with ideological fast food, yet without one's having to assert that it is (as SF authors used to argue) a great literature overlooked by an establishment of aesthetes who never heard of *Scientific American.* To imagine an American identity based on a whole range of ideas about war, nature, sexuality, technology, and history; to create this identity in a condensed mythic grammar resonating with dreamlike ease and materializing in our technological systems—this feat has something in it of both technology and magic.

Man-made Wonder

The Lady in the Enchanted Garden

There used to be a television advertisement showing a dignified, middle-aged woman dressed in a sort of green and brown toga, eating a slice of buttered bread. Told by an unseen announcer that what she was enjoying was really butter-flavored margarine, the matron set her arms akimbo, and, as fierce, howling winds started to blow around her, shouted, "It's not nice to fool Mother Nature!" I liked this advertisement because it counted on our stock belief in the antagonism between nature and science. We may not know anything about food processing, but we know why Dame Nature doesn't approve of it. We have worried about our troubled relationship with nature, in the language of myth, for the past four hundred years.

Before the Scientific Revolution people in the Western world believed that nature was a living being, Mother Nature. She was "a nurturing mother: a kindly, beneficent female who provided for the needs of mankind in an ordered, planned universe,[1] as the historian Carolyn Merchant tells us. In pagan religions Mother Nature had the rank of a goddess. The ancient Greeks worshiped Gaia, the earth goddess and mother of all living creatures; the Romans called the same deity Tellus. Christianity demoted the goddess to semidivine status. A sixteenth-century picture of the cosmos shows Mother Nature standing astride the earth, her wrist fettered with a long chain that leads up to a cloud representing God. Well into the Renaissance period nature was envisioned as a maternal spirit providing for her creatures, and manifesting God, who had imprinted his design on the Creation.[2]

The belief that the earth was a living, semidivine being tended to restrain ecologically disruptive industries. Mining, for example, was criticized in the sixteenth century for injuring and defiling the sacred body of Mother Earth. With the growth of industry-dependent technology, however, the traditional view began to erode. As mining, deforestation, and the enclosure of common land spread, so did a new view of nature as inanimate matter, acted upon by technological forces. The Scientific Revolution replaced the mythic mother with the concept of a passive, dead nature, over which man, empowered by science and technology, exercised dominion.[3] Descartes and Newton envisioned nature as inanimate matter ruled by predictable forces and organized in the form of a mechanism. In Descartes's opinion not only was matter, generally speaking, mindless and dead, but even live animals were mere automata. Although twentieth-century science has almost no use for the mechanistic model, the popular modern view of nature is still that of a dead world. We think of our bodies as machines and of the natural environment as a storehouse of material resources, stuff to be technologically shaped and used. Science fiction is the product of the death of nature and the emergence of modern science.

What does science fiction have to do with these sweeping changes of four hundred years ago? The images of nature and technology in science fiction not only reflect the death of nature but also show in considerable detail how modern Western culture is still beset by fears and anxieties that accompanied the replacement of the divine mother with a dead, mechanized world. To understand science fiction's nature imagery we need to know where it came from. The myth of Mother Nature came to science fiction via two literary genres, the romance and the utopia. But before looking at these literary sources, let's sharpen our sense of the changed attitude toward nature that the Scientific Revolution fostered. In 1627 Francis Bacon published a utopia called *New Atlantis*. Bacon described an imaginary society entirely devoted to maintaining a giant scientific research institute, called Salomon's House. The influence of Bacon's ideas was direct and powerful; within thirty years of *New Atlantis*'s publication, the Royal Society was founded, and Britain gained a scientific establishment. Today we recognize many of the goals of modern science in the research activities of Salomon's House, and most strikingly familiar is the Atlantean scientists' relationship to nature. A tour of Salomon's House takes us through a series of hollowed-out mountains. Inside the mountains laboratories produce artificial imitations of every possible natural environment. The scientists have created artificial lakes, seas, waterfalls, and weather, including thunder and lightning. Artificial minerals enrich the lodes of artificial mines. In artificial orchards and parks the scientists breed new species of plants and animals. We begin to feel chilled by the power hunger that the Atlanteans display when talking about their biological research. They boast that their products are better than nature's and tamper with animal species for no other purpose, it seems, except that of gratifying their pride: "We make them taller or greater than their kind is, and contrariwise dwarf them and stay their growth; we make them more fruitful and bearing than their kind is, and contrariwise barren... we make them differ in color, shape, activity, many ways." Live creatures are no more than putty in the hands of the researchers, who also describe the vivisections that they perform on their animals, in order to observe "continuing life in them, though divers parts, which you account vital, be... taken forth," and experiment on them with "all poisons, and other medicines."[4] The attitude evinced here is remote indeed from the view that certain human activities are injurious to the sacred mother. Bacon's utopia promotes the relationship to nature that characterizes modern applied science and technology—a relationship that we can say consists in the *technological appropriation of nature.* Technology appropriates nature's powers for itself, taking over nature's generativity, while nature becomes dead material, grist for the mills.

New Atlantis is a hard-sell promotion of the Scientific Revolution's new concept of nature, and, at a literary level, it initiated the first stage of transformation that led ultimately to science fiction. Bacon, who was writing for an audience familiar with the literature of the romance, altered the romance's traditional images of nature in order to give extra power to his vision of Salomon's House. By placing a scientific laboratory inside a mountain, Bacon cleverly subverted an important figure of romance literature, the Earthly Paradise. The best way to become acquainted with the properties of nature in science fiction is to look at the romance's Earthly Paradise and see what survives of it half a millenium later (science fiction being, as many critics have shown, a version of the romance).[5] By the time of the Renaissance a long line of Christian and classical sources had gone into the making of the Earthly Paradise, but for our purposes a simplified description will serve.

If you happen to have a picture of Botticelli's masterpiece *La Primavera,* look at the beautiful nymph wearing a translucent, flower-embroidered dress and scattering flowers. She sets the mood of the Earthly Paradise. On top of a mountain there is an enchanted garden in which it is always spring. Flowers bloom, a fountain overflows its basin, and someone is playing a lute, while another figure sprawls on the grass, indolently listening. Usually sacred to Venus, the garden has a presiding genius who is either the goddess herself or a lady who resembles her closely. A lover of wandering knights and a weaver of magic spells, she is the vital presence who makes the garden grow. In Spenser's romance *The Faerie Queen* Venus presides over a garden on a mountain's summit; she passes the time making love to her companion, Adonis, within a grove of myrtle trees. Around and below her grove are neat flowerbeds, which contain the "infinite shapes of creatures that are bred"–even fish!–before they go out from paradise into the world.[6] Although most Earthly Paradise gardens bloom with fewer varieties than Spenser's, they are always lush. The genius's seductiveness, and her magic, are both aspects of nature's generative power.

Where does this charming fantasy come from? The Earthly Paradise is a variation of an ancient myth, known to us as the myth of the Golden Age. Ovid's version of it tells how the world passes through several ages—Golden, Silver, Brass, Iron, and so on—each with its special qualities. In the earliest epoch, the Golden Age, human beings lived in perfect harmony with nature and one another. They did not farm, own property, or make war; laws were unnecessary, and the institution of government was unknown. Nature freely supplied all human wants. Harry Levin, a scholar of Renaissance literature, calls the Golden Age an etiological myth, a story about the origins of things, or "how men came to be alienated from nature and why they have lived too seldom in peace and plenty, justice and freedom, leisure and love."[7] The Earthly Paradise is the geographical equivalent of the Golden Age. In the enchanted garden warriors can rest, forgetting the missions and duties imposed on them by king, church, and chivalric code, returning to an earlier human freedom in love play and contemplative leisure.

While keeping its essential qualities, science fiction's Earthly Paradise assumes odd disguises. In Kurt Vonnegut's *Slaughterhouse-Five* the Earthly Paradise genius is a pregnant porn starlet named Montana, living in outer space—and she is the least bizarre of the enchantresses to be met with in this book. But the quality that always distinguishes the Earthly Paradise, throughout its literary history, is its embodiment of an ideal of love and harmony.[8]

The temporal Golden Age is definitely and irretrievably past, but the geographical Earthly Paradise has always been considered part of this world—here, if hard to discover. It appeared on medieval maps and in tales of imaginary voyages. And real travelers set out to find it.[9] Today any travel brochure for a tropical resort will sell you the Earthly Paradise complete with banquets, music, flowers, Golden Age natives, and loving enchantresses; this Western tourists' fantasy dates back to the exploratory voyages of Europeans who projected the Earthly Paradise myth upon other lands and peoples. Christopher Columbus, sailing up the Orinoco, actually thought that he had come within close range of Eden, the biblical version of the Earthly Paradise, during his third expedition in 1498. Not daring to venture any further without divine permission, Columbus wrote a letter back to Ferdinand and Isabella, in which he gave his evidence for the location of the garden, together with his latest theory about the shape of the earth. Levin has an interesting comment on this otherworldly episode. Columbus "was now of the opinion that the earth was pear-shaped ... that the newly discovered hemisphere was shaped like a woman's breast, and that the Earthly Paradise was located at a high point corresponding to the nipple.... Columbus, seeking the aboriginal site of human generation, would nostalgically envision it as a maternal archetype."[10] Columbus's geographical theory provides a picture of the relationship between the myth of Mother Nature and the literary Earthly Paradise. Just as the earth and Eden were physically contiguous in Columbus's mind, so the images of Mother Nature and the Earthly Paradise tend to overlap. The Earthly Paradise combines mundane and ideal qualities into one complete representation of maternal nature, as "she" was imagined in the Renaissance. What are the qualities of mythic nature in this literary representation?

Nature is an animate, feminine, and numinous being. She manifests in an unmediated way as natural generativity, the lush fertility of the garden, or she can assume the shape of a feminine genius. Whatever her form, Mother Nature always inspires wonder. Hers is a divine power; her generativity is numinous, or magical. Love, harmony, abundance, and eroticism are also associated with the Earthly Paradise. These are the qualities that science fiction will alter and turn upside down, making a witches' brew of the garden's bouquets.

From Romance to Utopia: The Lady Vanishes

It is no accident that *utopia* can mean either a tale or a real experiment in living. According to Richard Gerber, a critic of utopian fiction, the idea of utopia was not only a product of the Renaissance's "new social consciousness, but also the proper outcome of the humanist theories of literature applied to society in general."[11] Humanist poetics, the theories about the writing of poetry promulgated by Renaissance humanists, gave the Renaissance romance a new significance, one that prefigured the ideology of early modern science. The poetics of earlier eras held that the function of poetry was to imitate nature, or to illustrate metaphysical truths. But according to humanist poetics, poetry created an autonomous world, detached from nature. Sir Philip Sidney, author of the substantial romance *Arcadia,* called the poet's creation "an other nature," a man-made world superior to the original. In fact, Sidney imagined the poet bringing forth a "golden world" to devalue nature's brass.

> Onely the Poet . . . lifted up with the vigor of his own invention, doth grow in effect into an other nature: in making things either better than nature bringeth foorth, or quite a new, formes such as never were in nature. . . . Nature never set foorth the earth in so rich a Tapestry as diverse Poets have done . . . her world is brasen, the Poets only deliver a golden.[12]

Sidney's poetics endowed the poet with the power to do better than nature, the selfsame power flaunted by the scientists of *New Atlantis.* The poet's creation is a *heterocosm*: an alternative cosmos, a man-made world.

The heterocosm made possible the conception of fictional and real-life utopias.[13] For if the Earthly Paradise garden was not a poet's imitation of nature but, instead, his own independent invention, then it logically followed that human beings could independently realize the pleasant qualities of the Earthly Paradise. By applying the theory of the heterocosm to society in general, the utopian attempted to create an improved human condition that owed nothing to powers outside human reason and will. A man-made system, utopia, appropriated the abundance and social harmony of the garden and replaced Mother Nature as their source. In utopia the lady vanishes: the figure of feminine nature no longer enchants the Earthly Paradise.

The aesthetic price of casting the lady out of the garden is high. Having eliminated the garden's genius, utopia loses the mythic force that makes the Earthly Paradise such attractive reading in the romance. Although utopia is realized on earth, it has an abstract, lifeless quality. All its perfections are reducible to a plan. While the enchanted garden springs from deep within the human imagination, utopia is "a device, a construct." Every utopia is scientific, because it is constructed on the basis of a scientific analysis of social conditions.[14] Utopia's heterocosm is *rationalized.* Every detail has been reasoned out. No mysteries go unexplained, as the reader plods through the utopians' typical speeches about how they are born, fed, clothed, instructed, mated, and employed and about how they are happy.

Another way to describe what's lost in utopia is to call it the sense of wonder. Deserted by its genius, the Earthly Paradise garden can no longer inspire wonder's mix of surprise and awe at nonhuman powers. We may scoff or feel wistful at Gonzalo's utopian scheme in *The Tempest,* but our wonder is reserved for Prospero's magic. (There are good feminist reasons for dividing the title of genius between Miranda and Sycorax, but that's another story.) Wonder is our tribute to nature's numinous aspect. Unlike the other pleasures of the Earthly Paradise garden, it cannot transfer into the utopian heterocosm.

The science fiction writer Ursula Le Guin, credited with breaking some of utopia's generic limits, deals with utopia's deficiencies, among them the absence of the nature myth.[15] In her acclaimed novel, *The Dispossessed: An Ambiguous Utopia,* a utopian society settles on an arid moon, previously inhabited by a colony of miners. Over the course of years the utopians launch an ambitious desert reclamation project. In this conversation two young people, working in the lunar sand, disagree over a song:

> "She brings the green leaf from the stone,
> From heart of rock clear water running..."
> Gimar was always humming the tune...
>   "Who does? Who's 'she'?" asked Shevek.
>   "...It's a miner's song."
>   "What miners?"
>   "Don't you know? People who were already here when the Settlers came.... They still have some feast days and songs of their own...."
>   "Well, then, who's 'she'?"
>   "I don't know.... Isn't it what we're doing here? Bringing green leaves out of stones!"
>   "Sounds like religion."
>   "You and your fancy book-words. It's just a song..."[16]

Gimar's song conjures an image of feminine nature, that of the enchantress who makes things grow. As Shevek suspects, the song is religious. It belongs to a preutopian, prescientific community, the colony of miners who celebrate suspiciously religious "feast-days." Gimar knows her preutopian history but cannot really say what or whom the song is about. She tries to impose a utopian interpretation on the song's lyrics. Nature's magic is "what we're doing here," by technological means. She knows that there is something irritatingly irrelevant about Shevek's "fancy book-words," his humanism in action, but she doesn't refute his criticism. "It's just a song," she shrugs, depriving the tune of its verbal content and meaning. The words of myth cannot refute the words of books, of scientific knowledge, once rationality has replaced faith in the nature myth. And the song's verb *brings,* with its aura of magic and generosity, disappears behind the famous utopian verb *work.* As Gerber remarks, "The Utopians are happy because more and more efficient work is done."[17] Work, a social action, replaces nature's magical action. The utopian heterocosm offers industrious happiness in place of wonder.

For utopia this is not a disaster. Even without feeling wonder, people can enjoy reading utopias and being convinced by their ideas. But for science fiction the absence of the myth poses a major problem. Science fiction inherits the poetic structure of the heterocosm: it creates an autonomous man-made world. Yet within its heterocosm it makes every effort to recapture the lost force of myth. Many science fiction authors believe that science fiction is myth, or should be. Lester Del Rey contrasts "backward-looking myths" that "looked back to a golden age ... to demons also" with science fiction's forward-looking myths.[18] Ben Bova declares that science fiction "serves the function of a modern mythology."[19] According to Olaf Stapledon, "We must achieve neither mere history, nor mere fiction, but myth."[20] Precise definitions vary, but the idea of myth that they all share involves science fiction's fantastic apparatus, its marvels, strange places, and weird creatures.[21]

By now you will have discerned that the Earthly Paradise's journey happened in three stages, and in each stage the ideological forces of the Scientific Revolution appropriated different qualities of nature. The mythic lady vanished gradually. The first stage occurred in the real world, where the Scientific Revolution influenced social and economic systems. As new technologies started exploiting the environment on a large scale, they were supported by a scientific ideology that called for appropriating nature's powers while reducing the figure of Mother Nature to dead, passive matter, the "natural resources" of man's creation. Participating in the new ideology, utopia—our literary, second stage—appropriated the qualities of abundance and harmony from the romance's Earthly Paradise, banishing the figure of feminine nature from the man-made, rationalized world of the heterocosm. (Bacon's *New Atlantis* is the convenient meeting point of form and content, a

utopian heterocosm based on the ideal of total technological appro-
priation, proceeding via what might be called the hysterectomy of
Venus' mountain, or by scooping the mother out of matter.)
Science fiction inherits the structure and the ideology of utopia.
Every science fiction novel, structurally, is a utopian heterocosm.
Nothing can happen without a sound, rational, scientific explanation.
But science fiction's ambition is *precisely* to make us wonder, to show
strange and marvelous things. And so, ironically, science fiction attempts the final stage: to appropriate the Earthly Paradise's magic, the
numinous quality of feminine nature. To re-enchant the heterocosm,
without the enchantress. To manufacture wonder.

Manufacturing Wonder in the Disenchanted World

Science fiction belongs to a world that has become, in Max Weber's
famous phrase, "disenchanted," as it becomes increasingly technicized
and rationalized. The global capitalist system requires that all aspects
of our lives be entered into the calculation of productivity and profit;
human activity, even identity, fits into networks of information and
exchange. Most of what we are, do, and see around us has a label and
a market value. Disenchantment means that the world becomes "de-
void of collective transcendent experience";[22] transcendence, an
awareness of being that is greater than the sum of its parts, has no
place in our daily routines and institutions. To a great extent our
society lost the basis for transcendent experience by losing the relationship with numinous nature. The myth of nature is the magic that
has gone out of modern life. As mentioned in the introduction, however, our sense of wonder in the presence of nature need not depend
on responding to this particular myth; nor is this sense, of course, the
only kind of wonder. *The nature myth is a cultural construct,* not a
real lost goddess, and, in discussing the nature myth and its modifi-
cations, I am not recommending a return to prescientific nature worship; rather, I am recognizing our collective wish for a spiritual experience of nature. The nature myth is deeply embedded in our common
consciousness, as are the repercussions of the myth's scientific undo-
ing.

Kurt Vonnegut's sad and funny book *Player Piano* is a technological dystopia—the grim opposite of utopia—that treats of this loss. *Player
Piano* was written around the time when a generation of authors, most
prominently Isaac Asimov, were setting new standards for "hard" sci-

ence fiction, incorporating scientific Ideas in ingenious ways. A look at the social and historical background of Vonnegut's novel will help us to understand the real-life meanings of disenchantment and technicization and to see how science fiction emerged from that background. The novel itself deserves attention because it makes explicit connections that science fiction leaves hidden. Vonnegut likes to write playful exposés of science fiction's ideological and psychological roots–one reason why he has frustrated all attempts to classify him as a science fiction author.

In *Player Piano* he holds up a funhouse mirror to modern technological society and technocratic ideas. The rulers of dystopia are managers and engineers, whom the author praises ironically in his foreword:

> It [this book] is mostly about managers and engineers. At this point in history, 1952 A.D., our lives and freedom depend largely upon the skill and imagination and courage of our managers and engineers, and I hope that God will help them to help us all stay alive and free.[23]

Player Piano pours its satire on an America enjoying the postwar boom. For the sciences it was an exciting time. Scientific research was growing rapidly in the areas of solid state and nuclear physics, biology, and astronomy. The scientific breakthroughs of the 1950s were nothing short of breathtaking, from the first thermonuclear explosion in 1952, to the Explorer satellite in 1958 (a year after the Soviet Sputniks); television, computers, drugs (among them Salk's polio vaccine), synthetic materials, and other products were creating wealth and seemed to promise a future of unlimited progress.[24] The boom produced an extraordinarily affluent, industrially advanced society, one characterized by an oppressive banality against which a lively counterculture revolted. In 1956 Ginsberg's poem "America" complains: "Your machinery is too much for me. . . . Are you going to let your emotional life be run by Time Magazine?[25] Herbert Marcuse's *One-Dimensional Man,* published in 1964, remains a classic diagnosis of the period's pervasive technicized flatness, which was mirrored in the nuts-bolts-and-filter-paper quality of the period's science fiction.[26]

Marcuse argued that contemporary life had destroyed an entire transcendent dimension of imaginative and conceptual thought and, with it, the possibility of resistance to the system. Whatever was non-functional in terms of technological capitalism was stamped out, or stamped on: "Ideas, aspirations, and objectives that...transcend the established universe of discourse and action are either expelled or reduced to terms of this universe."[27] Marcuse was one of several twentieth-century thinkers who share a vision of a monolithic technological production system, encompassing all the interlocking spheres of economic, social, political, and intellectual life. The chief characteristic of this system is that, driven by "technical reason," its totalizing principle, it continually expands. Another school of thought acknowledges the system's scope but avoids crediting it with anything like a life of its own, looking instead for the historical choices that, cumulatively, push us in one direction. Vonnegut blamed America's disenchantment and technicization on the actions and values of corporate managers and engineers. Underlying Vonnegut's satire is the influence of managers and engineers on the growth of "one-dimensional society."

David Noble's book *America by Design: Science, Technology, and the Rise of Corporate Capitalism* describes the rise of engineering in the early decades of the century. The profession was the object of strong ideological desires and hopes. Advocates of social engineering, such as Thorstein Veblen and later the Technocrats of the 1930s, had believed that engineers' creativity and problem-solving skills would make them better planners than corruptible politicians. Veblen thought that technical productivity might displace the values of the "money system," in which businessmen labored without making useful products. Far from replacing capitalism, however, increasing numbers of engineers in the early twentieth century were integrated into large-scale corporations, where they assumed managerial responsibilities. In this double role they were charged with developing profitable technologies and coordinating what Noble characterizes as the "human elements of the technological enterprise." Perhaps inevitably, the second half of their task began to look like the first. Managers began to view their work force as an engineering project. Once they recognized that technological production was a social as well as a mechanical process, they tried "to formulate a scientific way of managing that process.... On the one hand, social organization and human behavior became new foci of engineering theory and practice; on the other hand,...engineering itself began to expand as...social and psychological variables were deliberately introduced within engineering analysis and design."[28] This scientific approach to human labor, Noble claims, was the beginning of modern management, a major strain in American social thought.

What modern management meant, for the workers and managers

alike, was that difficulties posed by human beings were seen as glitches, bugs in the program. People were subjected to a one-dimensional discourse, which defined "the human element" as a technical instrument, not as a political force. An example is this passage from a 1910 engineering magazine, cited by Noble:

> When we purchase a machine tool and find it slightly unfitted for requirements, we can usually make a change in construction which will control the difficulty in it.... If the human machine could be controlled by the set rules that govern machine tool operation, the world would be a much different place.[29]

Obviously, a machine tool cannot feel solidarity with other machine tools. (Karel Čapek, whose play *R.U.R.,* was the first fictional work about "robots" using that term, predicted that they would be the ideal industrial workers, though his robots were biological, not mechanical.) Hence the familiar managerial tactic of improving, or appearing to improve, workers' conditions by making piecemeal adjustments, without addressing the condition of the worker as a whole. Since the aim of personnel management was to shape human behavior in order to enhance profits, it focused on the particular worker, the glitch, directly. A disaffected employee might receive an extra benefit or a lecture on attitude, but he or she might not "transcend the established universe of discourse and action" to redefine the worker's role, human needs, social worth, and political values. In the 1950s an article entitled "Fitting the Right Man to the Right Job" shows us the mechanical metaphor for the human being, confidently set forth: "Deep as they are, the factors that 'make a man tick' can be described and analyzed with much of the precision that would go into the making of dies for the side of a Sherman tank."[30]

The flattening of human experience that Marcuse deplored could not be better illustrated than by this crude reduction of the worker into a military hardware component. Judging the metaphor on its own utilitarian terms, it was a success: as Noble proves, it worked. People were persuaded to think of themselves as objects, as instruments for specific purposes, implementing specific routines. There are differences as well as connections between Marcuse's critique and Marx's description of alienated labor. Although the system's benefits are unequally distributed, everyone involved in the production system, workers and bosses alike, becomes its instrument mentally as well as physically. What Marcuse draws attention to is not only the historical practice in which people of all classes are engaged but also their inability to imagine anything different. The transcendent dimension, the freedom of thought and feeling unharnessed to profit and productivity, the discovery of new ideas about who we are and how we want to live—this, the "space for transcending historical practice" is "barred by a society in which subjects as well as objects constitute instrumentalities in a whole that has its raison d'être in the accomplishments of its overwhelming productivity."[31] Science fiction is part of the reaction to the one-dimensional character of the technological enterprise. The idea of a purely instrumental world has met with both fear and enthusiasm; the latter attitude, as Noble shows, directs the management aims and policies of those who employ the human machine. At the present time, with our economy's change from industry to information services, modern management controls the workplace, and technicization is part of our workaday experience, and of our disenchantment.

Technicization, clearly, was the most memorable aspect of Kurt Vonnegut's job as a public relations specialist at General Electric (GE). Vonnegut quit the company to write *Player Piano*. Although in the novel machines "frequently got the best of it, as machines will,"[32] they did not get the best of *him*. Anyone who has worked in a large computerized organization can share his wry response "to the implications of having everything run by little boxes."[33] Besides throwing a wrench into the frictionless gears of technological utopia, *Player Piano* predicts fairly accurately the problems that arise when modern management principles are combined with a mainframe.

The typical American town of Ilium, New York, has three neighborhoods. In one posh suburb live the managers and engineers; in another sector, the automated industrial machines; and everyone else lives in the slums. Whether an Ilium citizen will enter the ranks of the technocratic elite or fall among the great unskilled, depends not on the technocracy's rulers but, instead, on the "personnel machines." A central computer administers a battery of standard tests to each Ilian, then spits out a "personnel card" that gives him (women don't count in 1950s dystopias) a specialized job along with his economic and social status. The unfortunates whom the computer classifies as too dumb for employment become slaves of the state, working out terms in the army or on construction crews. So the elite are, in fact, subordinate to a computerized management system that fits the right man to the right job—except that, of course, it doesn't. Scientific management's often stated goal is that of preventing waste—waste of time, waste of talent, waste of materials—by treating the human element as machine components to be adjusted for maximum efficiency. Ilium overflows with wasted technical talent. An engineer driving through the slums is mobbed by test flunkees who are "good with their hands," begging for jobs. A genius loses his job forever when he invents a machine that fills his numbered job slot. The privileged men who become managers and engineers lead regimented, uninspired, niggling lives geared to the corporate bureaucracy. Vonnegut works out the implications of the technological utopia[34] combined with corporate capitalism, and the result is technicized totalitarianism. The novel's overall atmosphere is one of sadness;[35] extreme disappointment in the social promise of technology and frustration with a boring, conformist, disenchanted world.

In the interests of historical perspective we might want to recall that some change in technological corporate culture took place in the 1970s and 1980s, with the growth of a young, flexible, dynamic computer industry that encouraged creativity and informality. (In my own incarnation as a business consultant, I remember being warned not to wear a suit inside Lotus Corporation—especially not a navy suit.) Donna Haraway, whose work is addressed in chapter 4, has written an illuminating summation of the shift to postmodern technological capitalism. But I do not think that the basic problems of disenchantment and technicization have changed, or are likely to change, with the vicissitudes of Silicon Valley companies and the U.S. Department of Defense. On the contrary, such factors as the breakdown of the Soviet bloc, the economic unity of Europe, and the interest of Third World countries in acquiring advanced technologies make inevitable the burgeoning of a global technological capitalism and the fulfillment of some unpleasant predictions, Vonnegut's not least.

The Earthly Paradise and Magic in *Player Piano*

"Little boxes" do worse than steal jobs. They steal nature, taking for themselves the properties of fertility and omnipresence but, worst of all, nature's magical quality. Through the thematics of the Earthly Paradise, *Player Piano* mourns the loss of numinous nature and seriously poses the question of whether it can be recovered. The first machine that we see is neither a computer nor a dynamo, but an old player piano standing in a dark corner of a seedy bar. The keys are going up and down by themselves. Two men watch this performance: Dr. Paul Proteus, chief manager of the mammoth Ilium Works, and Rudy, a decrepit old machinist. Years ago Rudy's workmanship was so fine that Paul chose him to make a tape of manual task motions, off which the automata of Ilium Works run, exactly like a player piano's keys. Of course, the automata made Rudy obsolete. Paul, squirming with guilt, listens while Rudy mumbles drunkenly:

"Makes you feel kind of creepy, don't it, Doctor, watching them keys go up and down? You can almost see a ghost sitting there playing his heart out." (28)

Rudy's words are sad and accurate. The piano has eerily taken possession of a human soul, expressing what used to be in his living heart. The animating spirit has gone into the machine. When Paul goes on an inspection tour of Ilium Works, we see how the tape of Rudy's hands animates them:

Paul paused for a moment to listen to the music of Building 58. . . . It was wild and Latin music, hectic rhythms. . . . He tried to separate and identify the themes. There! The lathe groups, the tenors: *Furrazz- ow-ow-ow-ow-ow-ak! ting!* . . . It was exciting music, and Paul, flushed, his vague anxieties gone, gave himself over to it . . . he turned in his delight to watch a cluster of miniature maypoles braid bright cloth insulation about a black snake of cable. A thousand little dancers. . . . Paul laughed at the wonderful machines, and had to look away to keep from getting dizzy. In the old days, when women had watched over the machines, some of the more simple-hearted had been found sitting rigidly at their posts, staring, long after quitting time. (10–11)

The Works may seem distant from the Earthly Paradise enchantress, who plays a lute or sings to the spellbound knight in her lap, yet hers is the magic that the machines appropriate. Their music is really the sound of their productive activity, just as the genius's seductiveness comes from her generativity. Like her charms, the machines' music is erotic, both soothing and exciting to the flushed hero. When the maypole comes into the picture, distance vanishes and we are standing in, of all places, Arcadia. The images wind as thick and fast as the insulation. Traditionally, the maypole dance brought villagers together to crown the May Queen and to celebrate the earth's seasonal renewal. All the qualities of Earthly Paradise are here—harmony, fertility, eroticism, even springtime—when, suddenly, Paul experiences wonder. The machines are wonderful. Paul becomes dizzy and remembers simple women bewitched by the same sight. This adds the magic of Faerie to the scene. The little elfin dancers are dangerous for peasants to behold, as they were in the old days, "once upon a time." The automata of Ilium Works possess the wonder-inspiring magic of the Earthly Paradise. They have appropriated Paul's, and society's, experience of an animate, feminine, numinous nature.

I can almost hear the protests of readers who like handling machinery themselves. Why should it be a bad thing for the machines to have captured nature's creative magic? Why shouldn't Paul feel delight and wonder in mechanical skill and artistry? If Rudy's skills are any indication, Vonnegut appreciates the instinct of workmanship as much as Veblen did. The problem does not lie with machines themselves so much as with the technological production system as a whole. By usurping the human relationship with nature, it ultimately kills the creative and imaginative quality, the "space within," that is truly human. Technological corporate capitalism does not encourage gifted workers. On the contrary, the managerial structure of big science and technology tends to suppress inventiveness. The human element has to be geared to specialized tasks. Writing a decade after Vonnegut, the novelist Thomas Pynchon has one character, an employee of the huge but risible Yoyodyne Corporation, who complains bitterly about the frustrations of talented engineers:

> In school they got brainwashed ... into believing the Myth of the American Inventor—Morse and his telegraph, Bell and his telephone, Edison and his light bulb. ... Only one man per invention. Then when they grew up they found they had to sign over all their (patent) rights to a monster like Yoyodyne; got stuck on some "project" or "task force" or "team" and started being ground into anonymity. Nobody wanted them to invent—only perform their little role in a design ritual, already set down for them in some procedures handbook.[36]

Vonnegut and Pynchon are not criticizing little boxes but, rather, the ideology and social practice of technicization. The ideology aims not to complement nature but to replace it. As for the social practice: "Teamwork ... is one word for it, yeah," snarls Koteks, the squelched inventor. "It's a symptom of the gutlessness of the whole society." "Goodness," exclaims his interlocutor, "are you allowed to talk like that?"[37]

There are two attempts in *Player Piano* to revivify industrial society's relationship with nature. Both fail. The first takes place at The Meadows, a company retreat owned by Ilium Works. The source for this episode was GE's Association Island, closed by the company after Vonnegut's depiction embarrassed it badly. We can still find a model for The Meadows in Bohemian Grove, an important retreat for business and political leaders. Howard Segal has compared the real with the fictional retreat, coming to the conclusion that "the Bohemian Grove, like The Meadows, seeks to restore close relationships with nature, but like its fictional counterpart never achieves more than a superficial return to nature."[38] The Meadows is a green, lush island, framing the strained romps of corporate campers in the scenery of the Earthly Paradise. An oak tree grows on the island. The oak is the classical symbol of the Golden Age, and, strangely enough, it is also the symbol of Ilium Works. Tearful executives gather around the oak tree and sing the company anthem to the tune of "Love's Sweet Song." No wonder GE was embarrassed. The rationale for this silliness, however, is sound. Activities at the retreat try to recover the social harmony of the Earthly Paradise by "getting back to nature," a perfectly good way to do it. Unfortunately, you can't revive the relationship with nature in the name of corporate teamwork. The profound human longing to live in loving peace with nature and one another is of a different order from company loyalty, so we find the scene comical. A later scene elaborates the failure of the retreat even more dismally.

This time the junior executives gather by the shore. A middle-aged, flabby, white actor, wearing bronze paint and a war bonnet, makes a speech. He says that, even though his own Indian people have gone from the island, their spirit, the Spirit of the Meadows, lives on in the wind, the water, the thunder, and so forth. Then he asks the junior execs, whom he calls "braves," to take the Oath of the Spirit. What's going on? Practically since Plymouth, American popular mythology has identified Native Americans with nature and has viewed them as "noble savages," the innocent people of the Earthly Paradise. This particular ritual conjures up the numinous aspect of nature, the water-, wind-, and thunder-dwelling Spirit, along with community spirit. A group responsory follows. But it is interrupted by the air arrival of Ilium Works' CEO, a man described as "the priceless two hundred and fifty pounds of Dr. Francis Eldrin Gelhorne, and his know-how":

"By the lapping of the great blue water, by the whirr of the eagle
wing—"
The Old Man's plane had skated across the water...and was
roaring its engines.... (193)

The contrast of the rhetorical eagle's whirr and the actual plane's roar
over the water effectively punctures the already thin illusion of Golden
Age harmony and numinous nature. None of these white executives
is really interested in eagles' wings, even in bald eagles' wings. The
retreat's instrumentality totally contradicts its Earthly Paradise qualities: know-how abolishes magic.

"The machines are to practically everybody what the white men
were to the Indians" (251), says the leader of the Ghost Shirt Society,
a radical group aiming to destroy the technocracy. Their name, signifi-
cantly, is taken from a Native American movement: in 1890 the Paiute
messiah, Wovoka, prophesied that many Indian dead were soon to be
resurrected, and founded the religion of the Ghost Dance, among the
adherents of which were warriors who dressed in magically protective
shirts.[39] Like The Meadows, the Ghost Shirt Society plays on the
American association of Indians with nature.[40] In this instance magic
opposes know-how: the Ghost Shirters believe that noble, natural humanity must pull the plug. While the historical Ghost Shirt movement
was subdued by force, however, the Ilium uprising collapses from
within. It is a case of seduction and betrayal.

At first the Ghost Shirters throw Ilium Works into havoc. They
burn, axe, smash, and overrun the automated installations, gathering
momentum from the populace as they go. Ilium is suddenly full of
machines that have stopped functioning. The human wave hits the
railway station, where, on a mosaic floor depicting "an earlier slaughter of Iliumites by Oneida Indians" (292), a crowd gathers

as though a great wonder were in their midst...the center of
attention was an Orange-O machine...no one in the whole country, apparently, could stomach the stuff—no one save Doctor Francis Eldrin Gelhorne.... But now the excretor of the blended wood
pulp, dye, water, and orange-type flavoring was as popular as a
nymphomaniac at an American Legion convention. (292)

The Orange-O machine is another sinister mechanical appropriator of
the Earthly Paradise genius's qualities. The crowd calls it "she," and
Vonnegut's simile leaves no doubts about its erotic attraction. It is, in
its fashion, nurturing and bountiful. Above all it inspires wonder.

Perhaps taking revenge for its sister, the insulation-braider, the Orange-O machine successfully ends the rebellion. The would-be Luddites trickle away from the crowd, sipping Orange-O and forgetting the Ghost Shirt manifesto:

> Man has survived ... to enter the Eden of eternal peace, only to discover that everything he had looked forward to enjoying there, pride, dignity, self-respect, work worth doing, has been condemned as unfit for human consumption. (260)

The Earthly Paradise will belong to the machines as long as the Ilians queue up for a drink that only their CEO can digest. In the disenchanted world, Vonnegut tells us, human beings themselves cannot tell what is fit for their souls' consumption.

Ideologies of Man-made Wonder

Science fiction, because it has the structure of utopia, tows the utopian ideological line. You'll recall that the utopian heterocosm is the garden without the lady, a man-made nature that excludes the Earthly Paradise genius. Even before taking into account science fiction's special themes, we can see that utopia has an ideological orientation in favor of technology. This is so partly because of utopia's historical connection to the Scientific Revolution, which I have discussed, and partly because of utopia's inherent logic. Jacques Ellul, an important critic of technology in culture, observes that "all utopians of the past, without a single exception, have presented society exactly as a megamachine."[41] Whether we take utopia in its literary sense or in its social one, it means a system of rules for the smooth, seamless functioning of an artificial world. What science fiction inherits from utopia is *an ideological commitment, structurally created,* to keeping the lady out of the garden. Technical reason, not nature's spirit, must be the principle of (hetero)cosmic order.

Now, along with utopian ideology, science fiction has many conventional themes and devices that encapsulate the ideology of progress. A technological utopia can spend three hundred pages justifying the need for space colonies, for example, but a science fiction novel takes the reader's assent for granted, even if it is a limited assent. The instant that we agree to enjoy the images of Colony, Frontier, Space, and so on, we swallow an ideological vitamin capsule, loaded with assumptions. (This process is treated further in chap. 3.) Samuel Delany gives a funny example in explaining how science fiction compels its readers to make assumptions: suppose you were reading a science fiction novel and came across a winged dog. If you believed that what you were reading was only fantasy, then the most you would have to do is imagine wings on a dog, "merely a visual correction." For science fiction, however, as you make that "visual correction," you "must... consider... an entire track of evolution: whether the dog had forelegs or not... or if... grafting was the cause, there are all the implications... of a technology capable of such an operation."[42] You must assume a background of scientific and technological meanings. This assumption amounts to adopting an ideological stance. Things make sense, according to the novel's ideology, when they are rationalized, and the marvelous only points conspicuously to the rational. The flight of fancy, whether taken by Pegasus or by Spot, is meaningless, but flight in its technical aspect is another story.

American science fiction's most striking ideological commitment is to the technological enterprise. Many science fiction readers and writers believe, with some justification, that science fiction and technological progress go hand in hand. There are many instances of this attitude. My favorite is Robert Heinlein's advertisement for the L-5 Society, in a 1979 anthology of stories and articles about outer space: "If science fiction is simply fun to you, skip this. But if you believe as I do that our race can and will and *must* spread out into space, stick around."[43] Heinlein means that science fiction isn't just entertainment: it *is* the L-5 colony. Donald Wollheim, speaking of Apollo 11, puts science fiction on the same footing as NASA: "Science fiction and its followers can truly claim the right to say that we started it and we pushed it through."[44] Science fiction sometimes appears to back off from technology. Cyberpunk, which features brain-computer interface technologies, also specializes in high-tech social squalor and depressing futuristic cityscapes. Yet in Bruce Sterling's introduction to a major cyberpunk anthology, we read that cyberpunk writers use "objectivity... a coldly objective analysis, a technique borrowed from science, then put to literary use."[45] Just as earlier science fiction was compared to experimental laboratories, so cyberpunk is really scientific method between the lines. Machinery may lose its gleam, but science fiction is still a branch of the technological enterprise.

If it were possible to sum up science fiction's ideologies from a single story, I would choose this vignette. A group of people attends a funeral on their pioneering space station. When the preacher reads, "We brought nothing into this world," the stationers grow upset. On the contrary, they protest: "We had built this world ourselves.... We had brought *everything* into this world."[46] A comic but inevitable mis-understanding. What the liturgy means is that our births and deaths are mysteries, beyond the limited grasp of human understanding and will. All we have at the end of life is the knowledge that there was life. The statement is metaphysical. But to the stationers, the heterocosm builders, the space station is *everything* in the world—it is nature's replacement—and it is the world of every manufactured *thing*. The whole is the exact sum of its hardware parts, life is the instrumental process of getting the job done, and there are no mysteries. This is the disenchanted world of our technological society. It is in the terms of this world, not by "getting back to nature" or pulling plugs, that science fiction tries to appropriate nature's magic and to manufacture wonder.

On the Alien, the Other, and Wonder

> What writers are after here is what the fans call "sense of wonder"—an indefinable rush when beholding something odd and new and perhaps a bit awesome.[47]

Let's try to define that rush, which Gregory Benford, speaking here on the subject of aliens, makes the goal of science fiction writers like himself. We know that aliens and the future are part of it—"the strange, the exotic and unfathomable nature of the future,"[48] as Benford says. Strangeness, then, is the intoxicant. But does science fiction really show us what is strange and different? Current literary theory rejects the notion that we can represent what is truly Other, alien from us. At best we can make textual gestures toward strangeness, or signs that represent the idea of strangeness. We cannot directly portray "the alien in its radical otherness."[49] The Other can be indicated but not told: the essence of the alien is that language can render only our surface contact with it, exactly like the five blind men and the elephant. Literature can, indirectly, give a sense of otherness. Take this passage from the chapter "The Tail" in *Moby Dick:*

> The more I consider this mighty tail, the more do I deplore my inability to express it. At times there are gestures in it, which...remain wholly inexplicable....Nor are there wanting other motions of the whale in his general body, full of strange-ness....Dissect him how I may, then, I go but skin deep; I know him not, and never will. But if I know not even the tail of this whale...how comprehend his face, when face he has none?[50]

The literary sense of otherness has to happen in the context of the familiar. In this case several preceding chapters have described the whale, with five pages on the tail alone, so that by now we know all we're going to know about cetacean anatomy. In the context of our expert knowledge, inexplicable motions of the tail are disturbing and suggest something truly alien. The problem of language and the alien is neatly posed: Does the whale have a face? Any answer will reveal our own linguistic and cultural definitions of "face," while the whale eludes us, unknowable on our terms. Again, the sense of strangeness must occur in a familiar context; you miss the point of the question if you have never seen a whale's head. Otherness is not the same as arbitrary monstrosity. It is a gap in the fabric of the familiar, given meaning by what surrounds it. The human Other is someone whose meanings make gaps in our own. So, for example, Thoreau conveys the otherness of the Native American craftsman in *Walden* who protests when a white lawyer will not buy his baskets:

> "What!...do you mean to starve us?"...Thinking that when he made the baskets he would have done his part, and then it would be the white man's to buy them.[51]

The craftsman's indignant response to a buyer's market is a gap resonant with meaning. It suggests a different economy, a diffcrent view altogether of life's balances. But for us to experience a true sense of otherness from his words, rather than dismiss them as nonsense, they must occur within the familiar context of colonial history (which Thoreau supplies).

Science fiction's sense of wonder cannot possibly stem from such a literary encounter with the Other. The technique that I have just described is off the genre's limits, for structural reasons. In fact, I would argue that *science fiction denies the possibility of otherness.* The utopian heterocosm deliberately excludes the familiar contexts of reality, such as history. It is a pseudoreality, a game, with automatically limited depth. Let me put it another way. Samuel Delany's winged poodle is not a gap in the familiar context but, rather, a product of the heterocosm's artificial evolutionary theory, the rules of the game. Any element in the game points to its rules, and that is its whole meaning. We don't get a sense of otherness, for example, from a strange creature like Pac Man. We know what he's about.

Robert Silverberg's story "Schwartz between the Galaxies" demonstrates how science fiction, looking for the alien, denies the possibility of otherness. Schwartz, a frustrated anthropologist, lives in science fiction fantasies about interstellar travel because cultural difference has disappeared from Earth:

> You visit the Zuni and they have plastic African masks on the wall. You visit the Bushmen and they have Japanese-made Hopi-motif ashtrays. It's all just so much interior decoration, . . . and underneath there's the same universal pseudo-American sensibility, whether you're in the Kalahari or the Amazon rain forest.

Science fiction is the only way out, Schwartz insists.

> Only one planet . . . one small and crowded planet, on which all cultures converge to a drab and depressing sameness. . . . Look to the stars. . . . Speculate with me on other ways, other peoples, other gods.[52]

The idea that technology will eventually homogenize, Westernize, or Americanize all cultures is an accepted part of the critique of industrial society.[53] Schwartz's problem, however, is in his own head. He cannot recognize cultural otherness that is not part of the decor. His frustration is that of the tourist who demands what looks different because he or she has no time to learn what is different. By seeing only universal technological culture, Schwartz really champions the ideology of the heterocosm. Fleeing "interior decoration," all he can do is to re-create it; he cannot step outside the ideology's projected man-made interiors. Generally, science fiction tends to cultural myopia, representing other peoples by their American stereotypes: vodka-swilling Russians, xenophobic Japanese, romantic Spaniards, patient Chinese. The cultures treated most seriously in science fiction are invented ones. This myopia is a telling symptom of science fiction's structural, and inherently ideological, denial of the Other.

What creates the rush of wonder, then, if not an experience of otherness? It's tempting to dismiss Benford's rush as a superficial response to exoticism, but such a cavalier dismissal hardly does it justice. At a deeper level the sense of wonder is the appropriate, culturally constructed response to science fiction's mythology. We experience wonder in the presence of the numinous. In science fiction what inspires wonder is the appropriated magic of the Earthly Paradise.

The Alienated Earthly Paradise of Science Fiction

In a short story by Isaac Asimov, "Misbegotten Missionary," a space-ship crew is placed in desperate peril by aliens who have nothing but good intentions. The alien planet displays the chief characteristics of the Earthly Paradise. Besides being entirely covered in pleasant green vegetation, the planet lacks carnivores, gives no evidence of biological competition for survival, and possesses no technology. The aliens, who are telepathic, share one vast, happy consciousness. They have no concept of the individual. When they come into contact with the crew's separate minds, they feel shock and pity. They say to themselves—or to their Self—with some astuteness, that human beings

> strove to find in the control of inanimate matter what they could not find in themselves. In their unconscious yearning for comple-tion, they built machines and scoured space.[54]

The aliens decide to absorb the pitiful human beings into their harmo-nious organic unity. They send the "misbegotten missionary," a small caterpillar, to contaminate the spaceship with a substance that causes parthenogenesis in females; parthenogenesis, here, is a figure for the magical fertility of the Earthly Paradise. The ship's laboratory animals give birth to offspring that have fuzzy green spots instead of eyes and communicate telepathically, through their green spots, with the alien consciousness. Let's consider this metamorphosis of the eye. From Galileo's telescope to the electron microscope, the eye is both a part of scientific observation, and the sense organ symbolically associated with science.[55] In Asimov's story alien contamination transforms the eye into a cross between grass and fur, an image suggesting the inti-mate sense of touch, the animal, and the vegetative. The fuzzy green former eye also becomes the point of connection between members of the great organic whole. We can say, using metonymy, that the labora-tory has been reabsorbed into the Earthly Paradise garden.

What does this deformed version of the nature myth mean? In the spirit of the cold war Asimov interprets his story as a parable of Ameri-can individualism, but underlying his treatment of the social organism is the problem of human relationship with nature. Consider the aliens' psychological diagnosis of the human beings: the human spacemen strive to control inanimate matter, to make up for something missing in themselves. This is a description, in a nutshell, of our modern human relationship with the dead, inanimate nature bequeathed to us by the

Scientific Revolution. We strive to control inanimate matter by techno-logical means, and we're missing something—the sense of wonder, the enchantment of the garden. Our scientific knowledge and technologi-cal power come at the price of the death of nature and chronic spiritual hunger. The aliens propose to give us back what we're missing. *What if Mother Nature came back to life?* What if we could return to the enchanted garden? This possibility takes the form not of a promise but of a threat. Asimov's story transforms the enchanted garden of the Earthly Paradise into an alienated, monstrous nature, a familiar fan-tasy of green, invasive aliens. The story expresses a fear of inanimate nature coming back to life and of our reunion with Mother Nature.

This fear has a history. It originated in the Scientific Revolution, eventually to become a mass nightmare in our modern culture. I come to my interpretation of science fiction's imagery by way of the work of Susan Bordo, a philosopher who writes about Descartes's *Medita-tions.* By applying psychoanalytic theory to Descartes's work, Bordo finds that his philosophy reacts in very specific ways to a profound change in the psychology of Western culture. Taking her clues from history and psychology, Bordo writes the "psychocultural story" that framed the writing of the *Meditations:*

> That narrative framework, as I develop it . . . is a "drama of parturi-tion": cultural birth out of the mother-world of the Middle Ages and Renaissance, and creation of another world—the modern.[56]

Descartes was reacting to the great shift from the view of nature as maternal being to nature as dead, inanimate matter. The death of nature affected Western culture on many levels, psychological as well as ideological. Compensating for separation from the benevolent "mother-world" of the nature myth, Western culture, the newborn "child," adopted an aggressive individuality. The concept of inanimate matter was part of the compensation mechanism. Simply, it allows us to deny that nature was ever alive. In addition, while Mother Nature had a will of her own, inanimate objects have no such inscrutable inner life, so that separation from the mother-world was rewarded by the possibility of scientific knowledge and control. Bordo's psychological analysis of Descartes's dead mechanistic cosmos is subtle and brilliant:

> "She" [maternal nature] becomes "it"—and "it" can be understood and controlled . . . by virtue of the very *object*-ivity of the "it." At the same time, the wound of separateness is healed through the

> denial that there ever "was" any union: For the mechanists, . . . the
> female world-soul did not die; rather the world *is* dead. There is
> nothing to mourn, nothing to lament.

Once the mechanical philosophy is established, cultural anxiety fo-
cuses on keeping nature safely dead! In my terms, we are anxious to
keep the lady out of the garden. The suggestion of a reunion with
Mother Nature becomes a threat to the very foundations of knowledge,
since scientific objectivity depends on treating nature as objects. Any
memories or feelings that interfere with objectivity are dangerous.

> Indeed, the "new" epistemological anxiety is evoked, not over loss,
> but by the "memory" or suggestion of *union;* "sympathetic," asso-
> ciational, or bodily response obscures objectivity, feeling for na-
> ture muddies the clear lake of the mind.[57]

Descartes's philosophy created a new human identity. This human
identity is the subject of the famous statement *"cogito, ergo sum"* (I
think, therefore I am). We can call the new human identity "the Cartesian subject." The Cartesian subject's existence is based on the division
between itself and the objects of its thought. The subject is pure mind,
nonmaterial; the rest of the world is made up of dead, mindless matter
(which Descartes called *res extensa*). The rules of Descartes's world say
that subject and object must be distinct entities. They cannot merge.
If they merge at all, if subjects start getting more material, and objects
begin to think, the whole thing is no good. Mind and body are separate: mind is the subject, body is *res extensa,* an object. There is the
human I and the nonhuman It. Logically, this also means that the
human subject cannot be a part of nature, because nature is inanimate
matter. Nature is It. One of the most frightening moments in any
science fiction tale is when the boundary of the Cartesian subject
becomes blurred—when the human I and the inhuman It begin to
merge. Haunted by the lost magic of the mother-world, science fiction
imagines the possibility of nature's reanimating herself, challenging
our dominion over dead matter. What if It suddenly turns back into
She? Side by side with that magical possibility comes the dreaded
blurring of the line between subject and object, and the loss of modern
human identity.

In Asimov's story the alien planet is the Earthly Paradise garden,
the lost mother-world of animate nature. It is a world of complete
union between maternal nature and her children, a world blessed with

the Earthly Paradise qualities of love, harmony, and fertility. Yet these qualities of the Earthly Paradise now belong to the alien. They're not paradisiacal anymore; they're creepy. Reunion with the mother-world is menacing, because animate nature, having a mind of its own, threatens to blur the Cartesian boundary between subject and object. The blurring of the Cartesian subject's boundaries produces monsters, horrible hybrids of I and It. No matter how much we may hunger for the lost enchantment of the mother-world, the possibility of being reabsorbed into Mother Nature is terrifying. It threatens us with losing our human identity. The suggestion that nature has come back to life menaces the pure, detached, Cartesian subject, the human self so painfully born in the denial of the mother-world.

"Misbegotten Missionary" tell us that humanity exists in a state of permanent cold war with nature; we depend for our identity on boundary control. In this situation the only good nature is dead nature. Technology becomes essential to the end of keeping nature safely dead. Back on the spaceship, the arrival of fuzzy, green-spotted telepathic hamsters has gotten everyone depressed. One crew woman is parthenogenetically pregnant, or so she says, and nobody wants to think about that. Meanwhile, the missionary caterpillar disguises itself as a piece of wire in the ship's engine. No sooner are the engines activated than the alien burns up, leaving a little gap of ash. Technology restores control over human boundaries—symbolized by the crucial gap in the wire—and makes nature safely dead again. In the modern era the spaceship is a more "natural" environment for human beings than the garden. Periodically purging itself of nature's crawly invasions, the technological environment is home, where normal matter is mechanical and one can relax.

"Misbegotten Missionary" shows us how science fiction transforms the Earthly Paradise into the alienated Earthly Paradise, nature into alienated nature. The myth's transformation occurs when science fiction attempts to manufacture wonder, to appropriate the magic of the Earthly Paradise, by creating images of the strange and wonderful. Science fiction's marvels are images of the nature myth, which, evoked in the context of the utopian heterocosm, raise the specter of nature's reanimation and the loss of human identity. Over and over science fiction reenacts the parturition drama: the death of nature and the birth of the modern technological world. Science fiction readers experience a "rush of wonder" triggered, sadly enough, by images of the *alienated* Earthly Paradise and breath a sigh of relief when the source of wonder inevitably submits to de-animation. (As we shall see, this happens even in science fiction written with a conscious intent to challenge the prevailing ideology.)

Alienated Nature is Feminine, Fertile, and Monstrous

What about that pregnant crew woman? Pregnancy gone awry is a main theme of the story, as its title suggests. The reader may already have deduced that the Cartesian schema works better for men than for women, best of all for people without bodies. The body is an object, not a subject. As Bordo notes, bodily response threatens to muddy "the clear lake of the mind." That's problematic enough. But how is it possible clearly to demarcate the boundaries of subject and object in a pregnancy? The lack of any satisfactory answer to this question would be enough to account for one of science fiction's stock plots, which Joanna Russ has called "The Weird-Ways-of-Getting-Pregnant Story."[58] Pregnancy is monstrous in science fiction because it threatens human control of the boundary with nature. "Weird" pregnancy expresses the fear of nature's re-animation.

Monstrous pregnancy is also the image of a strong cultural anxiety about fertility. We noted that parthenogenesis represented the Earthly Paradise's fertility, in alienated form. Nature's generative power is the source of wonder and nightmare. Like the fear of blurred boundaries, this fear has a history, too. Descartes's philosophy was written in an era obsessed with "the untamed natural power of female generativity, and a dedication to bringing it under forceful cultural control." The witch, as Bordo and Merchant tell us, was the central figure in the period's "nightmare fantasies of female power over reproduction and birth." Scientific writings project onto nature the image of the wild, sexually insatiable witch. Francis Bacon accuses matter itself, or rather "her"self, of being "a 'common harlot' with 'an appetite and inclination to dissolve the world and fall back into the old chaos.' "[59] The Scientific Revolution passed through a stage of unrationalized misogyny, demonizing feminine nature on the way to de-animating matter. Grotesque images associating generativity with the monstrous—and with the feminine—survive in science fiction's alienated nature. A womb of her own, as well as a mind, makes Mother Nature a menace, an alien Bug-Eyed Monster (BEM) lusting to dissolve the modern technological world and its human masters. It should scarcely be surprising, when alienated nature is feminine and monstrous, that women and pregnancy are problematic.

The horrific fantasies of seventeenth-century witch-hunters reappear with secular cool in the movies *Alien* and *Aliens*. In these films an alien species uses the bodies of living human beings to gestate its young. Even before the BEM enters *Alien* we're alerted to the problem. Let's sit back and watch the first scene. Slowly emerging from clear, egg-shaped containers, the crew of the spaceship *Nostromo* revives from suspended animation. As the containers open in a dead hush, we're reminded of coffins in a vampire's vault. We sense that where there are eggs, there's going to be trouble. Now the crewmen discover that they haven't arrived at Earth but were revived automatically in response to a summons from a nearby planet, one of those mysterious, seductive, come-hither signals that are the fairy music of outer space. Interesting! Like Columbus nearing the Earthly Paradise, they expected to return to humanity's birthplace. Where have they gone instead? Upon landing, the exploration crew enters what at first appears to be a cavern. It is the cavernous interior of an abandoned spaceship, which, in contrast to the sleek *Nostromo,* has a disturbingly organic, cartilagenous look. There they discover a cache of giant alien eggs, bathed in the purple light of a numinous force (I think of Eden's angel with the flaming sword, whom Columbus feared to encounter). A crewman plunges through the force barrier. Ignoring our uh-ohs, he tampers with a fuzzy, pulsing egg, which opens like a sectioned fig, oozing mucus and all but reciting Freud's remarks on the uncanniness of the female genitalia. Then a thing, a skeletal hand, flies out of the egg and, smashing the helmet's glass, melds itself onto the crewman's face. The other human faces are protected by bubble helmets, like personal observatories, but this victim has suffered the first slap in the face to the Cartesian subject. Later, after the bony hand-thing vanishes and the victim recovers, he is sitting at the mess table, strangely hungry. Suddenly he goes into spasms, bellowing with agony, and out of his belly bursts a snake-headed, fully formed alien. It gives one businesslike screech and promptly embarks on the "harlot" matter's career of voracity until the world of the spaceship is dissolved, literally blown to atoms by the crew woman Ripley, who hits the spaceship's self-destruct button after everyone else on board has been devoured. How can modern humanity be born from demonized, alienated Mother Earth? This is the problem that the sequel, *Aliens,* tries to solve.

In *Aliens* the problem is explicitly represented by women and mothers. The heroine Ripley, who witnessed the crewman's "delivery," dreams that the same thing happens to her. Ripley's nightmare "pregnancy" appears more like a normal one, because she is female and lying on a hospital bed. She tears the bedclothes from her bare abdomen, which juts outward as if at full term, before the alien explodes from inside. In both movies the "delivery" scenes play rather like a fearful child's misinformed notion of what pregnancy and childbirth are like. They suggest an area of cultural imagination that has been detached from life and stunted. Recalling Christa Wolf's question "What immense fear insulates the star warriors against life?" I find a partial answer in these grotesque images. *Aliens* tries to find an alternative to natural generativity by pitting two very different kinds of maternity against each other. One mother is Ripley; the other is her enemy, the alien.

Sole survivor of the *Alien* ship, Ripley has to fight the marauding monsters again. This time she also saves the life of an orphan child, Newt. Ripley acts maternally toward Newt, tucking her into bed, soothing her nightmares away, and promising to protect her. But Newt is not Ripley's biological daughter. In fact, Newt *chooses* to be mothered after an initial period of withdrawal, entering the relationship from a position of control. The problem of natural fertility does not arise. Better yet, Newt keeps Ripley ideologically sound. During a bedtime conversation Ripley picks up Newt's baby doll and tells the child not to have nightmares; after all, Dolly doesn't. Correcting Ripley's motherly attempt to animate matter, Newt replies in a let's-get-this-straight manner that Dolly doesn't have nightmares because "she's just a piece of plastic." Yet Newt's worldview has been shaken. Why, she asks, do grownups say that monsters don't exist, when they do? "It's usually true," Ripley answers, with sterling precision. The rarity of monsters is not geographical but epistemological. They don't exist in the universe of inanimate matter. The relationship between Newt and Ripley defines one kind of maternity, in which the Cartesian boundaries are firmly fixed against maternal nature.

The second kind *is* maternal nature. In the film's final sequences Ripley rescues Newt from the monster's egg-laying grounds. There is a moment of science fictional wonder, as Newt and Ripley gaze upon the rows of alien eggs, then Ripley torches them, with the same Promethean technological fire that purges Asimov's spaceship. At this point something interesting happens. The huge, dragonlike alien lunges at Ripley in ferocious counterattacks. But we're convinced, despite the alien's repellent appearance, that she's an enraged mother instead of a wild beast. Lest we miss the point, Ripley yells, "You bitch!" Besides telling us that the alien is a big bad mother, the epithet also lets us identify with Ripley as the antagonist of feminine nature, even though Ripley herself is a woman.

Mama Alien, seeking revenge for her brood, pursues Ripley and Newt on board the spaceship. Ripley steps into a mechanical exoskeleton, a "loading machine," that encases her in metal and gives her superhuman strength. She manages to grab the alien and eject her through the airlock. Battling in steel armor against the alien's thrashing scaly body, Ripley resembles Saint George the dragon fighter, in all but one important respect. Ripley's only weapon is her own body, *technologically redefined*. She uses the mechanical body-object, which is her "birthright," as a Cartesian subject. Her victory over the alien reasserts technology's control of nature and natural generativity. Her own female body is no more than a source of mechanical energy, safely locked into the mobile machine. The body of maternal nature is ejected from the man-made world of the spaceship. Under these conditions— female body controlled by technology, maternal feeling kept within Cartesian boundaries, maternal nature safely expelled from the inanimate world—humanity can reproduce itself. The mechanized environment of the spaceship must replace the fertile gardens of Mother Earth.

The images of science fiction's alienated Earthly Paradise, as they appear in the stories I have just discussed, are fairly typical. Nature's animate, feminine, numinous qualities are alienated, literally turned into the alien who inspires the "rush" of manufactured wonder. The Earthly Paradise's remoteness becomes that of alien planets or distant times, while the ideal of love and harmony becomes the menace of reunion with Mother Nature. Nature's generativity sprouts scales and tentacles and fosters an inclination to dissolve the world into chaos. More important than the consistency of alienated nature's images, however, is the cause of their consistency. Science fiction continually reenacts the "drama of cultural parturition," the loss of the mother-world and emergence of the modern world. The images of the alienated Earthly Paradise impress upon us how deeply our culture continues to be affected by the historical shift in our view of nature.

Science Fiction's Fundamental Ambivalence

As I have mentioned, this book is not an anatomy of science fiction. Its purpose is not to predict all possible plots and images. What the images of alienated nature show, if anything, is science fiction's thematic instability. Science fiction is fundamentally *ambivalent* toward the psychocultural drama that it reenacts. On the one hand, it wants to reawaken wonder in the disenchanted world and, to this end, imagines nature coming back to life. On the other hand, it is ideologically committed to nature's death and replacement with the technological heterocosm. As a result, the images of alienated nature change nuances of meaning easily, sometimes from one sentence to another (see chap. 4). The pattern of these changes, in each story, is like an ideological stress map.

We can now identify the anxieties in George R. R. Martin's story "Sandkings." The protagonist buys some aliens, sandkings, for terrarium pets. They look like small beetles, but they are mobile, telepathic extensions of a single female creature, who gives birth to them, predigests their food, and endows them with sentience. The sandkings erect a tiny medieval castle over their queen, whom the pet seller calls the "maw": "A pun . . . the thing is mother and stomach both." She looks like "a mottled, half-spoiled chunk of raw meat. With a mouth."[60] The maw is an alienated Earthly Paradise genius. She has the qualities, in alienated form, of fertility and genital eroticism; she also supplies her brood with abundance and social harmony. Her world resembles a romance setting, as the sandkings construct a kind of miniature Middle Ages in the terrarium. They hold court, stage tournaments, and decorate their towers with mosaic portraits of the protagonist, whom they think is God. Clearly, we may expect a battle over reabsorption into the prescientific mother-world. But God's replacement, Man the heterocosm-builder, is far worse than alienated nature. The protagonist is a nature-hating sadist. He slaughters his alien pets in exotic cockfights, tortures a puppy, and murders his ecologically aware ex-girlfriend. He mistreats the sandkings so badly that we feel sympathetic when their portraits of the human god become unflattering. When they escape from the terrarium and gobble up the villain, we're inclined to think that God is on "Maw Nature's" side. The story of the sandkings bringing their human owner to justice is a representative example of thematic instability, caused by ambivalence. Although Earthly Paradise nature is alienated and monstrous, it still exerts numinous authority, in contrast to humanity's merely technical transcendence.

The Alienation of Love

In Damon Knight's classic novella "Stranger Station" a new anxiety accompanies the figure of the alien. Once every twenty years a member of an alien species comes to a human space station and spends a few months in solitary confinement, during which it sits dripping a golden exudate into vats. The fluid prolongs human life. For no known reason, the aliens have been providing it voluntarily. During each alien's visit one man must occupy "Stranger Station." The hero, Wesson, takes this post determined to find out why the aliens donate their elixir and why all the previous stationmen went insane.

As Wesson explores the station, the alien's imminent approach inspires him with terror of space itself. Alone, treading a catwalk through the station's unlit, airless cavity, he "had the appalling sense of something so huge that it had no limits at all, descending, with a terrible endless swift slowness. . . . The alien was coming . . . he seemed to himself like a tiny insect."[61] Space is an alien vastness that can only be named by "a meaningless number, a cry of dismay, 0,0,0. . . . " Taking a not-so-inevitable step, Wesson grapples with the fear of space by splitting the universe into two opposable halves: "Here . . . was the outermost limit of man's empire: here the Outside funneled down to meet it . . . the two worlds came near enough to touch. Ours—and Theirs." Now the alien embodies the previously formless threat of space.

Wesson's anxiety is of a different order than the others that we have identified. The mother-world has vanished. The new world, an indifferent, alien emptiness, overwhelms him with the sense of his own isolation and helplessness.[62] Although "cultural parturition" has been accomplished, a new drama ensues, a struggle that Bordo describes in her commentary on Pascal's *Pensées*:

> If the impersonal, arbitrary universe of the early modern era is capable of physically "swallowing" him [Pascal], like a random bit of ontological debris, *he* is nonetheless capable of containing and subduing it—through comprehension, through the "grasp" of the mind.[63]

It is a case of Inside versus Outside, man's mind versus the universe, swallow or be swallowed. Wesson fights for the human empire, for "our" world, by mentally conquering "theirs." Stranger Station is a battle post, and scientific knowledge is Wesson's weapon. His need to comprehend the alien is extreme. As he tells his artificial intelligence companion, "*We'll die* unless we can find out what makes those aliens tick!" On the face of it this is a curious thing to say about beings who have given humanity the gift of lengthened life. A gift, however, creates and acknowledges bonds of feeling and interdependence;[64] the

giving and the receiving of gifts takes place between emotionally connected subjects.

Proper scientific "grasp" of the alien precludes any emotional
bond; objectivity requires that subjects and objects remain distinct.
The alien must be treated as an object if its behavior is to be scientifically understood and controlled. Wesson must reduce the alien to a
ticking clock, a part of the mechanized material universe; otherwise,
humanity will continue trusting the aliens to donate the elixir, and
such a bond of trust threatens the foundations of "our" empire. During
the next stage of the encounter Wesson fights the alien's telepathic
pressure to communicate. Visions of the alien's body remind Wesson
of "all the loathsome, crawling, creeping things the Earth was full of,"
as well as "the recurrent nightmare of Wesson's childhood," a trick
played one Halloween, when he was blindfolded and made to touch
some unidentifiable soggy thing. Wesson's obsession with creepy creatures suggests a historically earlier figure of a disorderly and demonic
nature. The chaos-spreading witch seems to lurk behind images of
earth's ugly spawn, and behind the Halloween trick's horror, almost a
horror of matter itself. Pitted against the impersonal modern universe,
Wesson has regressed to the Baconian demonizing that preceeded, and
justified, the death of nature. This Baconian view accounts for Wesson's scientific aggressivity: "In Bacon, most dramatically—the dream
of knowledge is ... imagined as an explicit revenge fantasy, an attempt
to wrest back control from nature."[65] "I'm *the stronger,*" Wesson mut-
ters at his computer.

Finally, the alien mind contacts his own, in a moment of erotic
communion, "a piercing sweetness ... a melting, dissolving luxury.... A pull, a calling." Through the breached boundary Wesson
learns the alien's secret. The elixir causes an intermingling of human
and alien minds. The aliens provide it so that, when human beings
enter space, the two species will be able to live together in harmony.
All the previous stationmen appeared insane because communication
with the alien transformed them. Wesson, appalled, launches into a
furious soliloquoy, the last line of which reverberates through the
whole story:

> The two minds, the human and alien, they stop fighting each
> other ... the bleary men ... come out of here not even able to talk
> human language any more. Oh, I suppose they're happy—happier
> than I am!—because they've got something big and wonderful
> inside 'em.... When we start expanding out to the stars—when

we go a-conquering—we'll have already been conquered! Not by weapons ... by love! Yes, love! *Dirty, stinking, low-down, sneaking love!*

A seduction has occurred. Immediately afterward the threat of losing human identity is conveyed by the familiar telepathic alien. Our suspicions are confirmed when Wesson measures the harvested elixir, checking the amount in the storage vats on "golden indicators," gold being the color of the Golden Age. The storage vats are "brimming, *gravid,* a month before the time. Wesson shuddered" (my emphasis). You may already have reached the conclusion that I will spell out. The alien's elixir, a once-per-generation gift of life, is a figure for nature's generative power, with the "gravid," shudderable-at vats suggesting monstrous pregnancy. The alien's seductiveness and harmonizing influence pose the threat of absorption into the reanimated mother-world. In other words, Wesson's friend is the alienated Earthly Paradise genius. But here the story parts ways with our previous tales.

Wesson kills the alien by answering its telepathic contact with hatred. He hopes that his murder will stop the aliens' visits; humanity, deprived of the elixir, will hate the aliens and, upon entering space, will eradicate them. Withering in the mental blast of Wesson's hate, the dying alien thinks, "*We might have been brothers.*" Why does Wesson choose this recondite murder weapon, instead of doing the usual thing with a blowtorch? Until now the defense against boundary-threatening nature was technology. "Stranger Station" is different because its greatest anxiety is not about keeping nature safely dead but, instead, about keeping modern humanity sane. Obviously, the "postpartum" universe is emotionally intolerable. The main reason for the alien's first appearance, it seems, was to give the dark, cold, maddening void a shape, called Inside versus Outside. This is the Cartesian schema: inside, the mind of man; outside, all the other stuff. But the alien offers us a different possibility. Humanity can acknowledge bonds of trust and dependence with the natural universe, which may be beyond our total comprehension but which overflows with life, including our own. Such a choice would mean breaching the boundary between Inside and Outside, mind and matter, subject and object. It would mean abandoning the philosophical basis of scientific objectivity and technological power. Since this is out of the question, love, the great temptation in the impersonal, disenchanted universe, must be alienated. Love becomes "dirty, stinking, low-down, sneaking"; the brotherhood of the Golden Age is the target of strategic hatred. Permanent cold war between humanity and the alien—whoever or whatever it may be—resolves the crisis of nature's death. Hate is the Dutch courage of the postpartum world.

What happens when a science fiction writer, aware of the genre's ideological commitments, decides to change them? Ursula Le Guin has written several novels dealing with the choice between love and hate of the Other, the alien. Her short story "Vaster than Empires and More Slow" is an example of writing science fiction against the heterocosm's ideological grain. The title, a phrase by the poet Andrew Marvell, describes a slowly growing "vegetable love," which death fails to interrupt. Le Guin literalizes this image. Her story continues the great tradition of green, telepathic garden planets thinking peaceful green thoughts—until the spaceship lands.

Le Guin's garden planet has never encountered another mind before. Confronted with the spaceship crew's otherness, it panics and begins broadcasting waves of terror. Unlike our other telepathic aliens, however, this one is far from monstrous. The hero, an empath named Osden, calls the alien mind: "Awareness of being, without subject or object. Nirvana."[66] Osden seeks mental communion with the planet to calm it down. While Wesson's mind contact was a threatening breach, Osden's union with nature actually gives him integrity:

> He had given up his self to the alien, an unreserved surrender, that left no room for evil. He had learned the love of the Other, and thereby had been given his whole self.

This attitude seems the very opposite of alienated "dirty love," but, despite the good intentions, Osden's love is a mirror image of Wesson's hate. The reason for Osden's volunteering to love the alien Other is that he can't stand human beings.

We have seen in "Stranger Station" how love is considered treacherous and contaminating, because the modern subject must remain untouched by the objects it controls. Evelyn Fox Keller gives the name "masculinism" to the scientific taboo on sympathetic feeling. In her view modern science requires an "epistemological stance" that places prime value on the "radical rejection of any commingling of subject and object."[67] Osden is an object lesson (no pun) in the masculinist stance.

The empath belongs to a team of exploring scientists. His role is "Sensor," and his appearance symbolizes the misery of this function.

An albino, he looks "naked" and "flayed," like "an anatomy lesson." The feelings that he must continually sense so endanger his boundaries that he resembles, instead of a properly self-contained subject, a displayed object. When a colleague asks him the interesting question "What is human feeling?" Osden answers, "Animal excrement." In this concise reply there are familiar resonances. *Animal* implies that feeling is nature's breach of human integrity (otherwise, *animal* would not be derogatory). *Excrement* puts feeling in the category of "dirty, stinking love," and the typical slime of the Bug-Eyed Monster. We do not wonder that Osden prefers absorption into a nice clean lettuce. He is not, however, ultimately reconciled with the Other. Settling alone on the garden planet, Osden enters an undifferentiated union that amounts to tranquil detachment, not erotic communion. His bachelor paradise is what Marvell, in another poem, called the "happy garden-State / while man there walked without a mate."[68] Human feeling, the threat to masculinism, is the real alien of this evasive tale. Although the story calls for a bond of empathy with the Other and with nature, it breaks its own promise.

Conclusion to Man-made Wonder

Most readers would probably say that the goal of science fiction is to integrate technology with the life of the imagination, a claim that is superficially true. This chapter should have made clear the limit of such an integration. Because of science fiction's commitment to the ideologies that produced modern science and technology, and because this commitment is built into its very structure, there are idols that it cannot break, ideas and attitudes that it cannot subvert. Perpetually invoking the myth of nature in order to alienate it, science fiction promotes the dichotomy of subject and object as well as, to quote Josette Féral, "a type of political economy which spares itself the burden of taking difference into consideration."[69] Science fiction nurtures a hostile cultural attitude toward nature and the Other. Yet, within its limits as philosophical romance,[70] it plays wittily with the idea of our technological being.

The stories and films analyzed in this chapter show three persistent fears that we owe to the changes in our view of nature wrought by the Scientific Revolution. The fear of nature's reanimation is one; the fear of nature's and of women's generative powers is another; the fear of love, or empathy, is a third. Around this trio a cloud of anxiety takes different shapes depending on the unstable balance of the science fiction story. Each reenactment of psychocultural drama is based on the same situation, with varying nuances. The power of the reenactment is in a sense timeless, since the crisis of nature's death is embodied in mythic images. In another sense the genre's power is historical, because it draws on philosophical ideas and metaphors that are part of modern consciousness.

Science fiction is an addictive popular literature, as most of its fans will admit, with a loyal following that varies in its degrees of cultishness. Like chocolate bars, it feeds an appetite without stilling hunger. From the analyses presented here, I conclude that the addictive ingredient is man-made wonder, the promise of numinous nature without the fulfillment. The need for man-made wonder recalls Marcuse's description of false needs, the "products of a society whose dominant interest demands repression." Readers' craving for the "rush" of man-made wonder is a false need, the satisfaction of which gives only "euphoria in unhappiness,"[71] while actually reinforcing the condition of disenchantment. Although science fiction's liveliness comes from its reaction against a world without marvels, the "rush of wonder" may be possible only in a society that cannot afford awe.

Wonder: Made in USA

The Great American Paradise Machine

How the Earthly Paradise Myth Affects American Culture

I remember a trip that I took to Mono Lake in California, together with some Italian friends. We drove through Yosemite National Park, joking and arguing about what we would eat for dinner. One couple had just finished wishing that they could pick up *una buona mortadella* when we parked near the salt lake and stepped out into moonrise. Beyond a shore of tall, dry grasses the lake stretched shining pink, gulls and other waterfowl that paddled on its calm surface leaving trails of blue. All around the water rose gently contoured mountains, the near slopes a dense ash color and the ridges behind them fading to smoke but clearly outlined against the sky. In one saddle of the mountains a huge full moon sat, without any pollution to color it, and poured a solid white stripe across the pink water. I heard the rare sound of five Italians simultaneously struck speechless. After a while someone ventured to say, "In the ancient times, when the Indians were here, this must have been a very holy place."

All of Western culture is heir to the Earthly Paradise, the myth of a wondrous nature. Americans, however, have a very special connection with the myth because, in the minds of its "discoverers" and settlers, the continent of America was supposed to *be* the Earthly Paradise. Columbus was the first in a long line of European explorers and political thinkers who endowed the New World and its native peoples with the lost innocence and happiness of humanity in paradise. Today the American wilderness still creates a deep impression of freshness and grandeur, and its presence is a major theme in our literature. The hero of Fitzgerald's novel *The Great Gatsby,* a rich young speculator, exemplifies a type of American optimism that has its roots in the experience of a paradise found. Leo Marx calls Gatsby's "hopefulness" a national characteristic and explains how it derives from the Earthly Paradise myth:

> Gatsby's uncommon "gift for hope" was born in that transitory, enchanted moment when Europeans first came into the presence of the "fresh, green breast of the new world" [Fitzgerald's phrase]. We are reminded of Shakespeare's Gonzalo and Miranda, of Robert Beverley and Crèvecoeur and Jefferson: in America hopefulness has been incorporated in a style of life, a culture, a national character.[1]

The "fresh, green breast of a new world," the American coast as the European settlers saw it, has yet to fade from our collective memory. That first encounter with the New World, Fitzgerald wrote, was the only thing commensurate with man's "capacity for wonder." The experience of wonder at animate, feminine, enchanted nature—the American Earthly Paradise—has persisted in the national consciousness long after industrialization made return to the garden impossible.

The echo of wonder persists in a culture that believes in returning to the garden, not against the odds but against the facts. In his typically optimistic way, Jay Gatsby believes that history can be "fixed," made over as if it never happened. Scheming to take his old love, Daisy, away from her husband, he's certain that returning to paradise is simply a matter of will. When a friend warns him that he cannot undo the past, "Gatsby is incredulous. Of course he can. 'I'm going to fix everything,' he says, 'just the way it was done before.' . . . Gatsby is destroyed by his inability to distinguish between dreams and facts."[2] American hopefulness is the attitude that life sets no limits, nothing has irrevocable consequences, or, in mythic terms, that the American Adam can always return to Eden. Such a belief originates from a position of power. Gatsby's dreaming is born at the expense of other Americans whom *The Great Gatsby* does not represent, like the Chinese railway workers of Maxine Hong Kingston's *China Men* or the former slaves of Toni Morrison's *Beloved*. Since, however, hopefulness is what fuels the production system, it influences everyone: both those who believe in life without limits and those whose labor supports the effort to attain it.

Paradoxically, our belief in returning to the garden expresses itself in the national penchant for expecting technology to solve human

problems, regardless of political and social contexts.[3] The Earthly Paradise myth is behind American faith in the benevolence of nature, or
the world-as-given.[4] We cherish the notion that the world we live in
is essentially good. On the other hand, misfortune, especially failure,
violates America's natural laws. We react to bad news with feelings
not only of sorrow but of betrayal: we've been let down by a world
that is behaving unnaturally. The next step is our resolve, like Gatsby's,
to "fix everything." If nature is a lemon, then let's replace it with a
version that works. Thus, we arrive at New Atlantis by way of American overland route. Replacing nature is the familiar ideology of the
heterocosm, and technology is the most potent way of replacing facts
with (realized) dreams. We invest in technology as the means of replacing fallen nature, fixing the past, and returning to the American
Earthly Paradise.

This explains the American fascination with Disneylands, malls,
space colonies, virtual reality games, and technological environments
of every description. I think of such environments collectively as the
American paradise machine, the technological heterocosm that we
manufacture in order to start afresh, like Adams and Eves in a new
man-made garden. Ironically, the attempt to fix everything and return
to Eden guarantees that technology will replace more and more of the
natural world. Jay Gatsby's car, for example, is "a sort of green leather
conservatory."[5] This green car with hothouse windows is a witty image
of the machine that replaces the garden, and there are many less subtle
examples—later in this chapter we'll look at a virtual reality replacement of a California redwood forest.

Like the characters in Kurt Vonnegut's *Slaughterhouse-Five*, the
American heterocosm makers are "trying to re-invent themselves and
their universe. Science fiction (is) a big help."[6] For future reference, let
me explain the difference between a technological heterocosm and the
American paradise machine. Both are heterocosms: "other natures,"
or man-made worlds, independent from nature. A technological
heterocosm is created by technology, as, for example, a space colony.
The American paradise machine is a technological heterocosm that is
supposed to recreate the American Earthly Paradise. If you built your
space colony just to hang around Arcturus, you're living in a technological heterocosm. If you built it because you decided that Earth was
old and used up, but you shivered with wonder every time you orbited
the New World of Arcturus, then you're probably living in the American paradise machine. If you also decorated your space colony with
Astroturf carpeting and plastic fruit, then you definitely are.

What does science fiction have to do with trying to reinvent the universe? Everything. To be more specific, let's employ a helpful idea from genre theory. Genres are a bit like uniforms that alert us to a book's social function; we expect to get certain uses out of them. One critic describes genre as a "social contract" specifying the use of the literary artifact.[7] *Science fiction's use is as both model and symbolic means for producing heterocosms.* I began this book by discussing SDI: the science fiction-based vision of a protective umbrella over the United States is a prime example of the American paradise machine. What does the Star Wars project attempt to do? Exactly what a paradise machine does. It replaces the nuclear weapons–containing and Soviet Union–containing world with a new, better world, "fixed" to be just like it was before the cold war started, before warheads were stockpiled and the logic of deterrence began to work. Under the SDI umbrella, where bombs cannot fall nor Russians penetrate, technology gives us a fresh replacement for fallen, history-tainted nature. I am tempted to see maternal imagery in the umbrella's dome. Imagine living in the technological womb of a Reaganite Earthly Paradise. Dogs sleep undisturbed in the middle of Main Street, innocent Adams and Eves stroll by hand in hand, all of them Young Republicans, etcetera.

Power, Value, and Solace in the Heterocosm

Any technological heterocosm is not a world that is but, rather, a world that power has made possible. Power is its raison d'être and defines its values. When the space station colonists in the story say, "We had built this world ourselves ... we had brought *everything* into this world," they mean that they had the technological power to bring in all the parts. In the movie *Citizen Kane* we find a man-made world less related to technology, yet perfectly exemplifying the heterocosm's values. Kane, the character based on the publishing tycoon William Randolph Hearst, builds himself a private castle called Xanadu, a fictionalized version of the Hearst mansion in Southern California. We see huge crates being lifted by cranes, containing massive quantities of imported art. Then we see a completed room: a cavernous hall filled with objects tastelessly jumbled together from every style and period, a kind of Ellis Island of art. At one end, before a giant medieval hearth, Kane's young bride sits languishing under the weight of jewelry and boredom. Unable to enliven her mausoleum-like surroundings, this sad genius exposes the pseudoparadise that owes its existence entirely to her husband's financial power. The only object in Xanadu that has a value beyond dollar power is a child's sled, painted with a word, *Rosebud,* and an emblem. Kane's final word on his deathbed, *Rosebud,* is a tightly wrapped image of nature and love, animating Xanadu briefly as reporters search for its meaning. But the clue they need lies undiscovered among Xanadu's wilderness of objects, until the estate's inventory is taken, when the "Rosebud" sled is priced as worthless and burned. None of Kane's would-be biographers see the emblem that symbolizes his last memory of his mother. Financial power, the means of creating Xanadu, defines its values. According to these values, the sled has no worth, no meaning, to preserve it from destruction. *Citizen Kane* reveals two sinister aspects of the heterocosm. It doesn't re-create paradise. Worse, it reinforces and contributes to *anti*-paradisiacal forces in the lives of its makers. In other words, the heterocosm escalates the conditions that brought it about. The more we invest in artificial worlds, the more our values are defined by power. Other values, having to do with experiences beyond the use of power, like love or wonder, are less and less available to us. To paraphrase the song by Joni Mitchell, when you build a tree museum, you stop seeing the forest, if only because you're busy handling chainsaws.

While the American paradise machine comes from our relationship to the Earthly Paradise myth, it is also part of a broad cultural tendency to blend reality and dream by technological means. The phenomenon of "Nintendo war" is one example: the same TV set that broadcasts video game–like images of the bombing of Baghdad is also used to play video games that simulate bombings. When military software developed for training pilots becomes home recreation, the line blurs between real war and fantasy. TV programming alone, without augmentation, supplies sufficient examples: "infomercials" confuse documentary formats with commercial messages, audiences have trouble distinguishing news from entertainment, and candidates for political office are notoriously packaged as TV images. During the October 19, 1992, debate of the presidential candidates, former president George Bush made an extraordinary remark. Describing his decision to wage war on Iraq, he declared, "*I looked right into the camera,* and I said, 'This aggression will not stand.'" No one laughed! It's no news in Hollywood that Americans like large doses of illusion, expertly produced. With our ever-increasing power to blur reality and illusion, however, a kind of bewilderment attends us. The eminent American historian, Daniel Boorstin, states that the "efficient mass production of pseudoevents," or media-generated reality, "is the work of the whole machinery of our society . . . our ambiguous experience is so pleasantly iridescent, and *the solace of belief in contrived reality is so thoroughly real.* We have become eager accessories to the great hoaxes of the age"[8] (my emphasis).

The phrase in italics tells a sad story. Solace, that mixture of consolation and amusement, is the one durable reality left—the feeling that we seek to comfort us for having lost reality to the machinery of mass-produced illusions. If Americans are eager to pull the electronic wool over our own eyes, it is because the hoax itself is the antidote to feeling cheated. Boorstin compares the technological processing and packaging of American reality to a house of mirrors: movies, books, "real" events, products, and celebrities mirror one another, and all reflect consumer fantasies. "Experience becomes little more than interior decoration."[9] Like the anthropologist turned science fiction fan, in Silverberg's story, those who experience reality as interior decoration—a prisonhouse of commodities—will keep "buying into" that experience, *for solace.* The circularity cannot be understated: Americans buy reality-product and enhance the machinery of its production, because, as Umberto Eco says, we want reality, with the "iridescent" high polish of man-made wonder.

Science fiction enters this state of affairs as a special case but also the quintessential one. Its system of images, or "frozen pseudo-events," is integral to the technological production system that we inhabit and that processes our reality.[10] As model and symbolic means for technological heterocosms, it constitutes a national mode of thinking. To get a vivid sense of science fiction's "contract" with the American paradise machine, imagine a man walking through a building that does not exist. Although his legs, eyes, and hands seem to explore an ordinary office corridor, he is actually sitting in a chair, connected to computer-generated "cyberspace" through a virtual reality program. Here is what he has to say about it:

> Although it sounds like science fiction, and the word "cyberspace" originated in a science-fiction novel, virtual reality is already a science, a technology, and a business, supported by significant funding from the computer, communications, design, and entertainment industries worldwide.[11]

Science fiction does more than predict, inspire, and express, although it does all of these. By naming and imagining cyberspace, William Gibson's novels provide the model concept for virtual reality.

Furthermore, there should be no *although* at the beginning of Howard Rheingold's sentence: the science, technology, and industry of virtual reality "sound like science fiction" because they *are* it. Don't like your body? Step into cyberspace, which will replace the natural you with something better, like a twelve-foot purple lobster or a robot through whose eyes you see your old body across the room.[12] This imagery—the familiar man-made wonder and Cartesian mind-body dichotomy of science fiction—is not only a dream inside a machine but also a dream realized *as* a machine. If corporate-funded science is the institutional means of the virtual reality business, science fiction is the symbolic means of this technological heterocosm par excellence. Science fiction is an integral part of the American flight from history toward paradise, a flight that ironically takes us farther and farther toward a world in which the technological system defines all values—or, in Rheingold's words, "a new world where reality itself might become a manufactured and metered commodity."[13] As Vonnegut says, if you want to reinvent yourself and the universe, science fiction is a big help.

Slaughterhouse-Five: The Mind of an American Wonder Maker

If you're a science fiction reader of a certain age, then you know about Kilgore Trout. In Kurt Vonnegut's *Slaughterhouse-Five* the ex-GI Billy Pilgrim, back from the bombing of Dresden, becomes an avid Trout fan. But not uncritically so:

> I don't think Trout has ever been out of the country . . . he writes about Earthlings all the time, and they're all Americans. Practically nobody on Earth is an American.[14]

Billy's remark reflects Vonnegut's own unique use of science fiction to probe and reflect upon the American character. In 1969 *Slaughterhouse-Five* had immense popular success as an antiwar novel. Like many of Vonnegut's works, while science fiction is at its heart, it isn't science fiction. War—Billy's experiences in World War II and the Vietnam War going on as Vonnegut wrote—is the occasion for this story of an ordinary American turning into a wonder maker, because he's unenthusiastic about living.

While *Player Piano* showed us the social forces around science fiction's Golden Age, *Slaughterhouse-Five* depicts a mind-set behind American science fiction. Of course, it's not the one and only such mind-set. Billy's traumatized personality does not typify science fiction writers and fans in general. What Vonnegut portrays is the extreme case of the drive to replace the world, not just to imagine its possibilities. So if the view that I'm offering via Vonnegut's seems negative, the reader should not see this as a condemnation of science fiction. Billy Pilgrim's cast of mind is an American mode of thinking—the flight from history toward paradise—that utilizes science fiction's images.

The narrator, let's call him Vonnegut, sits with a friend, discussing the war novel he's about to write (*Slaughterhouse-Five*). Suddenly, his friend's wife gets very angry and tells him off:

> "You'll pretend that you were men instead of babies, and you'll be played in the movies by ... John Wayne.... And war will look just wonderful, so we'll have a lot more of them. And they'll be fought by babies.... " ... She didn't want her babies or anyone else's babies killed in wars. And she thought wars were partly encouraged by books and movies. (*SF* 13)

Vonnegut sympathizes. After all, he has been advising his own sons not to work for defense-related industries. As a concession, he subtitles his novel "The Children's Crusade" and makes its hero so innocent and dumb that he's just a big baby in fatigues. Billy Pilgrim is such a baby that, as a POW, he keeps from starving by eating malt syrup made for pregnant women. The book's epigraph implicitly compares him to baby Jesus—"no crying he makes." There's something strange about this. When Vonnegut advises his own sons, he doesn't treat them like babies but, instead, like responsible young adults who have moral choices to make. Why pretend that the Vietnam War, or any war, is fought by babies?

Partly for the antiwar sentiment stirred by maternal tenderness. Beyond that, however, a baby can be defined as a person to whom history hasn't happened. The American Adam, who can always shed facts and return to Eden, is basically a baby. But faced with Dresden's lunar rubble, or My Lai, how can he shed the irrevocable consequences of war? What "fix" can he find to preserve his innocence and the possibility of returning to the garden, unscathed? This is the question that Vonnegut poses. Billy Pilgrim's answer is an American paradise machine. Whether this solves the problem is up to the reader to decide.

Betrayed by Nature

> The most important thing I learned on Tralfamadore [Billy says] was that when a person dies he only *appears* to die. He is still very much

alive in the past. . . . All moments, past, present, and future, always have existed, always will exist. . . . It is just an illusion we have here on Earth that one moment follows another one. . . . When a Tralfama-dorian sees a corpse, all he thinks is that the dead person is in bad condition in that particular moment, but that the same person is just fine in plenty of other moments. Now when I hear myself that somebody is dead, I simply shrug and say what the Tralfamadorians say about dead people, which is "So it goes." (*SF* 23)

For a couple of years at the beginning of the 1970s it was not possible to mention Kurt Vonnegut without hearing someone say, "So it goes." This refrain repeats throughout the novel, spoken by the narrator, as a kind of coda to the unpleasant. Billy's father dies in a hunting acci-dent—so it goes. In a nursing home Billy looks at the corpse of an old man who was once a famous marathon runner—so it goes. Billy prophesies that Chicago will be "hydrogen-bombed by angry Chi-namen"—so it goes. A soldier describes torture. The narrator mentions his father's death, from natural causes. Billy's German captors give him a civilian's coat. Lucretia Mott, the famous suffragist, died long ago. A guide at the Grand Canyon admits that three people per year commit suicide by jumping over the edge. And so it goes.

The trigger for the repetition of "So it goes" throughout Billy's life does not seem to be death alone. The phrase randomly embellishes anecdotes of bad luck, common mortality, and human violence. No distinction is made between the kinds of trouble caused by deliberate evil and natural circumstance. With angry nonchalance "So it goes" lays at nature's feet the question of why evil exists, along with why misfortune happens, and why we have to grow old and die. If the purpose of the refrain is to shrug off pain, Billy is in pain from more than his wartime experiences. And if, as I suspect, the refrain is a protest, then it is not only an antiwar protest. Nature, the world-as-given, is to blame for Billy's pain, and "So it goes" is the American Adam's cry that nature has betrayed him.

The betrayal consists in his having to enter history, that frequently distressing process of one moment following another one. As R. W. B. Lewis points out, "There has been a kind of resistance in America to the painful process of growing up, something mirrored and perhaps buttressed by our writers . . . issuing repeatedly in a series of outcries at the freshly discovered capacity of the world to injure."[15] The worst thing ever to happen to Billy wasn't his father's death, his dog's death, or even his captivity in Dresden. It was being born. He is uncomfortable with his mother, who upsets him "simply by being his mother...because she had gone to so much trouble to give him life, and to keep that life going, and Billy didn't really like life at all" (*SF* 88). So it goes—when the "it" that goes is time, which man born of woman has to go along with. Billy's thanks-but-no-thanks attitude toward maternity seriously undercuts Vonnegut's compassion for all worried mothers. What has happened to concerned parenthood and the political dimension of "the Children's Crusade"?

Billy's personal protest against war takes the form of fantasy, as he imagines a war movie run in reverse:

> The American fliers turned in their uniforms, became high school kids. And Hitler turned into a baby, Billy Pilgrim supposed....Everybody turned into a baby, and all humanity, without exception, conspired biologically to produce two perfect people named Adam and Eve, he supposed. (*SF* 64)

It's always touching to be reminded that we start out harmless. In political terms, however, Billy's movie is a disaster. It implies that the opposite of deliberate evil is not deliberate good but, rather, infantine innocence, and returning to paradise is the only way to recover it. On Billy's office wall hangs the familiar motto about accepting what you cannot change, and the narrator tells us that among the things Billy cannot change are the past, the present, and the future. This extraordinary claim of powerlessness, and Billy's unenthusiasm for life, make sense, if the only change he finds meaningful would be to reinstate the condition of Eden—an impossibility, or at least a very tall order, the logical consequence of which is political and moral paralysis. Frustrated by Earth, Billy reinvents his universe on Tralfamadore.

Artificial Innocence

Like all science fiction, Tralfamadore represents nature with both fear and longing; colored, however, by the special American tie to the Earthly Paradise. To begin with, Billy's world is a paradise machine. It's a domed chamber in a Tralfamadorian zoo, to which Billy has been abducted, together with the lovely porn starlet Montana Wildhack. The dome is decorated with stars. The accomodations are three-star hotel cosy, with wall-to-wall "federal gold" carpeting, a mint-green tiled bathroom, a refrigerator, and a TV. Montana gets pregnant and lolls happily in bed. Green and gold, the colors of the Earthly Paradise, combine with an erotic enchantress whose name evokes the fresh, mountainous American wilderness. The American Adam can preserve his innocence in this artificial Eden. What more could anyone want?

But Tralfamadore still conforms to the structure of the science fiction heterocosm, which determines that animate nature must be alienated and threatening. Montana can't "send Billy out for strawberries or ice cream, since the atmosphere outside the dome was cyanide, and the nearest strawberries and ice cream were millions of light years away" (*SF* 153). Outside pseudoparadise, the "real" Tralfamadore is not reassuring. The Tralfamadorians, who sometimes peek through the dome, resemble green plumber's helpers, with a hand at the top of the handle. An open eye is set in the palm of the hand. As you might guess, their main occupation is seeing. Observing all of time—past, present, and future—as a simultaneous pattern, they're passive onlookers even at the moment in which a Tralfamadorian test pilot presses a button that will cause the end of the universe. Billy and Montana are part of an obscure breeding program whose outcome is already seen. The Tralfamadorians, architects of Billy's little human space, represent the nature who betrays. They are the nature who imprisons human beings within irreversible linear time; the time of biological reproduction (including Montana's pregnancy), of history (including the button-operated Bomb), and of mortality (including the heat death of the universe). While Billy preserves an artificial innocence in his chamber, the Tralfamadorians encompass all knowledge and experience in the poisonous atmosphere of alienated nature.

Tralfamadore demonstrates American innocence preserved artificially in the science fiction heterocosm. We see, on the one hand, its unfallen American Earthly Paradise and, on the other hand, its alienated nature in which the wonder maker locates the painful threat to innocence. But Vonnegut also lets us ask the questions: *Why* is Billy so invested in the state of infantine innocence? How does his science fiction world reflect his view of life?

Back on Earth, we see Billy walk into an adult bookstore in order to buy a science fiction book displayed in the window. Science fiction seems to be window dressing for pornography. As Billy leafs through a magazine, reading an article about Montana Wildhack's death, he "knows" that she's really alive, on Tralfamadore. The magazine, however, "published for lonesome men to jerk off to," reports a sensational account of her murder, as an occasion to print pictures from her old movies. The photographs are grainy, anonymous, and "could have been anybody" (*SF* 176–77). Billy watches one of Montana's movies in the back of the store. Who and where is Montana? We don't know.

Obviously, the real woman, if she exists, has no more connection to Billy than to the other lonely masturbators. Tralfamadore is the fantasy of a voyeur—or, rather than a simple sexual fantasy, *the universe reinvented on the principle of voyeurism.*

Billy's paradise machine comes from the same voyeurism that produces blue movies. Both kinds of fantasy operate on the principle of denying the reality of others; the Other is turned into images for the voyeur's entertainment. Montana's death is "promised" by the magazine as an occasion for spectacle, rather than asserted as a painful fact. Billy doesn't believe it because it's not meant to be believable: the porn star's real life is meaningless to the voyeur. Her pictures are images of a body that represents nobody. When Billy (back at the zoo) mentions Montana's former profession, her "Tralfamadorian and guilt-free" response is to remind him of a wartime comrade who "made a blue movie with a firing squad" (*SF* 179), that is, was executed. Tralfamadore mirrors Billy's view of life as a movie, in which all experiences, like frames in a film, are equally illusory and painless: 'The most important thing I learned on Tralfamadore was that when a person dies he only *appears* to die. . . . All moments, past, present, and future, always have existed, always will exist. . . . It is just an illusion we have here on Earth that one moment follows another one" (*SF* 23). Billy's artificial innocence amounts to the voyeur's abdication of the capacity to feel and the will to act. He clings to his innocence because of what the omniscient Tralfamadorians have "taught" him: that the stance of ultimate power is the shrug.

Slaughterhouse-Five casts some light on the mind-set behind the American paradise machine. The drive to make artificial realities is akin to the voyeuristic withdrawal from feeling and action. The difference is that the heterocosm maker ultimately aims to transform the world-as-given into a reality of images. Did I mention that Billy is an optometrist? "Eyeballs . . . are where brains meet the world,"[16] says virtual reality chronicler Rheingold. He could be speaking from Tralfamadore, where knowing is seeing and where emotion and action are obsolete.

The Psychology of the Paradise Machine

Slaughterhouse-Five offers a glimpse into the mind-set of the wonder maker, affected by the national nature myth. To understand how a myth can have such an affect, becoming manifest in people's attitudes and behaviors, we need to go further into cultural psychology. Jessica Benjamin, a feminist scholar and cultural critic, writes about the psychology of differentiation, the way children learn to think of themselves as individuals, separate from their mothers. Benjamin believes that certain patterns of differentiation result in a Western cultural tendency to deny reality to others and to divide the world into subject and object. Although her main topic is psychology more than philosophy, she is similar to Susan Bordo in attributing our notions of self and other to a "parturition drama," a denial of union or empathy with the mother. Benjamin's description of differentiation gives us a psychological explanation of the mind-set that Billy exemplifies, including his voyeurism and sense of betrayal by nature.

Overdifferentiation: Male Subjects and Female Objects

According to Benjamin, "our culture knows only one form of individuality: the male stance of overdifferentiation, of splitting off and denying the tendencies toward sameness, merging, and reciprocal responsiveness" (46). You define your individuality by splitting off from others: every man for himself, as the saying goes. The model for individuality is the way that male children learn to define themselves. As a rule, little boys are taught to become men by denying any identification with their mothers, cutting off empathy with mothers' subjective realities and points of view. This means relating to mothers and other female figures as objects. "If the child is able to become independent at all, it is through adopting the male stance of repudiating its identification with its mother . . . by objectifying her" (Benjamin 46). It's important to note that "the male stance" is really a stance, an attitude, *not* a biological attribute of males—and it affects both genders by being the model form of selfhood. This is the psychological background for the philosophical notions of rationality and scientific objectivity, which depend on a duality of (masculine) subject and (feminine) object.

We have seen this duality before. In chapter 1 we witnessed how the prospect of reunion with feminine nature threatens the modern self by blurring the boundary between subject and object. Evelyn Fox Keller criticizes the masculinist stance of modern science, which requires the scientist to repudiate any connection to or empathy with nature. Where actual men and women are concerned, Benjamin claims that Western individualism denies women reality as subjects: "To be a woman is to be excluded from this rational individualism, to be either an object of it or a threat to it." Men, on the other hand, are burdened with the cold war of the subject, with the endless task of drawing the defining boundary line around the masculine subject and defending its territory: "To be a man is not merely to assert one's side of the duality, the supremacy of the rational subject. It is also to insist that the dualism, splitting, and boundaries between the male and female postures are upheld."[17] In the pattern of overdifferentiation women must be objects or threats in order for men to remain individual subjects. On Tralfamadore, for instance, genders divide up like this. Masculine = Billy, the subject. Feminine = Montana, an unreal image/object + the Tralfamadorians, threatening alienated nature.

Incomplete Differentiation

Overdifferentiation is just half the story. Incomplete differentiation means that the child continues to rely upon the mother's nurturance, but without recognizing the mother as a separate person. It is precisely this continued reliance on a one-sided relationship with the mother as nurturer that makes overdifferentiation, the aggressive denial of the mother's selfhood, necessary. The child sees the mother as a mental projection of him- or herself, and insists on differentiation, while never really experiencing difference. The consequence of incomplete differentiation in adult life is a voyeuristic mind-set, a sense of unreality about other people and one's own life experience. The individual subject is rational but self-involved and lonely:

> The individual is quite able *cognitively* to distinguish self from other. The person knows that he or she is physically and mentally distinct and able to perform, socially, as if other people were subjects. But at the deepest level of feeling there is not that sharp and clear sense, that vibrant aliveness, of knowing that I am I and you are you ... emotionally and unconsciously the other person is simply experienced as the projection of a mental image ... the sense of aliveness that could emanate from mutual interaction with him/ her is diminished. It is only "as if" he/she were there, while underneath one feels alone ... feels "like in the movies." This inability to experience others as real, and concomitantly the self as real, is well known to clinicians today.[18]

The voyeurism of the rational subject is also part of scientific objectivity's psychological background. The stance of scientific detachment supposedly allows scientists to produce value-free accounts of what they observe. But as Sandra Harding argues, "It cannot be value-free [for social scientists] to describe such social events as poverty, misery, torture, or cruelty in a value-free way..., The use of objective language to describe such events results in a kind of pornography; the reader... consumes for his or her own intellectual satisfaction someone else's pain and misfortune."[19]

Differentiation and Betrayal by Nature

We can connect, at this point, between the psychology of differentiation, and the American Adam's relationship with maternal nature. (As Bordo and Merchant show, the mythic figure of Mother Nature is powerful enough to permit our applying psychology to cultural views of nature, as, for example, in the parturition drama.) Taking our cue from *Slaughterhouse-Five,* let's recall Billy's relationship with his mother. He is a big baby. His mother makes him uneasy "simply by being his mother." These two pieces of data fit the pattern of incomplete differentiation. Billy relates to his mother as a baby, experiencing her only as the projection of his feelings about being nurtured. Moreover, Mrs. Pilgrim isn't a person. The narrator calls her "a perfectly nice, *standard-issue,* brown-haired, white woman with a high school education... [a] dumb, praying lady..." (*SF* 88–89; my emphasis). This perception fits the pattern of overdifferentiation. The mother is a feminine, maternal object, "issued" from an assembly plant that turns out human things with whom no real person would care to be identified. Putting the two patterns together, we have the differentiation syndrome that Benjamin describes: the son remains incompletely differentiated from the mother, relying on her as a projection of himself while repudiating and objectifying her.

Now we can fully understand *why* the American Adam feels betrayed by nature. I have given an explanation in mythic terms— namely, that the original identification of America with the Earthly Paradise has persisted in American consciousness, so that we feel betrayed by the imperfect conditions of mundane life. Incomplete differentiation explains the cultural psychology behind the myth's persistence. Remember the blasé anger of "So it goes," the novel's "series of outcries at the freshly discovered capacity of the world to injure"? The American Adam holds nature responsible for his nurturance and relates to it as a projection of his needs. The ills of life are felt to be the fault of an unreliable Mother Nature, who hasn't kept her babies out of the traffic.

Differentiation and Artificial Innocence

At the same time that American nature is expected to provide a benign, nurturing environment, it is also regarded as the object of rational and technological manipulation. In fact, the two attitudes are complementary. Take, for example, the following notes for a virtual reality program. The speaker, a member of the Atari Systems Research Group, dictated this scenario as she imagined herself at the helm of a "voice-commanded, total immersion personal simulator":

> "Give me an April morning on a meadow," she said. . . . Patches of cerulean sky were visible between the redwood branches . . .
> "Uhmmm . . . scratch the redwood forest," Brenda continued . . . reclining in the middle of the media room. "The background sounds nice," she added: "Where did you get it?"
> "The birds are indigenous to the northern California coast," replied a well-modulated but disembodied female voice. "The babbling brook is from the acoustic library. It's digitally identical with a rill in Scotland."[20]

The entire double score of differentiation is played in this fantasy. The rational subject reclines comfortably, her every desire granted as soon as she utters it, by a mental projection of herself. It is hard to imagine a more infantilizing procedure. The depersonalized, disembodied genius of this garden indicates the degree to which nature, despite its continued role as nurturing paradise, is repudiated and objectified. The aliveness and real difference of the natural world are irrelevant to the "personal simulator"—the little surprises that come with every walk in the forest, flowers that close or open, birds that roost or migrate, the tussle of old and new growth, and the complex causes behind each minute detail, are all irrelevant. The "personal simulator's" forest is generic and arbitrary. Real redwoods mean as little to virtual reality as Montana Wildhack's real life to her appearance on Tralfamadore. Brenda's paradise machine caters to the passive voyeurism of artificial innocence.

The creation of an imaginary nature in this virtual reality scenario is strikingly analogous to the U.S. Forest Service's computerized management of actual forests. A writer for Sierra Club Books relates how Forest Service workers have stopped going into the woods to learn about them. Instead, they work with computer models and algorithms that treat forests like factories, with "management units" and "production goals": "So now the Flathead Forest in Montana has a planned 'output' of 200 grizzly bears. And old-growth forest is 'accumulated capital.'"[21] By reducing the environment to computer-processed data, we lose the kind of personal observation that adds up, over lifetimes, to a fund of empirical knowledge. We also lose a reciprocal relationship with nature. The "new breed" of Forest Service workers, the writer tells us, "does not come to the task with a basic loyalty to and personal involvement with the land."[22] Planning "output" from a forest for which you feel mere detached self-interest, which you have not recognized as an irreducibly different reality, is not so far from demanding "an April morning on a meadow." The same psychological dynamics account for both disenchanting attitudes toward nature.

Differentiation and Eros

Compared to science fiction, life is boring. Schwarz the former anthropologist thinks so; Billy Pilgrim thinks so; numerous fans think so. To that list add the hero of Robert Silverberg's "The Science Fiction Hall of Fame." I have ventured to say, in one way and another, that we become addicted to man-made wonder when we lose the ability to appreciate difference. This does not mean that science fiction doesn't stir the imagination in valuable ways, with speculation, satire, surrealism, and other kinds of fun. When I speak of addiction, I mean the chronic need for the ingredient of solace in science fiction. The psychology of differentiation helps account for the feeling that man-made wonder beats reality.

The fan of "Hall of Fame," like Billy, immerses himself in science fiction partly to evade the fact of death and partly to live vicariously. Comically grandiose, he declaims, "Never to die . . . to see the future millenia unfold, to participate vicariously in the ultimate evolution of mankind—how to achieve all that, except through these books and magazines?"[23] On the night of the Apollo 11 moon landing he brings a woman home to his apartment:

> I met an interesting woman. . . . her name is gone from my mind, if I ever knew it, but I remember how she looked: long soft golden hair, heart-shaped face . . . gentle gray-blue eyes, plump breasts, slender legs. . . . I remember, too, how she wandered around my apartment, studying the crowded shelves of old paperbacks and magazines. "You're really into sci-fi, aren't you?" she said at last. . . . "I guess this must be your big weekend, then! Wow, the moon!" But it was all a big joke to her, that men should be cavorting around up there when there was still so much work left to do

on earth ... [watching TV] for the men to come out of their module, and—very easily, without a sense of transition—we found ourselves starting to screw ... one of those impossible impersonal mechanical screws in which body grinds against body for centuries, no feeling, no excitement, and as I rocked ... on top of her ... I heard Walter Cronkite [say] that the module hatch was opening. I wanted to break free of her so I could watch, but she clawed at my back. With a distinct effort I pulled myself up on my elbows, pivoted the upper part of my body so I had a view of the screen, and waited for the ecstasy to hit me. Just as the first wavery image of an upside-down spaceman came into view ... she ... went into frenzied climax. I felt nothing. Nothing.... Eventually she left.... And still I felt nothing.[24]

One rule of interpreting science fiction: the more campy and obvious it looks, the more carefully you read. That upside-down astronaut-baby is as throat-clearingly blatant as you probably think, but there's more to him than meets the first glance. If we apply the double pattern of differentiation to this story, it actually becomes rather revealing and complex.

Let's begin with overdifferentiation. The young woman isn't a subject. The hero can't give her a name. He makes the oddly hostile remark about perhaps never having known her name, as though the very fact that she might have a name attached to a subjectivity is threatening and has to be treated with proper boundary-drawing disdain. The nameless female is objectified by her physical description, a list of fetishized items that sounds more like a collage of Penthouse Pet body parts than a living person. This kind of stance toward women and woman's body, fairly common in science fiction, has drawn its share of feminist fire. But to dismiss the description as sexist and leave it at that would be to miss the importance of overdifferentiation to the meaning of the episode. Standing naked beside the overcrowded bookshelves, uninterested to the point of caricature in the moon landing, the woman is an object that represents real life and Earth.

The pattern of incomplete differentiation begins with the nameless woman who is also "interesting." While the hero is not interested in her name, or her self, she is attractive as a mental projection of his needs. Literally attached to her through the sex act, the hero's incomplete differentiation shows in his weird pretense of innocence and passivity. He doesn't do anything. Sex just happens, in a phrase alighting between hyphens, without any help from his personal will or bodily desire. Although his position requires effort, he associates effort and physical volition only with looking up at the TV screen. He is not responsible for his intimate connection to the woman; like a baby stumbling over its toes, he "finds" himself involved. Eventually, however (and despite turning sex into a machine, a "mechanical screw"), he cannot deny the woman's response. Here lies the American Adam's grievance. In contrast to the futuristic moon shot, the woman involves him in the act that spans "centuries." She will not let him "break free" of the body's commitment to biological time, history, and mortality. Incomplete differentiation makes her both a mental projection and an imprisoning womb.

With both patterns in place we now ask the key question. What is this episode all about? Silverberg campily juxtaposes the woman's orgasm and the astronaut's appearance. Superficially, the plot implies that the moon landing is the sexual conquest of a new world, the fan is really interested in other planets, etc. But consider a new perspective. Connected physically to the woman, watching the screen and awaiting "ecstasy," the fan wants the orgasm to occur while (as the woman has earlier hinted) *his science fiction fantasy becomes real.* Of course, only astronauts experience this reality firsthand. To TV viewers it is spectacle. This is why the hero engages in a sexual encounter. He tries to project reality—through his connection to a body representing real life, Earth, and time—*onto the image.* What ecstasy does he anticipate? Orgasm, or the moon landing? Given the astronaut's "delivery," I would say that the fan awaits the ecstasy of being born into vicarious science fiction "life." Overdifferentiation provides him with the means for this, since he uses the woman as an objectified resource, a sort of all-natural reality concentrate. Incomplete differentiation provides the reason for the attempt, since the fan wouldn't need to live vicariously if his own life and other people felt real to him. Caught in a vicious circle, he "feels nothing," because his voyeuristic modus operandi is to escape feeling in the first place.

The story also satirizes the hero's desire to make science fiction "real" in a certain way. He wants a visceral, erotic sense of reality. This is the very sense that man-made wonder, the imagery of science fiction, does not satisfy. After all, science fiction is the symbolic means of making heterocosms, of replacing nature with mechanical and disembodied simulacra. Silverberg's story hints that the construction of man-made worlds is incompatible with an erotic connection to life. We have already seen the alienation of love in science fiction, based on the threat to the Cartesian subject. Benjamin's work further shows how Western attitudes toward the development of selfhood perpetuate the failure to connect vitally with others and with ourselves. Man-made wonder beats life—when life itself seems unreal. But the feeling of unreality, the underlying cause of boredom, cannot be exorcised unless the patterns of over- and incomplete differentiation are broken. Unless, that is, in one poet's words, we "give up the temptations of the projector,"[25] discover who's been running the film and who's been watching the show. Benjamin's theory of differentiation provides a psychological weft for the broad cultural patterns of the American flight from history toward paradise.

One aspect of "Hall of Fame" should not go unmarked. Trying to escape the cycle of generations and be reborn as an astronaut, the fan makes his bid to become an individual, immortal American hero. This wish also has antierotic repercussions. Generally speaking, the American Adam's innocence, for various well-known reasons including the legacy of Puritanism, depends on saying no to Eve. Erotic delight, especially in women, is subversive and even anti-American. For an example, we need only refer to former army general Dave Richard Palmer, who described the Vietnamese strategy of a people's general uprising as "the orgasm of revolution."[26]

A Connecticut Yankee in the Earthly Paradise

The Context of Technological Utopia

We have been looking at American science fiction in the large, sweeping contexts of cultural mythography and psychology. I would like to narrow the focus somewhat and look at a literary context, the technological utopia. Science fiction's next of kin, the technological utopia has flourished in America, inspired by an optimistic vision of science and technology bringing the cure for society's ills. Science fiction, by contrast, satirizes technology's abuses as much as it celebrates its advances. But whether the outlook is bright or jaded, science fiction relates to society in the particular literary context of the technological utopia, the vision of technology at the center of social organization. This context is important because of the questions it forces us to ask about technology. Does technology inevitably create certain social and economic structures, or does it happen the other way around? Is a totally benign technology possible? The ideas of the technological utopia have influenced us continuously since the late nineteenth century. They frame science fiction's fables of technology's impact and possible meanings.

Mark Twain's novel *A Connecticut Yankee in King Arthur's Court* was written in the late 1890s, in the wake of the post–Civil War industrial boom and at a time of increasing American enthusiasm for science and its products. On the one hand, *Yankee* shows a Colt Firearms company foreman who travels back in time and modernizes the agrarian society of Arthurian England along technological utopian lines. On the other hand, it displays this industrious character's motives and results in a very dubious light indeed. *Yankee* asks where America's technology is taking the country. Curiously, when it was published the novel was received as "a glorification of American technology."[27] Modern readings, more sensitive to the novel's pictures of technological warfare, tend to see doubt instead of glory. What I find staggering in *Yankee* is the vengeance taken on technology by the Earthly Paradise, in a final scene that might be the sequel to *New Atlantis*.

In the coming sections we'll look at technological utopian ideas in *Yankee* and in the first volume of Asimov's *Foundation*. Having seen the continuity of the technological utopian tradition, we'll observe the negotiation that Twain sets up between the Machine and the Garden, and its disintegration into chaos.[28]

Society as a Machine

One of the foremost elements of technological utopia is the concept of society functioning as a machine, made up of interchangeable human components. Hank Morgan, the Yankee, has this in mind when he sets up the scarily named Man-Factory, an education and indoctrination center to turn medieval Englishmen into standardized "up to grade" citizens. When Hank looks at people, he sees material. In one funny episode he visits the renowned Saint Stylites, who spends day and night on top of a pedestal, bowing from head to foot in worship. All Hank makes of this is the sorry spectacle of pedal motion, "one of the most useful motions in mechanics,"[29] going to waste. He times the saint with a stopwatch, jots down the number of revolutions per minute, attaches elastic cords to the unfortunate man, and uses him to run a sewing machine. The saint's desire to glorify God by mortifying the body is utterly irrelevant to the engineer. Over a century later, Marcuse would describe Hank's view of the human being as one-dimensional, flattening the transcendent dimension of experience in the interests of technological corporate productivity.

Human Perfectibility

Yet the technological utopia doesn't strive for productivity alone. Hank and other technological utopians really believe that their system will make people happy. In any utopia happiness is the expected outcome of perfecting the human race, in whatever direction the utopian thinks perfection lies. In this case machines, not saints, are the model for human perfectibility: "The very efficiency of technology inspires men and women to emulate the perfection of the working of the machine."[30] King Camp Gillette, a utopian writer at the turn of the century, innocently used the phrase "cogs in the machine" to mean happy workers and managers. The phrase sounds sinister in the 1990s, but the difference to the modern ear may not mean that we are less willing to emulate the machine. The gigantic wheels, gears, levers, and pistons of *Modern Times* and *Metropolis* make us think of fascism. But consider computers, which for some decades have inspired fantasies of human perfectibility. Hans Moravec, director of the Mobile Robot Laboratory of Carnegie-Mellon University, states that, within the next thirty years, we may be able to program our minds into intelligent machines, which will replace human bodies and make us immortal.[31] The basic idea is not so far from Hank's: society geared to the machine achieves human perfection and utopian transformation.

Technocracy and Democracy

Technological utopias are run by elites of technicians, or technocracies. As I mentioned in the last chapter, during the early stages of U.S. technological corporate capitalism, there was a hope that technical experts would make better rulers than corruptible politicians. In this spirit Hank and his Man-Factory grads, headed by his chief assistant, Clarence—a boy who first appears in tights and a plumed hat but later gives the impression of going nowhere without a pocket calculator—resemble the corps of engineers whom Thorstein Veblen believed would best govern the state.[32] The technological utopia nullifies politics. In the words of utopian writer Harold Loeb: "Political government ... would be showmanship. The routine of its executives would be made up of receiving distinguished guests, laying corner stones, making speeches about the rights of man, American initiative, justice." Howard Segal, an expert on the genre, adds, "As technicians rather than politicians run the utopian government, the government is technical rather than political in nature."[33] What is a technical government? To begin with, it is a government in which scientific knowledge

is power. Scientific and technical education is what creates the govern-
ing elite.[34]

This idea has both democratic and antidemocratic possibilities. If
the ruling class consists of the best brains in society, then the technocracy is democratic in the sense of sanctioning upward mobility. At
Hank's modern military academy, "West Point," smart boys from peasant and artisan backgrounds are admitted, while ignorant scions of
nobility are shunted into a militarily useless corps of ogre-hunting
knights-errant. As his favorite innovation, West Point helps Hank
build an elite of military-industrial brainpower, while reducing the
political aristocracy to the ornamental status of a tapestry hung in the
boardroom. But the technological utopia's contempt for traditional
politics has the antidemocratic effect of refusing representation to
groups and values that do not advance the project of the social machine. To Hank civilization is synonymous with the military-industrial
base. "Our civilization" is Clarence's collective name for "our vast
factories, mills, workshops, [and] magazines."[35] The people, as a political and as a cultural entity, have no voice in a system whose overriding
goal is efficient production. Loeb's list of speech topics for showcase
politicians could easily include "freedom of expression" among the
rhetorical phrases that don't merit the technocrats' attention. That war
and technological development are inseparable and that the social
machine is also a military machine are further facts noted by *Yankee*
but avoided by most technological utopias.

Technocracy and Socialism

One reason why technological utopias overlook the tie between war
and industrial development is that they're focused elsewhere, on commodity production and consumption. The technological utopia measures its success not by private accumulation of wealth but, rather, by
the ample and equitable distribution of goods. Most technological utopias have economies under strong state control. The most famous
American technological utopia, Bellamy's *Looking Backward,* is socialist. Abundance is the keynote of Bellamy's futuristic Boston, which a
character compares to "a gigantic mill, into the hopper of which goods
are constantly being poured . . . to issue at the other end in packages
of pounds and ounces, . . . pints and gallons, corresponding to the infi-
nitely complex needs of half a million people." The education of technocrats stresses commodity production as the prime value. Gillette's
ideal society "will want its children to learn its business; the miracle

of scientific production; the fairy tale of flour; the romance of rubber; the wonder of wool and silk. The child will get his education in the midst of production."[36] Whatever you may think of rubber romance, it's clear that the young technocrat isn't brought up on Horatio Alger. Which brings us to a puzzling fact about *Yankee*. Although, as Henry Nash Smith says, Twain's novel is "the first literary effort of any consequence to treat the entrepreneur sympathetically," Smith nevertheless regards the book as failing to deal seriously with nineteenth-century industrial capitalism. Hank appears to operate a national system of factories without any mention of "wages, conditions of work, unemployment, strikes. . . . The industrial system seems to operate with no internal friction." Moreover, the factories are not part of a market economy.

> All fixed capital belongs to the state; [Hank] simply does business with himself. He administers the industrial complex for the common good, presumably reinvesting the profits and distributing consumer goods without regard to prices. For all we are told . . . the sewing machines and typewriters that he mentions are simply issued to the inhabitants of the kingdom instead of being sold.[37]

Smith blames these inconsistencies on Twain's having overreached himself, in trying to telescope an entire economic system into the single character of a Hartford mechanic. We can take a different view, however; rather than having failed to represent Gilded Age capitalism, Twain has quite adequately represented the economy of the technological utopia. Hank himself is a qualified technocrat, displaying far more technical than business ability, while scientific knowledge gives him the run of a system in which money has no relation to power.[38] The knights who wander around Hank's England wearing sandwich boards over their armor, advertising mouthwash and toothpaste, are the Yankee's version of "the romance of rubber." They replace romance with something greater, the commodity.

I don't think that Twain intended to endorse technological utopia, or a state-run economy. In all likelihood, as Smith suggests, these characteristics evolved more or less out of the quirky narrative logic that the figure of Hank engendered. Yet it's perfectly natural that Hank's program would closely match the important technological utopian ideas of the period. Both *Yankee* and the technological utopias are trying to achieve the same goal: integration of the Machine and the Garden. Physically, technological utopias attempted to integrate the American wilderness with the urban setting and pictured a continent-wide landscape of garden cities and corporate parks. The tension between the Machine and the Garden would be resolved by landscaping the Garden, modernizing rather than abandoning it.[39] With the choice of Hank as hero, Mark Twain "was asking himself whether the American Adam, who began as a representative of a preindustrial order, could make the transition to urban industrialism"[40] Naturally, technological utopian ideas would accompany Twain's thinking about such a transition.

I find it more surprising that of all technological utopia's distinguishing characteristics, the one least apparent in science fiction is its economy. Galactic corporate capitalism seems to be science fiction's norm. A book might easily be written about the economics of American science fiction, and I don't propose to tackle the subject here. But within the framework of questions that the technological utopia raises, it's worth pondering whether science fiction reflects the impossibility of a utopian socialist technology or the assumptions of its audience.

Traders of the *Foundation:* Asimov's Yankees

By 1951, when Isaac Asimov's much loved *Foundation* was first printed, there was enough new technology around to build utopia, and more was coming. *Foundation* seems to be inspired partly by the need to explain the continued importance and function of political and social institutions during an unprecedented scientific and technological boom. On many levels it is a fascinating fable about technology and society, influenced by the assumptions of technological utopia. The Foundation itself is a remote outpost established by scientists, during the collapse of a galactic empire into pockets of feudalism and barbarism. Dedicated to mitigating civilization's collapse by secretly controlling access to technology, over the centuries, the Foundation promulgates a "religion of science," which trains "priests" to perform technical tasks under the guise of ritual. The Foundation's religion promises—what else—"a return of the Earthly Paradise."

It also employs the services of Traders, explorers who, like Hank, are self-interested entrepreneurial businessmen. "I don't scoot about space to save the Foundation," one of them says upon accepting a dangerous diplomatic mission; "I'm out to make money, and this is my chance." But as with the Yankee, money scarcely makes an appearance. The Trader's mission is to persuade a culture with a taboo against sophisticated technology to buy "atomic engines," so that the Foundation can acquire a foothold there. Profit is an unimportant sideline to the main business of expanding the empire of technology. In fact, hard cash is so uninteresting that the Trader doesn't know gold is valuable and has to be instructed in its monetary worth by the planet's native dignitaries. He thinks that their gold standard is a funny, exploitable superstition and seduces them into purchasing a tin-into-gold "transmuter." What they end up buying, along with taboo-breaking machinery, is the absolute value of technology. The Trader transacts his business on behalf of a technocratic system, in which money has little relation to power.

Like Hank, as soon as the Trader starts reeducating the natives, he is brushed with the rhetorical gilt of industrial democracy. Demonstrating a steel cutter, he asks for someone to give him a length of steel pipe.

> An Honorable Chamberlain of something-or-other sprang to obedience in the general excitement... and stained his hands like any laborer.[41]

In technological utopian terms, a superfluous politician is transformed into a useful worker, obedient to the imperatives of production. And the dubious "chamberlain" associates old world culture—like Twain's dimwitted English nobles—with politics, ceremony, religious taboos, in short anything peripheral to the streamlined, single-minded technological and scientific dynamism identified with America.

In Asimov's Galaxy, as in Twain's England, technology is civilization, and the signs of technology are consumer commodities. One Trader explains how a planet, formally at war with the Foundation while using the Foundation's technology, will capitulate by popular demand after its household gadgets break down:

> The small household appliances go first... a woman's atomic knife won't work any more. Her stove begins failing. Her washer doesn't do a good job. The temperature-humidifier control in her house dies on a hot summer's day.... They'll bear up under enemy bombardment, if it means they have to live on stale bread and foul water in caves half a mile deep. But it's very hard to bear up under little things when the patriotic uplift of imminent danger is not present.... It will be annoying and people will grumble.[42]

Although factory equipment is eventually included in the list of failed items, consumer annoyance ranks high as a war strategy. Lost profits aren't depicted half as vividly as lost conveniences, the fruits of the technological civilization.

Foundation repeats the themes of the technological utopia. It shows us the rule of a technocratic elite. It equates civilization with technology, wealth with abundance of consumer commodities, traditional social and political institutions with "something-or-other." Like *Yankee,* it foresees the prospect of a scientific and technological Earthly Paradise but wonders how and if we'll get there. *Foundation* has a pessimistic cast. In its cyclical history of civilizations, technological and scientific progress are always at the mercy of human irrationality. This opposition of know-how and human folly comes, however, from a technological utopian outlook. We can understand how Asimov and his readers, in the 1950s and 1960s, might have felt that technology was the most reliable, and most gratifying, measure of man. *Yankee,* on the other hand, questions whether technological utopianism isn't just as irrational and dangerous as other forms of faith—anticipating critiques of scientific rationality, such as Jessica Benjamin's and Susan Bordo's. The treatment of religion and magic in these two books indicates the implications of the difference between them. In *Foundation* religion is an empty ceremony designed to trick those who don't have a firm, scientific grasp of reality. Myths are just distorted versions of facts. In the following exchange a scientist asks for information about the Foundation's ritualistic concoction, the "religion of science":

> ". . . what kind of a religion is it?" . . .
> "Ethically, it's fine. . . . High moral standards and all that. There's nothing to complain about from that viewpoint. Religion is one of the great civilizing influences of history, and in that respect, it's fulfilling—"
> "We know that," interrupted Sermak, impatiently. "Get to the point."[43]

Those in the know aren't fooled by flummery—high moral standards "and all that." The Foundation's religion is a mask for the real civilizing force, science and technology, the only kinds of human knowledge that are real because they make real things tick: "It is the chief characteristic of the religion of science, that it works."[44]

Hank would be at home in *Foundation*'s grindingly one-dimensional universe. In the Yankee's opinion there is a simple functional distinction between his scientific know-how and the magic of the court sorcerer, Merlin: "Every time the magic of fol-de-rol tried conclusions with the magic of science, the magic of fol-de-rol got left" (*CY* 359). But the plot proves Hank wrong. In the end magic works, and magic wins. No such conclusion can occur in science fiction, because the laws of the science fiction heterocosm preclude unrationalized phenomena. (Even when the science is made up, nothing remains scientifically unexplained.) What this implies is that science fiction cannot make us face, as *Yankee* does, technological utopia's main stumbling block: the irrationality that explodes from within the technological project.

New Atlantis II: The Enchanted Garden Strikes Back

A Connecticut Yankee in King Arthur's Court isn't a utopia but, rather, the story of a utopian, revealing that there is more lurking in the depths of Hank's personality than utopian tidiness. Utopia's relation to the Earthly Paradise is one of simple appropriation, seizing the material and social comforts of the garden while expelling its genius. But Hank's relationship with Earthly Paradise nature is complicated, irrational, and finally disastrous.

Hank calls King Arthur and his subjects "white Indians." This epithet summarizes his ambivalent attitude toward the pastoral setting. He's "an avatar of the American Adam dwelling in the Garden of the World,"[45] in the American Eden. At the same time, he's the representative of the Machine, ready to transform or destroy nature and the "savages" to create his "civilization." These two opposite sides of Hank, the Garden and the Machine, begin a dialogue. At court Hank meets the damsel Melisande, the genius in the Garden of the World. Encouraged by the Round Table, Hank embarks with Melisande on a long, Monty Pythonesque quest. During their travels through the English countryside, voluble Melisande entertains Hank with lengthy speeches lifted verbatim from Mallory. Upon returning to Camelot, Melisande refuses—spouting more Mallory—to leave Hank's side. Hank marries her to regularize the situation, then falls in love with her. The synthesis between the Garden's genius and the Machine's agent seems confirmed with the birth of a baby daughter, whose name says everything.

One night Melisande overhears her sleeping husband sigh the name of an old love. Hank has been dreaming of a young Connecticut switchboard operator, whose voice used to send him into romantic raptures. For that, he says, she was worth what she was paid. Such a

romance is appropriate for a technological utopian. It is highly rationalized, in Benjamin's sense of the term. The girl was objectified and
paid for as part of the telephone service (overdifferentiation). Her voice,
controlled by Hank's calling in, was a vehicle for projecting his fantasies without facing her individuality (incomplete differentiation). Melisande doesn't realize that the dreamer's whisper isn't a proper name—a
mark of individuality—at all but, instead, a signal. She tries to fuse the
world of Hank's dream with her own world by naming their daughter
"Hello-Central."

The naming of Hello-Central Morgan represents a hybridization
of two languages from her parents' opposing worlds. Melisande speaks
the language of preutopian romance: free, uncontrollable, full of wonders and miracles—an erotic language, in which the romance heroine
expressed her love and made herself an irresistible presence. Hank
speaks the language of technological rationalization: it doesn't express, it controls, as we're acutely aware whenever we have to converse
with a computerized voice message system. Hello-Central compensates
for her father's denatured, sterile relationship with the switchboard
operator. Meanwhile, Hank has been installing a telephone system
throughout the country. His little girl could be the emblem for a harmonious and humane balance of technology and nature.

Sadly, the promising synthesis falls apart. Hank upsets the balance
in order to fulfill his utopian program. He becomes the copy of an
unsympathetic character first drawn in the original technological utopia, Bacon's *New Atlantis*. The director of Salomon's House, the
preeminent scientist, wears the garb of a magician. By adopting the
magus' dress, he asserts total control of nature, from which he has
wrested magical powers.[46] The technological utopian project stands or
falls on the outcome of the struggle between Hank and the numinous
power of the Garden, embodied in the magician Merlin. In the frequent
clashes with his sorcerous competitor, Hank doesn't expose Merlin's
pretensions to magical power; rather, he rivals them, using fireworks,
dynamite, and various special effects. Instead of educating the superstitious crowd, he himself earns the reputation of a supreme wizard.
Since Hank and Merlin fight on "equal footing," Twain often gives us
the impression "that both Merlin and the Yankee actually do have
magical powers, even though the Yankee's may be the stronger."[47] One
of the Yankee's most awesome demonstrations, the blowing up of
Merlin's tower, depends at the last moment on fire from heaven, in the
form of lightning that the Yankee uses (via lightning rods) to ignite
gunpowder. The necessary spark leaps from the clouds to the rod at the

precise moment called for in the Yankee's grandiose staging of the event.[48]

The conflict between Hank and Earthly Paradise nature comes to a head in the "Battle of the Sand Belt." After the church imposes a sudden ban on Hank's schools and factories, he challenges all the chivalry of England to a giant battle. His new, modern society cannot progress, he believes, until its predecessor has been wiped out. On one level this rationale for mass slaughter is patently a version of manifest destiny; Hank is determined to eliminate the "white Indians" of the American Garden, with their preutopian "religious" worldview and their connection to Earthly Paradise nature. On another level Hank plans a typical Baconian assault on nature, intending to reduce her to dead matter and seize her magical powers. He recruits fifty-two of his West Point graduates, all young boys, as technical assistants. Alone with them, he sets up military headquarters in a cave, isolated inside a sand belt of buried torpedoes, alternating with electric fences. Is it pure accident that Hank's nickname for his absent wife Melisande, whose name comes from *honey,* is Sandy?

During the preparations, a subtle skirmish between the Machine and the Garden takes place on the same linguistic level as their earlier reconciliation. Hank erases the language of romance, replacing it with the language of command and control:

> I watched my fifty-two boys narrowly; watched their faces, their walk, their unconscious attitudes: *for all these are a language ... given us purposely that it may betray us ... when we have secrets which we want to keep....* They *had* to speak ... in the neat modern English taught ... in my schools. (*CY* 390; my emphasis)

Like any smart manager, Hank looks for signs of incipient rebellion in the labor force. He imagines that the boys' body language exists for his benefit, betraying their secret thoughts to his methodical scrutiny. Products of the Man-Factory, the boys are in the last stage of being transformed from denizens of the Garden into Hank's instruments. Hank turns their physical expressiveness into a means of control and further curtails the boys' ability to think disobedient thoughts by restricting their expression to a rational dialect. "Factory English," as tidy and modern as the Sand Belt, guarantees that the boys will not revert to the Garden's passionate language. They definitely won't start spouting Mallory. Alongside his cold-blooded account of managing the assistants, Hank effuses: "Ah, they were a darling fifty-two! As pretty as girls, too." He projects the spooky affection of incomplete differentiation onto the boys, as onto the girl whom they most resemble, the nameless telephone operator who was also an instrument of the Machine.

Hank's psychology in this chapter is entirely that of the heterocosm maker. As we saw in "The Science Fiction Hall of Fame," the construction of man-made worlds suppresses an erotic connection to life. Bearing in mind the fact that Twain was a great reader of Cervantes, we can see how the images of the Sand Belt invert the erotic images of romance. Hank's cave was formerly a retreat of Merlin's. Like the mountain, the cave is a favored setting of romance eroticism and the nature myth. In *Orlando Furioso* a pair of lovers meet in a cave, leaving the walls scrawled with verse, delicately alliterative, in which can be heard the sound of echoing water drops. In ancient mythology the cave signified the maternal earth's womb; the Greek Titans came out of the earth's caves. By installing his operation in a cavern, Hank begins the Baconian appropriation of nature; in addition, his deployment of technology banishes the romance's erotic associations. Like the Atlantean scientists, Hank has also created an artifical body of water, diverting a stream to

"bring it within our lines and under our command, arranging it in such a way that I could make instant use of it." (*CY* 394–95)

The stream or fountain is an essential part of the Garden—water, of course, being a venerable symbol of life. In the romance, as in the tradition of Western art, bathers in a pastoral setting evoke a sense of erotic pleasure and harmony with nature. Earlier in *Yankee,* when Hank goes traveling with Melisande, he enjoys reaching the end of a hot, dusty day and having Melisande pour cool spring water under his hauberk. Now Hank uses his stream to flood the Sand Belt after the battle, sweeping away a wall of shattered corpses. The contrast speaks for itself. The inverted image of the Garden is most shocking in Clarence's report on the Sand Belt's buried torpedoes: "It's the prettiest garden that was ever planted. . . . It's an innocent-looking garden, but let a man start to hoe it once, and you'll see."

A modern audience can instantly label Clarence's attitude. He's a scientist in love with a problem, an engineer delighting in a technical challenge, oblivious to the human consequences of his work. We are sensitive to this in a way that Twain's first readers could not be. We have also begun to articulate the deep irrationality in the technological utopian project itself. In the novel's last scenes, as the American Adam turns the Garden of the World into a sterile and deadly battlefield, and calls it "pretty," Twain seems almost involuntarily to expose us to the presence of madness.

While *New Atlantis* celebrated technology's victory over nature, *Yankee* shows its defeat. Hank succeeds in destroying the kingdom's massed warriors, but after Armageddon he falls ill, trapped inside his cave. While Clarence is attending to him, an old woman comes—the only woman who has yet appeared in the Sand Belt. It is Merlin, Clarence relates,

> disguised as a woman ... a simple old peasant goodwife ... he offered to cook for us ... saying her people had gone off. (*CY* 403)

The pronoun switches gender, from *he* to *she,* as if cooking were the essentially feminine thing about Merlin's disguise. And it is. By cooking, providing nurturance, the old peasant woman embodies maternal nature in action. The next thing Merlin does—casting a spell of sleep on the Yankee—represents Mother Nature's numinous aspect, her magical power. Merlin stays feminine while he's casting the spell, the pronouns switching back only when it's finished:

> About midnight I [Clarence] awoke, and saw that hag making curious passes in the air about The Boss's [Hank's] head. ... The woman ceased from her mysterious foolery. ... I called out:
> "Stop! What have you been doing?"
> She halted, and said with an accent of malicious satisfaction:
> "Ye were conquerors, ye are conquered! ... I am Merlin!" Then such a delirium of silly laughter overtook him that he reeled. (404)

I confess that this scene gives me gooseflesh. Till now, whenever Hank and Merlin have clashed, they've both been dignified wizards. A certain pomp surrounded each, whether it was the technological splendor of the Machine or the sorcerous aura of the Garden. Now the mask has been stripped away, and in place of the solemn bearded magus stands a witch. We know which witch, too. She is the Scientific Revolution's demonized version of the myth of Mother Nature, the world-dissolving, chaos-spreading "wanton matter" whom Bacon depicted in arguing for dominion over nature. Her spell casts the Man-Factory's

Boss into a sleep that lasts till the nineteenth century. For the moment magic has won.

On the level of myth, then, Twain shows us that the Machine and the Garden cannot coexist. The Earthly Paradise's numinous power triumphs over the technological utopia. If the book's question is whether the American Adam can make a harmonious transition from an agrarian context to an industrialized one, clearly the answer is no. The reason for the forecast of failure, however, isn't that angry witches will come out of the Connecticut scenery and hex Colt Firearms. In Clarence's frightened contempt for the witch's "foolery," we apprehend the nightmare of the rationalist, an Other to whom the laws will not apply. She is attended by infirmity, delirium, mystery—or, in a word, by pandemic irrationality. But if we switch our cinematic view from a close-up on Merlin to a pan across the Sand Belt, we see a nightmarish chaos of cadavers and spent artillery in a dead landscape. We are forced to admit that the disorderly Other is a mere projection of the world-dissolving chaos underlying Hank's "neat and modern" rationalism. The Yankee's utopian design is the product of alienation from nature, the self, and others, and, as such, it carries the seeds of its own destruction. Cultural psychology, not the nature spirit, turns technological utopia into a charnel house: the alienating psychology of the heterocosm maker turns nature into a demon, eroticism into a threat, the boundary of the subject into a battle zone. In Twain's negotiation between incompatibilities we see that the Garden's vengeance is the same story as the alien's threat in "Stranger Station": these nightmares represent our culture's self-induced terror of "dirty, stinking, low-down, sneaking *love*."

Conclusion to Wonder: Made in USA

Through a series of misunderstandings punctuated with alcoholic binges, or binges punctuated with misunderstandings, Lister finds himself at the farthest remove possible from Earth. He's aboard a spaceship drifting in deep intergalactic space, he's been in suspended animation for three million years, but, worse than that, he's just become aware that he's locked into a virtual reality (VR), a software implant imprisoning him in a seamless world of his own fantasies, while his body (which he can't feel) withers away and dies. "Ever since he'd left Earth," he reflects sadly, "every step had led him further away from the dirty polluted world he loved. . . . It was hard to imagine how he could ever be further away from home."[49] In Lister's computer-realized fantasy, however, he lives contentedly in a small midwestern town called Bedford Falls, where it is always Christmas Eve.

Lister's interesting predicament, in the new novel *Red Dwarf,* traces the American flight from history to paradise. It begins with the urge to abandon Earth rather than make an effort to clean the place up. It takes the American Adam into more and more technologically dominated environments: his final companions are a robot, a genetic mutant, and a dead man's computer-stored personality, hologramically projected. And to think that all he wants is Bedford Falls, population three thousand, where nobody ever locks the front door![50] When Lister discovers that his Eden is really the American paradise machine, he has to make a choice. But he can't leave his family on Christmas Eve. A classic case of incomplete differentiation, attached to his projected fantasies, he forgets that "in Bedford Falls, it was always Christmas Eve." Lister decides to stick with the VR software, which bears the sinister brand name, "Better than Life." Man-made wonder beats life, when life itself seems unreal—but, the novel signals mutely in the final ellipsis, the only genuine alternative to life is death.

This chapter has looked at the American national mode of thinking that science fiction constitutes: the cultural investment in technology as a means of returning to the American Earthly Paradise. We have looked at this mode of thinking in its mythic form, the metaphors for nature that appear in literature and are also embodied in such technological projects as SDI or virtual reality. To understand the persistence of the myth, we have looked at the psychological background that produces science fiction, the paradise machine, and the technological utopia. The psychology of Western rational individualism explains how, as a culture, we develop an alienating stance toward others. It also explains how this alienation undergirds the philosophical notions of rationality and scientific objectivity.

Our excursion into cultural psychology leaves us with a new approach to an old question: Can science and technology ever be completely benign? Twain's answer is to expose the madness at the heart of the technological project, which seems to guarantee that science and technology will always carry the seeds of war and death. But what if the mind-set itself changed? What if Western cultural psychology were altered by new concepts, alternative ways of rearing children, different political and social realities? Feminist philosophers have called for a new science, promoting emancipatory relations between scientists and the "others" whom they study. The task of creating, and identifying already existent, new scientific practices requires a philosophical reformulation of scientific concepts and the revision of political agendas. Harding, for instance, takes issue with the idea that pure scientists are "innocent" of the human consequences of their work. While no one can guarantee that research applications will always be beneficial, she argues, scientists should not be complacently ignorant about their work's political and social stakes: "If the law finds avoidable ignorance culpable, why shouldn't science? . . . The 'innocence' of science communities . . . is extremely dangerous to us all."[51] Scientists' artifical "innocence" is analogous to that which we have observed in *Slaughterhouse-Five,* "The Science Fiction Hall of Fame," and elsewhere: the absence of feeling and action oriented toward the reality of others. Clarence's "innocent-looking" garden of buried torpedoes is a case in illustration of Harding's point. By claiming moral responsibility, she asserts, scientists can help cause political change and exercise control over the political agendas of research. With such a key change in our technological-scientific culture, Eden could begin to look less attractive than Earth.

The study of science fiction, as the symbolic model and means of constructing technological worlds, can contribute to this movement of criticism and change. In a politically and culturally fluid America the changing connection between dreams and machines will be worth watching.

Myths of the Final Frontier

How Space Became the Final Frontier

The Numinous Dimension

In the only Western epic poem beginning with the word *Ladies,* the noble knight Orlando deserts Charlemagne's army in order to pursue the elusive princess, Angelica of Cathay. After many adventures he finds, inside a cave, a wall scrawled with love poetry, composed by Angelica's chosen mate, a Moorish page. Orlando, beside himself, makes his way out of the cave only to discover that the trees are also covered with poems. He attacks them and, during an arboreal scrimmage, loses his wits. He literally becomes a lunatic: his wits fly up to the moon, and there they sit, bottled and labeled "Orlando's Wits" by the lunarians who attend to such matters. His friend Astolfo travels to the moon and fetches them back. On the way up Astolfo stops to meet with Saint John in paradise.

Astolfo's tale is one of many romance stories in which a hero goes to the moon, stopping first to meet with Saint John, whose ascension in the Book of Revelations qualified him to be the official guide for romance space travelers.[1] Through this tradition the Earthly Paradise became a feature of the space journey, appearing sometimes as a way station in the heavens, sometimes as the summit of a moon-high mountain. The historical distance between romance tales and modern space fiction isn't measured only by the amount of information that we have about the heavens. Before the Scientific Revolution, space, although visible to the eye, was qualitatively different from Earth. Space was a separate and perfect reality that did not suffer physical change or the passing of time. Like the Earthly Paradise that it sometimes enveloped, space was a domain of myth. Now it is difficult to imagine what it must have been like to stand on the earth at night and look up into a sacred dimension. (Science fiction readers might think of Isaac Asimov's tale "Nightfall.")

The Objectification of Space and the Map of Conquest

Our view of space began to change during the Renaissance. European explorers of the New World and other lands discovered strange realities on the surface of the Earth, blurring the line between the credible and the marvelous; Columbus did not have to stretch his imagination to believe that he had found the Earthly Paradise on the Orinoco. The Scientific Revolution had as great an effect as the voyages of discovery. Galileo found new stars in the supposedly unchanging heavens and earthlike topography on the moon. Newton proved that the laws of gravity were the same in space and on Earth. In keeping with the tendency of science to objectify the natural world, space, the numinous dimension, was gradually stripped of its mythic qualities and made an extension of earthly reality. An atlas of the year 1652 illustrates a halfway point in this process. Peter Heylyn's *World Geography* places the moon in the same dimension of reality as the new territories of Australia, New Guinea, and the Solomon Islands; alongside them are maps of Utopia and Fairyland.[2] New conquests and colonies fueled dreams of conquering space. In 1638 the Bishop of Chester published a book predicting the inevitable conquest of the moon by some airborne Drake or Columbus; what concerned the author was the pressing need for missionaries able and willing to convert the lunarian heathen. In the same year, and in 1659, popular romances by Francis Godwin and Cyrano de Bergerac described voyages to the moon that included the traditional layover in the Earthly Paradise setting. Instead of Eden, however, the paradisiacal locations were St. Helena's Island and Canada. The numinous dimension had been thoroughly assimilated to the expansion of colonial empires.

The changing view of space paralleled the cultural transition from the belief in maternal nature to the modern concept of inanimate nature. With the objectification of space, nature is physically appropriated, while its numinous aspect is pushed off the map of a newly rationalized world. (An interesting side effect of all this involves the sense of time. The numinous dimension was timeless and changeless. But when space became conquerable territory, time was also objectified. History became a charted map of exploration and conquest, while the future was more of the same, an automatic extension of the map of conquest. In other words, if you looked at Peter Heylyn's map, you saw lands that had already been conquered, history, and lands that hadn't yet but would be, the future.)

The Final Frontier: Meditations on American and Human Identity

Science fiction's images of alienated nature come from beyond the borders of science's map. Before peering over the map's edge, let us consider the metaphor that seems so natural in the opening words of each "Star Trek" episode, the metaphor of space as a frontier. What exactly is a frontier? My *Webster's* has three definitions: (1) The border of one country abutting another; (2) The part of a civilized, settled region nearest to an uncivilized, unsettled one; (3) A new or incompletely investigated field of learning.[3] How does outer space resemble these?

Space isn't like the border of Massachusetts and New Hampshire; you can't even see it in the daytime. That leaves meanings (2) and (3). Meaning (2) is a description of places like nineteenth-century Fort Laramie, from the white settlers' perspective, but does it realistically apply to the Van Allen Belt? Meaning (3) may be taken in a figurative sense; space exploration has created new fields of learning. In this sense, however, any object worthy of scientific inquiry is a frontier. We endow space with all the above meanings, regardless of logic, not because the frontier is an inevitable metaphor for space but vice versa, because space offers a way of thinking about the American frontier. Space is a comprehensive metaphor that relates American imperial expansion to our myths of nature and technology.

Below, a cultural critic summarizes the themes of 133 science fiction films produced between 1950 and 1957,

> beginning, predictably, with *The Flying Saucer*.... They used an expanding stockpile of mythological apparatus to dramatize contemporary existence as an extreme extension of established frontier myth. In the form of endless routines of panic and relief, invasion and dispersal, collapse and recovery, they rehearsed the nightmare of defeat and destruction or vampiric absorption—personal, national, or global—and the dream of rejuvenating violence for security which the post-war state both encouraged and needed to constrain.[4]

Space fiction stories are meditations on American identity, in which the mythology of the American frontier is central. Like the science fiction nightmare of absorption, "rejuvenating violence" is a typical space fiction theme. It comes from the myth of the frontier hunter, a hero who achieves self-renewal through acts of violence against nature and native peoples. In an important book called *Regeneration through Violence* the Americanist Richard Slotkin has shown that myths of the frontier, since the beginnings of white settlement, have affected American attitudes by exalting violence into a purifying, redemptive, and even generative force. Space fiction reiterates, but also changes, the idealized violence of frontier mythology. In shaping an American identity, space fiction uses the frontier myths to connect two aspects of American experience: the natural wilderness and the technological system. What is the connection between the hunter and the scientist? How can we "civilize" the solitary frontiersman's violence into collective technological power over nature? How can we "naturalize" the technological system so that it becomes a second nature for Americans? These are the questions that space fiction raises, and answers, in the language of myth.

Although space fiction stories are frequently derided for being no more than high-tech westerns, this association of space fiction with the frontier is the least accurate. A scholar of the western rightly remarks that space adventure "depends on a mastery of technology that requires a group effort and an interlocking between man and machine very different from the violent individualism of the classic western."[5] There is a big difference between slinging a Colt revolver and managing a Death Star! Space fiction is a meditation on modern human identity. It searches for a human ideal to suit our disciplined and disenchanted life within the technological system. Each space adventure unrolls an incomplete map of conquest, bordering on the region "where no man has gone before." Each story widens the map with another tale of the encounter between humanity and the numinous dimension and decides what relationship to nature and to technology is properly "human." (Think of the ragging Spock takes from McCoy—either he's acting too much like a computer, or else his blood is too green.)

A word to the reader about my use of the first-person plural. Science fiction does not reflect Native American experience; it reflects white American fantasies about nature, machines, and the "frontier." But however narrow and one-sided the viewpoint that engendered science fiction's mythology, all Americans have experienced the concrete results of the national mode of thinking. "We" means the reader who is willing to grasp the myths, imaginatively, "from inside"—just as "we" includes women who grasp the alien monstrousness of animate, feminine nature "from inside." This American mythological apparatus must be comprehended thoroughly to be handled, or dismantled, effectively. It is a legacy that belongs to everyone affected by the problems of U.S. technological culture.

The Myths of Alchemy

Like the Earthly Paradise, the myths of alchemy originated in the old world but have an active life in the new. Alchemy furnishes science fiction with two myths of maternal nature, the Rock and the Abyss. These are part of a general myth about the alchemist's quest for immortality and the power of creating life. Alchemy represents an ancient dream of control over nature, persisting in the dreams of modern science. We will see how the myths of alchemy contribute to space fiction in two novels about desert planets, C. J. Cherryh's *The Faded Sun* and Frank Herbert's *Dune*.

Immortality and the Maternal Rock

Alchemy has its roots in the ancient nature myths of smithcraft. For millenia human workers in metal saw Mother Nature in stone. She was believed to have given birth to the human race in her caves, while metal ores and minerals were her developing embryos. (The Latin name for this myth is the *petra genetrix,* the generative stone.) According to Mircea Eliade,[6] smiths believed that they were practicing what amounted to interventional obstetrics. By heating ores in an oven, the smith speeded up nature's generative process, bringing her embryos to maturity in an artificial womb. Controlling the speed of nature's "gestation," the smith controlled biological time itself, while remaining outside it. Alchemy simply extrapolates the technological control of time. The alchemical operation follows this logic: since mineral nature must be developing toward a final form, and gold is the most perfect metal, then, by transmuting base metals into gold, the alchemist is helping nature reach the final and perfect form to which she ultimately aspires. By speeding up nature's ETA, the alchemist controls the very ends of time, while remaining outside it. The essence of the alchemical operation is a quest for personal immortality, or exemption from natural time. The two sought-after products of the alchemical operation, gold and the elixir of immortality, are really interchangeable. We see this in science fiction novels such as *Dune,* in which an elixir doubles

as a precious exchange medium. More important, gold often symbolizes the power to bring about millenium, the end of time, when the
human race reaches perfection. While the Earthly Paradise is figuratively golden in the sense of a blessed natural state—the Garden's
colors are green and gold—millenial gold implies that humanity has
gone through an alchemical operation or some equivalent technological forging process. Frequently, in science fiction the perfected form
of humanity is literally crafted metal: robots.

Initiatory Dismemberment and the Maternal Abyss

The alchemist's blazing furnace connects his art to archaic fire-magic.
Eliade's study of alchemy goes back to the training of shamans in the
mastery of fire. If the key concept in smithcraft is obstetrics, in shamanic magic it is the eternal cycle of dissolution and rebirth. The
aspiring shaman must undergo the ritual dismemberment of his body,
returning symbolically to the state of primordial matter in the maternal
Abyss, or cosmic womb, out of which all material forms emerge. Since
it was believed that the universe must descend into the Abyss in order
to become eternal, the initiate takes upon him or herself the task of
matter's perfection. In person he or she suffers dissolution and rebirth
on behalf of the cosmos. The shaman emerges from initiation with
magical powers.

The alchemist, on the other hand, substitutes his materials for
himself in the initiation rite. In Eliade's phrase, the alchemist "projects
onto matter the initiatory function of suffering," by cooking matter
beyond recognition in various tortuous ways, so that *he* can get magical powers from *its* dismemberment. A good exemplar of a practicing
alchemist is the original Dr. Frankenstein, the misguided monster
maker of Mary Shelley's novel. During an intense phase of his prelimi-
nary research, Frankenstein feels strangely indifferent to unusually
fine weather and lovely mountain scenery, finding himself obsessed
by his laboratory's ghoulish clutter of notes, equipment, and body
parts. At night he has a dream in which he reaches for his young wife,
only to embrace the decomposing body of his mother. The dream
reveals Frankenstein's relationship to nature. In place of biological
fatherhood, he obtains the magical power of generativity by submitting matter to the alchemical operation. It's fair to say that the alchemist's attitude toward nature is ambiguous. He can be nature's servant
and friend, accompanying the transformations of matter with his own
spiritual development. He can also be a power-hungry manipulator,

exploiting nature in the name of perfection. In the latter incarnation his actions and attitudes dovetail with those of the frontier hero, who is greedy to "improve" and perfect the land. The myth of the frontier

> enables us to exploit and lay waste the land as a means of trans-forming and improving it and converting it into the ideal world of our dreams. It enables us to express our love of the land and its potential by destroying it. The key term is *improvement*.[7]

Dune Messiah, at the end of this chapter, shows us how the myths of alchemy and the frontier can work together with devastating results.

In science fiction, space is the image of the maternal Abyss. But since traveled and charted space is a rationalized region, the Abyss appears most often as the dimension of faster-than-light travel, in which time slows down or stops. Hyperspace (to use one of its common names) is uncomfortable.[8] Passing through it gives sensations of dis-memberment: people feel like they're falling apart or being surrealisti-cally rearranged. At the very least they're nauseated. The hyperspace passage frequently coincides with mystical revelation or psychological crisis, in keeping with the Abyss's initiatory function. When the voy-agers sleep through the passage, hyperspace becomes dream space; its threatening alternate reality is contained in the unconscious but must still be traversed. The descent into the maternal Abyss endows travelers with routine but unmistakable magical powers. They control time—lightyears—to bring the new planet of their destination out of the abyss. And they gain the quasi-immortality of the relativistic shortcut across normal time.

American Meditations I: *The Faded Sun*

The Faded Sun, by the prolific novelist C. J. Cherryh, is a prolonged meditation on human identity, by which Kilgore Trout and I also mean American identity. A frontiersman is the hero of this story about a mysterious alien culture that first fights humanity, then assists in the human conquest of space.

History as Nightmare

The regul are too fat to fight. In their wars against humanity they hired the mercenary mri. The mri lost. Our story begins as Sten Duncan, a young human SurTac, or surface tactical officer, accompanies the regul during their evacuation of a desert planet, Kesrith, which they are surrendering to human occupation.

The regul conduct their bureaucratic lives according to a strict age hierarchy. We visit the regul in their offices. A "youngling" clerk, toadlike, neuter, and harassed, hisses a demand for our credentials and scurries to fill its elder's beverage cup. The obese elder, sitting strapped into a power sled, condescends to talk with us. The youngling spills the hot beverage. Piqued, the elder clobbers it with a dinosaurian fist, and the clerk's frightened siblings carry away its corpse. Meanwhile, the elder has no need to review memoranda for our meeting. He possesses eidetic memory and in a lifespan of centuries will never forget, lie, or imagine. The elder also knows everything that *his* elders ever knew, possibly by cannibalistic means. Information is his weapon. We have seen one regul clan obliterate a rival clan by withholding a single fact. Information is also the regul's supreme value. Regul will commit genocide cheerfully but balk at destroying data in computer banks: "It [is] the death of elders," they hiss: "It [is] murder."[9] Regul are disgusted by our heartless attitude toward the political assassination of an elder; we, on the other hand, are tired of their cavalier attitude toward our youngling troops. With their tyrannical elders, millenial memories, and total reliance on precedent, they make us feel suffocated. They are history as nightmare.

More precisely, they are *the nightmare of enclosure in history as the price of technological advancement.* Regul technology may be advanced, but it's all about being enclosed. The regul elder is enclosed in a sled; the regul colony is enclosed in its spaceship; the regul's mind is enclosed in history; and to underscore the undeviating order within which the regul live, the most uncomfortable sensation a regul can have under stress is the out-of-phase beating of his two hearts, which must be brought back into an orderly rhythm. Sten Duncan barely controls his resentment of "both their long lives and their exact memories" along with his loathing for "this . . . chromium-plated, silken-soft imprisonment . . . regul and regul machines, hulking beasts, helpless but for that automation . . . great shapeless parasites attached to appliances of steel and chromium."[10]

Regul technology doesn't impress Duncan as much as the regul's physical helplessness without it, as though somehow, by needing the machines, the regul don't deserve to have them. He resents the sight of these creatures—"beasts" and "parasites"—flying in the face of their obese and sedentary nature. Objecting to the reguls' beastliness, he also revolts, somewhat contradictorily, against their supercomputer memories and "silken-soft" civilization. The problem seems to be with the meaning of regul technology. The regul are a type of fallen nature, perhaps no more so than anyone who uses a wheelchair, brace, or glasses, but there it is—they're naturally imperfect. Their machines compensate, complement, and facilitate. Their technology doesn't make the world over, wresting a new Eden from fallen nature, escaping the taint of history. Here, on the contrary, technology exists in order to support the great collective act of memory that is one meaning of civilization—a meaning from which the American hero instinctively recoils.

The Motherless Soldiers of Humanity

> War was all [Duncan's] life: it had made him move again and again in retreating from it, a succession of refugee crèches, of tired over-worked women; and then toward it, in schools that prepared him not for trade or commerce but for the front lines.... He had allegiance for nothing now but his humanity.[11]

> ... [Duncan] knew the mechanics of ships and of weapons, and the working of computers—all in areas necessary for training in combat, in which he had been trained from a wartime youth, parentless.... All his knowledge was practical... rammed into his head by instructors solely interested in his survival to kill the enemy. (*SJ* 13)

Humanity is an army. The problem with the army is that it demands allegiance without natural ties. Mothers are absent. Fatherly authority rests with the top brass, who are as harsh as regul elders but more impersonal; even the horrid regul are true parents, while the human commanders have no familial loyalty to their troops. We feel the lack of natural roots in Duncan's upbringing. He is a technological weapon, guided across space toward a target—war—but he makes no meaningful progress. He just keeps moving. The orphan soldier is all instrumental purpose, without an origin to give his wanderings the shape of a quest, without a grip on the instinctual sources of power. He is a tool rather than a conqueror. But Duncan's forlorn upbringing does not suggest antiwar sentiment in *The Faded Sun*. The story will *naturalize* the role of the soldier by merging it with the myth of the frontier hunter, which "imagines the relationship between man and nature... as that of hunter to prey."[12]

Duncan has a frontiersman's affinity for wilderness. A specialist
in terrain, independent and irreverent, he is the type of hero, like Davy
Crockett, who abandons civilization for a solitary life, one of those
whom D. H. Lawrence called "integral souls venturing outward in
space."[13] The only peacetime occupation he could tolerate would be
opening the wilderness to settlers. Duncan's instincts give him a latent
connection to the feminine nature figure of American mythology—an
animal, person, or landscape, described in feminine terms. Among
Americanist scholars Richard Slotkin refers to an "archetypal nature-
goddess" of the American wilderness, while Annette Kolodny says that
the "land-as-woman" is a pervasive American metaphor.[14] Not as
clearly defined as the lady in the enchanted garden, the feminine spirit
of the land is still a persistent and unmistakable presence.

The feminine nature figure comes out of the woods in Elizabeth
Bishop's poem "The Moose." A bus drives toward Boston, through the
evening, and gradually the passengers fall asleep. Suddenly it stops.
A moose has stepped onto the road.

Taking her time,
she looks the bus over,
grand, otherworldly.
Why, why do we feel
(we all feel) this sweet
sensation of joy?[15]

The moose incarnates American nature. The instinctive joy that her
appearance gives the travelers is sadly missing in the deracinated culture of humanity's army. Duncan is due to meet a moose. He goes on
a short trek outside the spaceship and is promptly captured by the mri.

Mother Rock's Golden Children

The mri are governed by their old tribal Mother, Intel, the "she'pan,"
or "keeper of secrets." Among other things, Intel keeps secret the reason why she insisted on choosing Kesrith, out of all the planets that
the regul offered her tribe. The scorching climate has killed off the
Kath, the blue-robed caste of childbearing women, and all but one of
the Sen, the gold-robed caste of scholars. Of the black-robed Kel, the
warrior caste, a handful of aged veterans survive, along with a young
brother and sister, Niun and Melein. Melein, the last fertile female,
trains to succeed Intel in the celibate she'panate. These golden-skinned
mri are as beautiful as the regul are hideous, and as passionate as

humanity is impersonal. Their harsh, stubborn Mother is an avatar of the maternal rock of Kesrith itself. Eventually, the mri and Duncan between them will produce an ideal human identity, close to maternal nature yet serving science and technology's empire. But to reach perfection some alchemical work has to be done. Intel (better than Bechtel?) hints as much by calling Kesrith "the Forge of the People."

Kesrith's terrain resembles the calcination stage of alchemy, gray alkaline flats erupting in mud and acid geysers, a landscape of death. Duncan's hike onto the surface coincides with a regul attempt at genocide. Having lost the war, the regul act to prevent the mri from selling their services to the victorious human forces. They bomb Intel's stronghold. On his way there Niun runs into Duncan, grapples with him long enough to determine that he's human Kel, and takes him prisoner. Unheard of! Mri *never* take prisoners. But somehow, Duncan's being a "kel'en," a soldier, gives inexperienced Niun a moment of crucial hesitation. As a human fighter-pilot says later in the novel, the mri are "just soldiers behind their black robes and veils . . . a human could understand them." The soldier is the basis for the ideal human identity that Duncan will come to represent.

When the bombing subsides, Duncan helps to dig Melein out of a shelter and accompanies the two bereft mri, the last of their race, to a cave shrine. On the way he learns a few things. A face veil tied correctly helps you to breathe. If you throw a pebble into that wide circle of little holes, it produces a hungry land octopus. The white hunter begins his initiation into the ways of the native. At the desolate shrine the two kel'en camp in the entrance, while Melein disappears into Intel's inner sanctum and spends all night learning the she'pan's secrets. In the morning she emerges carrying a large, metal, egg-shaped container. She "bore it as she might have carried an infant, as something precious, though she staggered with the weight . . . and could not step over the stones bearing it" (*KE* 232). Anxiously, Niun supports his sister, finding to his dismay that her skin is very cold and that she's become oddly remote. Like the egg, which is "cold and strange in balance," Melein has "something else . . . contained inside her." She's pregnant, of course. Melein has become the new avatar of the maternal rock. She bears the shining, precious egg, the embryonic future of the mri. Yet although Melein is officially a Mother, she has no tribe and nowhere to go. The mri have no forward momentum, and in this respect they are Duncan's opposites. Where he was all sourceless motion across the map of humanity's advancing front, the mri are all suspension within their numinous maternal source.

Images of Science

An air battle breaks out, and Duncan, in the confusion, gets the mri aboard a human ship, where they are confined, sedated, and examined. The sacred egg is commandeered for study by a xenologist (anthropologist for aliens), Dr. Boaz, on the research ship *Flower*. Duncan cleans up and goes to visit the only human woman in the story.

The egg is "resting in *Flower*'s belly"; meanwhile, plump Dr. Boaz interviews Duncan with "naked interest" in her eyes. Bellies and blossoms seem to promise an Earthly Paradise, but—

> *Flower,* despite the name, was an ungainly shell,... an ugly ship, meant for plain, workman duties. She brought technicians, scientists, who were already beginning to sift through the remnants of Kesrith's records... to perform the myriad tasks that would begin to *appropriate the world* to human colonists. (*KE* 234; my emphasis)

Alas, "scholarly lust" for the sacred egg is the gleam in Dr. Boaz's eyes (*SJ* 32). This disillusioning fact, and the name of the research ship, betrays something about the work conducted on board. The scientists are interested in the secrets of Kesrith to *appropriate the world* and remake it in the image of humanity's expanding empire. Science is the business of appropriating nature and remaking it. Boaz's scholarly erotic drive and the misleading cluster of images around *Flower* testify to the appropriation of the Garden and its reshaping into the forms of scientific knowledge and technological power. The sacred egg, symbol of the maternal rock, also promises to become a part of science's project. But we are dealing with a different nature myth now; the rock belongs to the myths of alchemy. Boaz's experimental work on the egg is a picture of science as an alchemical operation.

She "cracks the egg," submitting it to the dismemberment process. (You can't make an omelette...) Opened, the egg contains thin leaves of gold covered with inscriptions. Boaz continues her operation on the materials, rendering down the egg's contents in various linguistics computer programs. At last the inscriptions are revealed to be navigational records and coordinates of all the planets previously inhabited by the mri, including their original home planet. Nature has yielded her powers to the alchemist: Boaz has discovered the golden genetic code. She is now in a position to assist in the development of the maternal rock's children and to give the mri a future. *Flower*'s military authority decides to send the mri back to their planet of origin, for further research. The mri records are programmed into a scout ship's navigational computer, then Melein, Niun, and Duncan are sent aboard. With *Flower* following, the scout starts a long, wandering journey across a desert of stars. When they reach their home planet at the end of time—the end of the navigational tape—the golden mri will make the human empire immortal.

Although the modern laboratory bears little resemblance to the alchemist's smoky workshop, in this key episode we see how images of science are drawn from the myths of alchemy. What do these images of science tell us? First, they firmly unite science with technology. They tell us that science is about the technological control of nature; the alchemist relies on instruments to gain his powers. Second, they imply that the powers that science seeks are control over time and over the generative process. A very important question to raise, at this point, is whether the scientist-alchemist has a friendly attitude toward nature. At first glance it seems that, without science's alchemical intervention, the mri would die in utero. Surely, we are observing science at its most benign, working to protect and nurture an endangered species.

But another development accompanies the alchemical operation. The sacred egg is turned into a data base, and its holy writ is transformed into coordinates on a map. Science's map of objectified space has been expanded, and numinous nature has been expelled from it. The episode reflects the fact that scientific research is conducted on behalf of the technological system, not outside it, and necessarily leads to expansion of the system. In the organizational framework of big science, at least, the scientist is the unfriendly type of alchemist, bent on appropriating and reshaping nature into forms of collective technological power, or *Flower* power. Is the image of the power-hungry alchemist an accurate reflection of nonfictional science? On the one hand, the dreams of alchemy might not be relevant to science that has no technological application. On the other hand, although the objectification of space accompanies the technological feats of crossing oceans and blasting off from the earth's surface, objectified space is a scientific idea: it is simply a description of the natural world according to certain criteria that exclude nature spirits from being considered real objects, or objects of scientific knowledge. The fact that the mass dream of science fiction identifies the scientist with the alchemist raises the question: To what extent are modern science and technology separable activities, with separable ideologies?

Ethnographies of Others, Allegories of Ourselves

Being taken POW and having their sacred objects desecrated were the best things that ever happened to the mri. Why? Science fiction adapts to its own purposes a kind of allegory that we find in the writings of Western ethnographers, like anthropologists and folklorists. Although ethnography has been regarded as an objective science, recently ethnographers have begun to call attention to the subjective quality of their work. Telling stories about other cultures, they claim, is a way of describing ours. What we value or dislike in our own culture often appears, disguised as allegory, in the ethnographer's report. Our dislike of industrial society's breakneck pace can be read in descriptions of leisurely, unhassled hunter-gatherer cultures; our descriptions of polygamy will differ depending on whether our views are Christian, feminist, or Marxist. This doesn't mean that ethnography is impossible. It means that the standard of scientific objectivity is questionable, and, as ethnographers have become aware, you cannot narrate a story about others without appearing in it yourself, as a value-laden voice-over. The allegorical tendency of Western ethnography has a historical background. When Europeans made the voyages of discovery, they projected their own myths onto the lands and peoples whom they encountered. Columbus's "discovery" of the Earthly Paradise is such a case. Montaigne's description of vigorously healthy and virtuous cannibals is an allegory of an idealized medieval Europe and its codes of honor.[16] Europeans observed or invented data that matched stories they already knew—stories about themselves. "More or less explicit biblical or classical allegories abound in the early descriptions of the New World,"[17] according to ethnographer and critic James Clifford.

Science fiction entertains us with imaginary ethnography. The illusion of ethnography, with its drama of unfolding clues, ensures that the aliens will seem like a real, different culture. A character who is an anthropologist, or a narrative proceeding by way of research materials such as field reports, diaries, and tape transcripts, gives the stamp of scientific rationality to the novel's allegory. Science fiction's alien cultures are the purest form of ethnographical allegory, because there are no real natives to limit the ethnographic "observations." For this reason they also reflect uninhibited fantasies about our culture's encounter with other peoples. Space fiction's question is always: Will the aliens add to humanity's map of objectified space, or will they threaten it? Even a book like Ursula Le Guin's *The Left Hand of Darkness*, which tries to question assumptions about human identity, boils down to the question: Will the natives accept our science and our *reader?*   *?*

government? Science fiction's "ethnographical allegory" can reveal our wishful expectations of others.

An example. In the real world it is difficult to study other cultures without interfering with them. An anthropologist usually sets up a relationship of exchange with a native culture; he or she provides Western commodities in exchange for access and information. But such exchange destroys handicrafts, disrupts customs, and "makes anthropologists constant contributors to what they see themselves as the destruction of their object of study."[18] If you give a tribe the plastic dishes that it covets, you can say goodbye to the local pottery. The conditions of study force the anthropologist, paradoxically, to participate in Western cultural domination. In *The Faded Sun* quite the opposite happens. At the novel's end Melein, aided by Boaz, is bargaining with human colonial officials. She offers the mri's mercenary services in exchange for a home planet and spaceships. The colonial governor reacts with suspicion:

> "So you offered the regul. What benefit did they have of the bargain?"
>
> "Ask," Boaz said.... "You are on the wrong track, governor. Ask *why*; ask why, and you will get a different answer."
>
> "Why?" Lee asked after a moment. "Why do you make such a bargain?"
>
> "For the going...the going itself is our hire...we are a sharp sword to part the Dark for you. So we did for the regul...giving them worlds....We are makers of paths...and the going itself...is the hire for which we have always served." (*KU* 254)

What a fantasy for the CIA! Provided with a home base and military assistance, the natives will fight for the government, because it fulfills their nature to do so. The mri take hire, as one regul puts it, "for no apparent reason...save that this arrangement seemed to satisfy some profound emotional need of the mri." The mri are motivated by something that can't be rationalized or objectified: a strong emotional need. Close to maternal nature, they are essentially irrational, yet their very irrationality is described in instrumental terms. The mri profoundly need to be a sharp sword—anybody's sword. By buying their mercenary services, humanity helps them to be their natural selves, while making the universe safe for democracy, as we used to say. And far from destroying the native culture, science, in the person of the well-informed Dr. Boaz, has guaranteed its integrity. Boaz's somewhat messianic role (*Flower* is the first new mri ship) recalls a common scene in ethnographic stories. Mary Louise Pratt, a literary critic who studies the writings of anthropologists, notes that scientists frequently report their first encounter with a native culture in images that, more or less subtly, glorify their mission. In Pratt's view these first contact reports draw upon a rhetorical tradition that began in the narratives of the Renaissance voyage. "Far from being taken for a suspicious alien, the European visitor is welcomed like a messiah by a trusting populace ready to do his or her bidding."[19] In science fiction's ethnographic allegory, whether the imaginary natives are hostile or friendly, their ultimate function is to help define who we, the "human beings," are and what we ought to be.

The Frontier Captivity Myth

Duncan's relationship with the mri culture is the "fieldwork" that adds realism to the ethnographic allegory. The combination of his personal experience and Boaz's professional expertise gives the imaginary ethnography a kind of stereoscopic depth. On another level Duncan's ordeal of going native among the mri introduces the myths of the American frontier.

Tales of white settlers captured by Native American tribes are "the first coherent myth-literature developed in America for American audiences." They are the earliest literature of the frontier, and they influenced later American fiction. The captivity tale is a religious drama with a simple outline. The hero suffers a fall. His soul is endangered by his ordeal in a corrupt, mortal world. If he resists temptation, he experiences rebirth and attains a new, cleansed soul. His great temptation is to accept being absorbed into the native tribe, an option chosen by a surprising number of real captives. The tribe represents the Puritan's externalized unconscious, his dark side, projected onto the wilderness and onto the Native Americans who were perceived as its extensions. Settlers believed that the Indians "enjoyed a special and more-than-human relationship with nature, which gave them a kind of demonic power."[20] Thus, this earliest frontier myth is about a fall into nature, which is also a fall into the unconscious. Later frontier literature modified the captivity tale, as the European settlers acculturated to their American surroundings. The captive's ordeal was gradually overtaken by the myth of the white hunter's initiation into the Indian wilderness. Duncan's story reflects both these versions.

Aboard the scout ship, Niun and Melein brusquely inform Duncan that mri do not take non-mri into space. He can die, or become mri. As the first step in his mri-fication, he has to strip the living area. "Niun's amber eyes swept the compartment 'F'nai,' he said, 'i.' Remove it all."

A Puritan woman in an early captivity narrative recounted the stages of her capture not in days and nights but in "removes," spatial and spiritual movements away from her life and into the tribe's. By discarding chronological order in favor of a series of shocks, she expressed the all-encompassing quality of captivity, an experiential microcosm "complete even to having its own peculiar time-space relationships."[21] Duncan's loss of identity also takes place through a series of wrenching spatiotemporal "removes." In the cabin's white, featureless compartment he becomes spatially disoriented. Then Niun throws away the medication that allows humans to survive hyperspace passages. Time in Duncan's captivity is now measured by the ship's hyperspace removes, immersions in the dimension that the mri call "the Dark":

> That initial feeling of uncertainty, and walls, floor, time, matter, rippled and shredded ... stomach-wrenching, like a fall to death. Duncan clung where he was, wishing to lose consciousness, unable to do so. (*SJ* 128)

Duncan falls into nature's darkness, and the mortal weakness of his own flesh. He clings to his rational mind like the good soldier that he is, but a natural temptation overcomes him in the shape of the *dus*. A bearlike animal telepathically connected with the mri, the dus represents the native's bond with nature as well as an externalized Id; this beast communicates feelings of fear, anger, or pleasure, and kills if it is told a lie. As Duncan starts collapsing during one hyperspace passage, he throws his arms around a pair of warm, furry *dusei*, who flood his mind with comforting animal thoughts. Afterward he is disgusted. "Human, who had laid [*sic*] down with them, no more than they" (*SJ* 129). He has yielded, figuratively, to the temptation of sexual union that is one of the captivity narrative's motifs. Dizzy, vomiting uncontrollably, Duncan lives the captive's "perception of sin and sinfulness as a total environment, a world like hell, in which one breathes [and] ... drinks one's own spiritual filthiness."[22] Unsympathetic Niun, leaning on a mri mop, chides, "You were kel'en.... Now what are you?" The most basic human identity—the soldier—has disintegrated, with the rational hero's absorption into the natural wilderness.

The Soul-dier: An Ideal of American and Human Identity

Like the Puritan captive, Duncan must acquire a new, clean soul. His salvation, however, lies in *joining* the tribe. Physically and spiritually, he must become mri to survive. Why? If we put on our shaman's mask, we see that Duncan has suffered an initiatory dismemberment into the Abyss, and his new identity will give him magical powers. Now, if we put on our raccoon-tail cap, we see that Duncan, the frontiersman, is going to learn the tribal ways and get an Indian name. These transformations of Duncan's identity work together, combining the myth having to do with technology, alchemy, and the myth having to do with America, the frontier. They are both transformations of the basic identity, the soldier, that will finally produce an ideal of human and American identity, the *soul-dier*. (There's one hat left in our act, but we'll leave it till the end of this section, with the rabbit.)

Niun and Duncan are sitting cross-legged on the floor. Out of his ample robes Niun produces two small wands, hands one to Duncan, and teaches him to recite a chant while tossing the wands back and forth between partners. Several months pass. Duncan learns the full chant, naming the genealogies of the mri castes, recounting the feats of individual members and giving instruction in caste duties, all to the beat of the passing wands, now doubled to four. Duncan understands he is learning the great Game of the mri. Circles of a dozen or more play it on ceremonial occasions. Nevertheless, he is nonplussed when Niun takes away his wands and substitutes two razor-sharp circular knives. Wands are for Sen scholars. Kel play with *these*. Duncan is still human enough to wonder what happens if you die playing the Game. You will be honored, Niun assures him, as if you had died in battle.

The Game cures Duncan of hyperspace sickness. When the jump into the Dark comes, Niun's words echo in his ears: "'*Play,*' Niun urged him, '*to deserve to live. Throw your life, kel'en, and catch it in your hands.*'" Something clicks, and Duncan

> knew how to let go and cast himself utterly to the rhythm of the Game, to go with the ship, and not to fear . . . the teaching of the Service had been *survive,* but that of the Game was something complexly alien, that careless madness that was the courage of the mri. Kel'en. (*SJ* 134)

Having endured his initiatory dismemberment, Duncan now has the magical power of entering and emerging whole from the Abyss. Let us look more closely at his new soul. What is the difference between a soldier in humanity's Service and a mri kel'en?

The Game literally makes a world of difference. The rhythm of the Game replaces the chaotic removes, and its chant reconstitutes an entire historical and social reality, including the identities of the players. This ritual recreation of identity is the factor that distinguishes a human rational instrument from a mri magical weapon. The human soldier is a missile hurled on an impersonal trajectory; his purpose is to survive and fight another day. The kel'en is a self-propelled knife; his purpose is to create himself anew by periodic immersion in the maternal Abyss. Death in the Game reaps military honors because war is what keeps the mri on the move, like knives flying across the Dark, perpetually "shedding each world's taint, renewing ourselves like something born always new, young again and strong," as Melein puts it (*KU* 179). Duncan's acquisition of a new soul is an ideal of human perfection. *The ideal human identity is a soldier for whom rootlessness would be no hardship but, rather, his very essence: a warrior-self defined by continual periodic motion through the empowering source of maternal nature.* No longer an orphan, he would remain a weapon.

Why is the naturalized soldier, the "soul-dier," an appealing human ideal? Probably because he is based on an American ideal. American frontier mythology gives us the original great game: hunting. Stories about frontiersmen exalt hunting as a form of self-expression and self-renewal. Besides taming the wilderness for civilization, a frontier hero like Daniel Boone loves the chase "for its own sake and the sake of exercising his skills, with an aura of religious sanctity. Crockett and Doggett likewise see their hunting as a self-expressing...self-validating activity."[23] The religious aspect of hunting consists in the hunter's communion with the land. The hunter renews himself in nature through "rejuvenating violence": the kill sanctifies a marriage between feminine nature and the frontiersman, giving him the same bond with the land's spirits that Native Americans were believed to possess. White hunters thought of their activities in terms influenced by Native American religion, but the myth of the hunter strayed from its religious sources. It preserved the aura of ritual, while discarding the Native American respect for the balance of nature that set limits to hunting and generally kept human beings in their ecological place. Instead, the frontier myth licensed greed and exploitation and, to our further misfortune, gave rise to an American tradition that sanctifies violence as a form of cultural regeneration.[24]

Frontier mythology is about the desire for limitlessness. This desire bears a family likeness to the American Adam's flight from history to paradise. But limitlessness in the hunter myth is a special kind, bound up with violence. If the hunter recreates himself through acts of violence, "what becomes of the new self, once the initiatory hunt is over? If the good life is defined in terms of the hunter myth, there is only another hunt succeeding the first one."[25] Limitlessness is the essential theme of space fiction's American meditation. It is the promise that the soul-dier is forged to fulfill. The regul, the humans, and the mri represented three versions of technological and natural identity, each acknowledging, in its own way, a form of limitation. The soul-dier, in his warlike person, unites the technological empire's wars of expansion with the "natural" cyclic hunts of the frontier. He is an ideal of American identity because limitlessness is the very basis for his personal integration of technology and nature. The violent character of perpetual expansion is idealized, so that the soul-dier seems to be a symbol of freedom, instead of a religiously dedicated technokiller.

To understand the soul-dier completely, as an ideal of human identity, we put on the alchemist's hat. Forging the soul-dier is the final stage of the alchemical operation performed by Boaz, with poor Duncan in the role of suffering matter. Duncan knows this. At the beginning of his trials, when scout's bare cabin makes him feel lost, he is overcome by a vivid memory of a chameleon-like creature that he once saw in Boaz's laboratory. Caged in a white metal box, desperate to camouflage itself, it turned every color in its repertory, went cinder-black, and died. Like the science fiction allegory itself, the scout ship is an extension of the scientific laboratory. The fate of the captive chameleon illustrates the sense that we adapt with difficulty, or not at all, to the technicization of life. *The Faded Sun*'s answer to this modern problem is a kind of mythological engineering. Organic nature myths, like the Earthly Paradise, draw our attention to biological rhythms, to birth and death, and to the limits of our organic selves. But the myths of alchemy accommodate a hope of breaking biological limits: our natures, the alchemist tells us, are such as can be forged or technologically recreated. By cracking the genetic code, we can create a golden race that is always young. Science also has a dream of limitlessness: the quest for immortality. And that's the rabbit.

Gods of Technology: The Megamachine and the Worship of Transcendence

Rabbits are notorious for appearing in large numbers out of other rabbits. Like eggs, they are an old symbol of *natura naturans,* nature generating itself. The point of the hat routine is that the rabbits come out of nowhere, and that act is God's. I have talked about disenchantment and our lost sense of nature's divinity. But the Machine has deities of its own; the gods of the stars, of armies, of cities, and of giant technological projects (like the Tower of Babel, arguably the first space program). They are gods who transcend all natural limits, and are immortal by definition. They are not new.

Between 6000 B.C. and 4000 B.C., in the regions of Mesopotamia and Egypt, the style of life that we call civilization developed. Out of the neolithic landscape of small villages and farmlands rose cities, with fortifications, towers, and monuments such as the Egyptian Pyramids. The work of the late Lewis Mumford, particularly his book *The Myth of the Machine,* traces the descent of our technological system from the ancient "megamachine," a name for the form of social organization that developed with, and made possible, the growth of cities. The task of building urban structures was accomplished by enormous labor forces, coordinated and organized in strict hierarchies, in which every worker was assigned to a specific task. This massive engine made up of human components is what Mumford calls the megamachine. Today, as in ancient times, Mumford argues, the whole standardized society of civilization is a megamachine, capable of achieving tasks far beyond the reach of agrarian, cooperative communities.

Human beings deployed in anonymous masses require a special religion, and the prime mover of the ancient megamachine was the divine king. Coinciding with the rise of astronomy, the institution of divine kingship represented the sky-gods on earth. The divine king was the incarnation of a godhead that transcended nature and wielded transcendent power. We still worship the divine king in the form of exalted corporate entities, of which the state is the most important. Statehood levies demands on our loyalty and strength for the production of monumental works, like NASA's space program. Although the state's projects are superficially secular, "communities never exert themselves to the utmost, still less curtail the individual life, except for what they regard as a great religious end. Only prostration before . . . some manifestation of godhead in its awful power and luminous glory, will call forth such excessive collective effort."[26] In Tom Wolfe's novel *Bonfire of the Vanities* a Wall Street firm provides a good example of a megamachine dedicated to a great religious end. The firm's senior partner, who imposes a strenuous discipline on himself and his employees, doesn't find compensation only in riches. At work he privately titles himself "Master of the Universe," and his staff prostrates itself accordingly. The divine king was and is the dazzling focus of a cultural hunger for limitlessness. "The desire for life without limits," Mumford claims, "was part of the general lifting of limits which the first great assemblage of power by means of the megamachine brought about. Human weaknesses, above all the weakness of mortality, were both contested and defied."[27]

The Faded Sun unveils the transcendent god-king. Arriving on the planet Kutath, ancient homeland of the mri, Melein enters an abandoned city and discovers a computer bank that is its sleeping brain. She alerts the machine and talks to it, then to all the city computers on Kutath. Her companions stare at the "pulse of lights welcoming Melein, mortal flesh conversing with machines that were cities . . . light bathed her white-robed figure until it blazed blue, like a star" (*SJ* 204). Melein forgets to eat and drink, turning too bright to watch. After this apotheosis she sweeps across the planet, gathering up lost mri tribes and consolidating them into an efficient, regimented, caste-conscious, blue-, gold-, and black-robed megamachine. Then, just before acquiring *Flower* and initiating the mri space program, Melein the god-queen of technology has a curious encounter with the all-but-forgotten Earthly Paradise. She and her troops stumble into the city of the elee, a race of beautiful, frail, utterly defenseless people living under glass domes. The innocent elee, who spend their time among fountains and flowers, making love and art, inspire profound disapproval among the mri warriors. The elee Mother hands Melein a perfect little flower, carved in stone, and explains that it is an artist's whole life. Melein, unimpressed, says that the human ships will bring a tourist market for such trinkets. After further cross-cultural miscommunication, the mri smash the glass walls with a collective sense of relief, because "mri hated barriers, borders, and locked doors." And then *Flower* lands on Kutath.

A conversation has taken place about the meaning of life, a very short conversation between an artwork that says, "Life is enough," and a spaceship that says, "Nothing is enough." There is no compromise between these points of view. The Earthly Paradise myth presents a dangerous, subversive alternative to the worship of transcendence. It makes limitlessness seem less important than peace. It seduces us into thinking that life in the megamachine is harsh, repressive, and sterile. Above all, it portrays mortality as an acceptable fact instead of as a weakness to be overcome at all costs. Our story demands that the enchanted garden be demolished and champions transcendence over the possibility of living with our mortality and within the balance of nature. *Flower* power brings the end of the garden.

The enchanted garden holds a suspect place, also, in the mythol ogy of the American frontier. Early seventeenth-century colonists who promoted the New World as an Earthly Paradise often cast doubt, in the same breath, on the character of the garden's enchantment. In their descriptions of the country the land-as-woman figure becomes a charming, dangerous seductress. Robert Johnson, writing in 1609, pre-sented Virginia as a feminine Eden. But he also warned that where the climate is sweetest and the soil most fruitful, "men are in danger of 'beeing in a golden dreame.'... The woman who had 'so ravisht' the early explorers, he seems to be saying, ought not to be trusted too completely."[28] Remembering that colonial Virginia was a mercantile venture, we can understand how an Earthly Paradise idyll might be dangerous to industry. Moreover, the "golden dream" that the colonists warned of, a harmonious and gentle frame of mind, breaks down the opposition of man and nature, hunter and prey, and subverts the my-thic meaning of the frontier. The myth defines our concept of *the American frontier: where the forces of limitlessness meet what has yet to be broken and recreated in their image.* A contented partnership with the land does not support the frontier myth's imperative, "the continual expansion of our power into new fields or new levels of exploita-tion."[29]

The Faded Sun envisages an ideal human nature that can be forged, a soldier whose soul is the push of limitlessness. Kutath, home base of the mri space program, is the only natural landscape compat-ible with technology's transcendent god. A ball of omnipresent sand, it has no seas. Water has vanished into the eroded deserts. The "ancient mother's" womb is empty:

> Sea-chasms gaped, empty in this last age of the world.... Some-where out there was the bottom of the world, where all motion stopped, forever; and that null-place grew, yearly, eating away at the world.... It was a place ... where one could look into time, and back from it; it quieted the soul, reminded one of eternity. (*KU* 15)

This is no innocent contemplation of eternity in the wilderness. A dead, empty desert, eventually to fade away in space, the impression of being released from time—this is a vision of the annihilation of nature. I am reminded of Galway Kinnell's poem about the atom bomb, called "The Fundamental Project of Technology." In a travesty of detached scientific style, the poet condemns the bombing of Hiroshima as an attempt to transcend mortality by eliminating mortals: "to establish deathlessness it is necessary to eliminate / those who die."[30] Kinnell writes that the dream of transcending nature by technological means is a murderous fantasy, adding his voice to those who criticize the explosive irrationality underlying the technological project. Technology is nothing but the "mechanisms of *pseudologica fantastica*," as Kinnell calls it, an insane defense against the fear of death. Whether or not we concur, space fiction is full of landscapes like the deserts of Kutath and the Sand Belt in *Yankee,* icons of transcendence, eradicating whatever appears to embody natural limits.

"Establishing deathlessness," however, oversimplifies technology's mythic project. Our myths of limitlessness and our worship of transcendence combine in *the dream of finding an alternative to generative nature.* Immortality depends on eliminating birth even more than on eradicating death. *The Faded Sun* uses the nature myths of the Rock and the Abyss to make the space program seem like an alternative to the Garden. The alchemy myth depicts the creation of life in a technological womb. With the god-king, however, we take the mythic step of transcending the womb entirely. The question that *The Faded Sun* does not address, and the *Dune* tries to, is this: How can humanity transcend the realm of Mother Nature, achieving the stature of the immortal gods, yet continue to reproduce? Space fiction seeks a hat that really makes rabbits: that is the final frontier.

American Meditations II: *Dune*

In an old castle, in a darkened room, a little boy lies half-asleep. His mother is watching him from the door, standing behind a crone robed in black. Who is she? The two women softly discuss the boy. He's small for his age, the witch observes, but that's typical of the Atreides family, says his mother, concubine to Duke Leto Atreides. The old witch hovers nearer and cackles, talking to him. She knows he's awake. And tomorrow he must meet something of hers . . . a word he doesn't understand. Already dreaming, he's in a dim cavern, surrounded with strange faces and the sound of dripping water. He knows that this is a future event on the planet Arrakis, where his family is going, because Duke Leto has been appointed governor. The waterdrops puzzle him, since Arrakis is a desert planet.

The Sky-God and the Nature Witches

The crone is Reverend Mother Mohiam of the Bene Gesserit (BG), a society of female witches who conduct a human breeding program some thousands of years old and who emerged at the dawn of space travel. Space travel, of all the unlikely things, filled the world with witches flying in the face of God:

> All through religion, the feeling of the sacred was touched by anarchy from the outer dark. It was as if Jupiter ... retreated into the maternal darkness to be superseded by a female immanence, filled with ambiguity and a face of many terrors. ... It was a time of sorceresses whose powers were real.[31]

Is this science fiction? What has happened to the rationalized world of the heterocosm, in which everything is explainable, even if the science is made up? Space travel created *real* witches. Even when we find out that the BG's spooky-looking powers are technical feats, Herbert hints that the technician-sorceresses were controlled by "an even higher plan of which they were completely unaware!" (D 510)

In *Dune*'s post-space travel Bible, Genesis reads: "Increase and multiply, and fill the *universe,* and subdue it, and rule over all manner of strange beasts ... on the infinite earths ... " (502). Human space-flight took the form of a religious mission. Bibles in hand, spaceship captains set out to fulfill God's commandment of ruling new worlds. While many space fiction novels are similarly based on the European voyages of discovery, *Dune* is the only one that makes divine will—the higher plan—an active agent of the plot. This violates the basic rule of the science fiction heterocosm (no unrationalized elements) and gives *Dune* a religious character. As *Dune*'s story unfolds, the values it espouses are part of a religious myth: the battle of the transcendent sky-god against the witches of nature. *Dune* retells this old world myth in the new world, on the American frontier. I stress the religious quality of the novel because of its enduring popular success. *Dune* is a living example of the worship of transcendence, in the guise of secular entertainment.

The identities of the witch and the god bear further clarification. Who is the "female immanence," and what kind of sorcerous anarchy does she unleash? We know that, as the Scientific Revolution progressed, scientific writing employed a type of rhetoric that gave personified nature the qualities commonly attributed to witches. The once benign Mother Nature was portrayed as a lustful, chaos-spreading harridan needing to be brought under the dominion of science. Interestingly, some important seventeenth-century scientists were among the most fervent believers in witchcraft. To these men the indisputable presence of demonic female nature spirits helped define the gender and the boundaries of scientific knowledge, or what might be called science's diplomatic relations. Science was masculine, actively refusing to recognize nature's spirit as a proper or worthy part of its enterprise.[32] On Earth and in space, as science's epistemological map expanded, witches—alienated nature figures—hovered in the map's margins. As the mechanical model of nature gained ascendence, the prospect of inanimate matter coming back to life, and space having its own spirits, remained a potent threat. *Dune*'s mythology returns us to the period when feminine nature was explicitly associated with witches and science with a godly masculine order. Jupiter, king of all the gods in the Roman pantheon, is the patron deity of science's imperium.

The expansion of colonial empires also bred witches along its borders. On the American frontier the witch was associated with the unconquered wilderness and its natives. Puritan opinion, as Cotton Mather expressed it, held that the continent had been the devil's territory until God's chosen arrived on its shores. In records of the Salem witch trials and Cotton Mather's "exorcism" of a "possessed" girl, Mercy Short, the supernatural phenomena cited as proof of the devil's presence took the form of "a sudden infection of the Christian soul by an Indian familiar or demon."[33] The witches of Hawthorne's *Scarlet Letter* met in the forest and could be identified by the stray leaves clinging to their hair. Patron of science, Jupiter is also the divine patron of the American empire, suddenly eclipsed by the vast "maternal darkness" of unconquered territory. Establishing Jupiter's reign over an obedient, despirited, and denatured New World is *Dune*'s religious mission.

A complication is introduced, however, by the novel's meditation on American identity. Our hero is fated to represent the New World's Jupiter, but he begins as the American Adam, known to have difficult relationships with the institutions of fatherhood and monarchy. Determined to stay innocent and unmarked by the passage of time, he is no candidate for biological fatherhood. And while the king of the gods transcends nature, the American Adam remains always ready for a fresh beginning in Eden.[34] If *Dune* is to elevate the hero to Jupiter's unchallenged throne, this story, unlike *The Faded Sun,* cannot permit periodic immersion in the maternal source. How can *Dune* reconcile, in one American identity, absolute transcendence with renewal in nature? On the level of cultural psychology Jupiter and Adam, the transcendent god and the dependent son, are halves of a complete dynamic that we have seen before (chap. 2): the differentiation syndrome. The hero relies on the nurturance of woman/nature, relating to the feminine Other as an extension of himself. Unable to perceive the Other as an independent subject, he insists all the more aggressively on his difference from woman/nature. In *Dune* this revolving-door syndrome gives rise to the hero's dilemma: How can man born of woman transcend the realm of the Mother? The only answer, seemingly, is to eliminate the feminine principle entirely and replace it with a masculine equivalent. Like *The Faded Sun, Dune* seeks an alternative to generative nature. While the former looked toward more accommodating nature myths, however, *Dune* imagines replacing maternal nature with a masculine mode of reproduction.

When science fiction calls for masculine parthenogenesis, a favored solution is the robot. In *Dune*'s imaginary future, however, robots are banned by religious law, as are computers and any machine modeled on human functions. You might think that, if such machines were no longer available, human emulation of machines would also disappear. Let's visit the court of the galactic Emperor.[35] We walk behind a Bene Gesserit Reverend Mother, who is stopped by imperial guards at the entrance to the great hall of the court. Before the guards can question the black-clad witch, she murmurs a phrase, and, with expressions of astonishment, the guards reflexively snap to attention, letting her pass. It's easy when you know how to use your vocal vibrations to manipulate people's nervous systems. As we approach the throne, the Emperor turns to a man standing below him and commands, "Compute!" The Mentat, a human computer, runs through all the possible logical scenarios resulting from our visit and whispers the final computation to the monarch. During the second or two while the Mentat is occupied, our Reverend Mother makes eye contact with the Emperor and, while bowing, uses a technique of interpreting body language to read some secret political information in the tense set of his eyelids. Meanwhile, a gentleman who thinks he's a merchant, but is really a spy operating under the influence of a mental block, presents the Emperor with a female slave, a belly dancer, whom our Reverend Mother suspects of being a seasoned practitioner of "neuro-enticement." A lady-in-waiting bows to us, catches the Mother's hand, and presses it with impulsive affection, while the very tip of her little finger imperceptibly traces a complex code onto the witch's palm. It's easy when you know how. Nearly every human activity in *Dune* becomes a technical feat. People are professionals. Very few of them do not have a specialization, an expert skill, and a standard of performance. The galactic empire may not be mechanized, but it is technicized; *Dune* is a world of thoroughly instrumental values, in which the meaning of both flesh and metal can be summarized in the phrase "See Instructions for Use." We can identify the vision of human society in *Dune* as the megamachine, the social engine made of specialized human components.

The novel goes even further, however, giving an instrumental interpretation of the nature myth. Instead of a wondrous mother goddess, Nature is a professional agency that controls every ripple in the genetic pool. Why does *Dune* imagine nature this way? In psychological terms the Bene Gesserit is a fantasy of motherhood that reflects the dynamic of incomplete differentiation. The goal of the Bene Gesserit breeding program, an effort of ninety generations, is to engender one male child with certain features. The fantasy suggests the viewpoint of a dependent child, endowing his mother with impersonal and terrifying power that is totally focused on himself. Like Billy Pilgrim, Paul Atreides is made uneasy by his mother for the sole reason that she's his mother—and that's all he thinks she is. Projected on the larger psychocultural screen, the fantasy is a misogynist paranoia centered on woman-as-nature. Just as seventeenth-century misogynist writing blurred the distinction between witches and all women,[36] so *Dune*'s opening scene tells us that in the dark all mothers are witches, out to *get* you in every sense of the word. At this level, however, *Dune*'s portrayal of nature aids the novel's invention of masculine parthenogenesis. Instead of the gentle enchantment of the "golden dream," *Dune*'s representation of nature stresses power and secrecy. The power of generativity is a professional expertise, and the secrets of generation are the key to nature's system of total control.[37] To become a god the American Adam must take possession of nature's secrets.

More Ethnography: Not-So-Free Men and Imperial Scientists

On a moonlit night, among sand dunes and rock outcrops, Jessica and Paul are captured by the Fremen, the tribal natives of Arrakis. Sand is their element. They live in caves. Venturing out, they glide over the dunes in black robes that distill moisture from the wearer's body, and their sharp noses are fitted with nostril plugs against dust. Under their hoods their eyes are blue without whites, from ingesting *melange,* a vegetable spice unique to Arrakis. They are thrillingly expert with knives. The nicest thing about the Fremen is their means of transportation: they ride standing on the backs of giant sandworms. To the imperial colonists the sandworms are a Loch Ness monster–sized nuisance that constantly threatens production by creeping up on factories and swallowing them. But as closeness to nature separates the allegory's "natural" native from the "civilized" ruler, so the Fremen way with sandworms is their distinguishing secret. Also unknown to the empire is the fact that sandworms are the source of melange, an elixir that lengthens life and makes spaceflight possible by giving navigators a prescient vision, like a map. On our mythographical atlas of space fiction, Arrakis and Kutath inhabit the same system, the nature myths of alchemy. The sandworms are avatars of the maternal rock and produce its elixir of immortality. The Fremen, like the mri, are the rock's children. The *petra genetrix* of Arrakis serves the conquest of space. But while *The Faded Sun* gave science the power to work alchemical miracles, in *Dune* science has to be directed by a higher religious authority.

The Fremen have a long-range ecological project. By trapping moisture in strategic locations, over the course of centuries, they hope to turn Arrakis into a green and flowering Eden. No one knows of their devotion to this plan except Liet Kynes, son of Kynes, the Imperial Planetologist, whose dream it was and who disciplined the Fremen to carry it out. To Kynes, "the planet was merely...a machine being driven by its sun. What it needed was reshaping to fit it to man's needs. His mind went directly to the free-moving human population, the Fremen.... What a tool they could be!" (*D* 493). Like Hank Morgan attaching a motor to Saint Stylites, Kynes sees instrumental potential everywhere. With utopian single-mindedness he sets up his own version of the Man-Factory, recruiting Fremen, but not in the spirit of industrial democracy that partially motivated the Yankee. While Hank's explicit mission was to replace ignorant feudal superstition with science, hygiene, and assembly lines, Kynes, less a technological utopian than a megamechanical one, is interested only in control. One day, as the scientist stands explaining his blueprints to a group of Fremen, a man approaches him with a knife. Kynes glances at him once, says, "Remove yourself," and goes on talking, his back exposed for the blow. The attacker withdraws three paces, then deliberately falls onto his own blade.

Talk about omens! From that instant, Kynes had but to point, saying, "Go there." Entire Fremen tribes went. Men died, women died, children died. But they went. . . . Water began collecting in the basins. . . . (495)

Kynes's charisma has nothing to do with science fiction. His eerie power is another of *Dune*'s "higher plan" supernatural phenomena. How does the "higher plan" affect *Dune*'s ethnographical allegory, the fantasy encounter with other cultures? We can take Kynes's colonial paternalism at face value and regard his project as a representative case of Western science bringing progress to the natives for their own good. If the sahib has a tinge of enlightening transcendence about him, so much the better. I am inclined, however, to take the "removal" of natives more seriously and to read in this anecdote a ritual retelling of how the West was won. Kynes descends to the level of his human tools, the Fremen, in two ways. He fathers a half-Fremen boy, Liet, whom he names after the "removed" knife fighter, Uliet. The frontier myth has a use for the names of people or animals whom the hunter kills. Often the hunter takes them himself. Identities are exchanged between hunter and prey, or a kinship is acknowledged between them, that symbolically reconciles them at the very moment of the kill. That is the moment in which all the frontier hunters, "from Benjamin Church, through Daniel Boone and Davy Crockett, to . . . Ahab—ultimately realize their identity and achieve their power to dominate events."[38] Uliet's death is the moment when Kynes establishes his control over human and natural resources. He acknowledges kinship with his prey by naming his son, who will inherit his status and powers. Inexplicable in the science fiction universe, this moment is one of *Dune*'s ritual gestures; it grants science the role of the frontier hunter and sanctifies the ruthlessly instrumental use of nature and people in the name of improvement, or of claiming the wilderness for civilization.

In *Dune*'s mythology, however, despite its importance, science alone is not capable of restoring the reign of Jupiter. The irrigation project is off the mark. A green and fertile Earthly Paradise is not the landscape compatible with the transcendent sky-god. On the topic of religion—it's a funny thing, but the Fremen, who speak Arabic, live in tents in the desert, sit on pillows, drink boiled coffee out of ornamental services, have a month of Ramadan, and go on jihad carrying green banners, aren't Muslims. Careful reading reveals that the Fremen religion is "Zensunni," which makes you wish you hadn't asked. The T. E. Lawrence paraphernalia seems to wind an exotic wrapping around the one indispensable Fremen quality: they're unequaled fighters. The harshness of life on Arrakis has toughened the Fremen till their chil-dren are a match for the imperial troops. Fremen are indeed a tool, but not, as the scientists believed, for desert irrigation; like the mri, they are natural weapons. Only the divine king appreciates and exploits their real potential. The dubious orientalism of the allegory tells us that there is just one hard fact about another culture: where it fits in our military policy.

War, the Alternative to Generative Nature

Lady Jessica has requested permission for Paul to be made a member of the Bene Gesserit society. Paul is introduced by his nervous mom to sardonic old Reverend Mother Mohiam, who takes his hand, inserts it into a metal box, then holds a poisoned needle to his neck. Inside the box his hand is burning. If he withdraws it, she will kill him with her needle. While Paul's hand chars, Mohiam explains that she is testing his humanity. "You've heard of animals chewing off a leg to escape a trap? . . . A human would remain in the trap, endure the pain, feigning death that he might kill the trapper and remove a threat to his kind" (*D* 9). Finally taking his hand, whole and unharmed, out of the box, Paul survives the dismemberment stage of his shamanic initiation.

What new soul has he acquired? Something like a hunting lodge membership. He is now officially human according to Mohiam's defi-nition: humans are hunters, not hunted. Inflicting violence is human, but suffering pain, Mohiam sniffs, is for animals: "A human can over-ride any nerve in the body." We recognize the dualism of the frontier hunter myth. The test of human identity is staying on the correct side (left side, facing you) of the opposition between man the hunter and nature the prey. And although Paul is being initiated into the witches' society—rather, *because* he is—he insists on reinforcing the masculine/feminine dualism as well. He may owe his existence to the nature witches, but nothing is going to make him one of the girls.

> ". . . Sit down, little brother, here at my feet" [says Mohiam].
> "I prefer to stand."
> "Your mother sat at my feet once."
> "I'm not my mother."
> "You hate us a little, eh?" (*D* 11)

If we compare *Dune* to *The Faded Sun,* we find that the novels start at opposite ends of a spectrum. Duncan starts from a technological hu-man identity, which is naturalized to produce the ideal of the soul-dier.

By contrast, Paul starts out as a hunter—too connected to nature for his own comfort. Yet we can see the beginnings of a technological subject in Paul's initiation. Denying or "overriding" pain can become a form of transcendence, a way of sealing your identity with invulnerable boundaries. Most of us have, at some point, denied pain in order to safeguard or fulfill a self-image. In *Dune* pain and violence are opposites. Pain is a form of weakness, associated with being mortal and a part of nature, while violence is a proof of power, associated with transcending natural limits, like the body's limitations. Paul's initiation gives us a rather trigger-happy type of human subject.

On Arrakis disaster strikes. Duke Leto is assassinated. Teenage Paul and his mother flee into the desert. Hiding in a small tent with Jessica, Paul cannot grieve. He sits in rigid silence, wearing the look of "*someone forced to the knowledge of his own mortality.*" Paul is dangerously close to the wrong side of the dualism, the painful, "natural" side (*D* 197). Jessica asks what's wrong. "You!" he shouts, "what have you done to me?" "I gave birth to you," she answers (195), detecting her son's essential grievance. Suddenly, Paul has a vision. He beholds himself riding at the head of a terrible army. He sees the green banners of legions waving as they pass his father's grave, thousands of warriors shouting his name and following him into holy war, jihad, against the emperor of the galaxy. He sees spaceships, filled with his troops, overrunning the galactic empire. Although the jihad avenges his father's death, Paul comprehends that the deeper, underlying casus belli is "the need of [the] race ... to cross and mingle ... bloodlines in a great new pooling of genes ... the ancient way, the tried and certain way that rolled over everything in its path: jihad" (199). War is in the genes.

At last Paul closes his eyes and allows himself to mourn. He understands that the commander of the jihad will be as powerful a broker of mortality as his mother, because his "genetic" war is the equivalent of the Mothers' breeding program. Paul is nevertheless not a nature witch. No! His war "overrides" the pain of being mortal, and the violence that he inflicts upon the universe is the proof of his transcendent power. Paul's vision shows us a hat that really makes rabbits. *War is an alternative to generative nature.* War creates a god-king whose transcendent power, manifested in destruction, rivals nature's awesome power of creation. Does this sound to you like a myth of some archaic people or the theme of a late-late science fiction show? You and I have also been led to believe that the power to destroy life rivals the power to create life.

"Congratulations to the parents. Can hardly wait to see the new arrival"—this is the text of a telegram from Ernest Lawrence to physicists at Chicago in 1942, responding to research work on plutonium. In July of 1945 Richard Feynman was summoned to Los Alamos "with a wire announcing the day on which the birth of the 'baby' was expected."[39] Evelyn Keller observes that "the metaphor of pregnancy and birth became the prevailing metaphor surrounding the production and the testing, first, of the atomic bomb, and, later, of the hydrogen bomb. If the A-bomb was Oppenheimer's baby, the H-bomb was 'Teller's baby.'" In Keller's view the extremely disturbing metaphor of the "birth" of nuclear weapons is directly related to the myth of maternal nature:

> Life has traditionally been seen as the secret *of* women, a secret *from* men. By virtue of their ability to bear children, it is women who have been perceived as holding the secret of life. With the further identification of women with nature, it is a short step from the secrets of women to the secrets of nature.[40]

Personified as a mother—or, in *Dune*'s case, as a mafia of mothers—nature holds the secrets of life. The successful bomb tests prove that the scientists have come into possession of nature's secrets, an appropriation celebrated by the pervasive birth metaphor—but "the secret of life," now owned by the scientists, "has become the secret of death." "He who can destroy a thing has the real control of it," says the hero of *Dune*. Although this definition seems eccentric if we think of displaying control over Michelangelo's David or a favorite armchair by destroying them, it makes sense if we think, instead, of annihilating nature with "her" own secrets, now in our hands. The fact that we can destroy the biosphere with nuclear weapons proves that we are the godlike masters of life. A transcendent masculine principle replaces the generative feminine one, or, as Keller puts it, "Fertility is countered by virility, measured now by its death-dealing prowess."[41] Against reason, though not against psychocultural logic, war, and the power to destroy life, can be understood as a masculine mode of reproduction. The Bomb has a father but no mother.

The Rape of Nature and the Secret of Life

A young boy when captured by the Fremen, Paul grows up among them, acquires a practical wife and a beautiful concubine, rides wormback, and has a good time. Meanwhile, his destiny approaches. Because of a slip in the Bene Gesserit breeding program, the aimed-for male child was born prematurely. He is called the "Kwisatz Haderach." This is Herberticized Hebrew for a concept in the Jewish cabbala, roughly translatable as "the shortcut," an ability of saintly rabbis to travel to the end of time and back. In *Dune* the shortcut is a person, a male Reverend Mother. The talent he has been bred for is the ability to see into a "dark place" in the human soul that the Bene Gesserit have not been able to fathom. Paul's prescient visions inform him that he will be both the Kwisatz Haderach and the future god-king who leads the Fremen to galactic dominion. But first he must undergo a final initiation.

Paul's childhood dream of a cave comes true when the Fremen hold a ceremony for Jessica, to make her the successor to their Reverend Mother. Jessica has never aspired to this highest rank among the witches, knowing that the initiation test can be fatal, but she decides to try. At night, following behind their shrunken old Reverend Mother, the tribe files into a cavern in which their water supply is stored. Torchlight quivering on the black surfaces of full cisterns, walls streaked with damp, and the surreal echoing sound of waterdrops create the ambience of a world separate from the desert planet. In an expectant silence the crone prepares a drug, the Water of Life, made partly out of melange. She gives Jessica a leather pouch with a spout and, when Jessica draws a very small sip, squeezes the bag so that the witch swallows a large dose and, immediately falling into a trance, perceives her mortal danger. In a moment of suspended time Jessica sees the molecules of the toxic drug taking effect within her own metabolism. She survives this biochemical dismemberment by mentally rearranging the drug's molecular composition. Completing the task, she hears the tribe's Mother speaking inside her head. The old woman's spirit has left her body and is entering Jessica's mind, bringing with her a string of ancestresses. Her life experiences—a cascade of sand off a cliff, a lover's body—pour into "Jessica's awareness as water is poured into a cup" (*D* 356-57). A warm affection accompanies this union. The Fremen Mother finds to her delight "a mind full of interesting things." Jessica feels another presence, her own embryonic daughter, woken to consciousness in the womb. She surrounds the mote of life with love and feels it reflected back. Coming out of her trance, Jessica hands the waterbag with its changed contents over to the Fremen. The Water of Life is now an aphrodisiac, which they imbibe on the spot, and Paul falls in love with a girl whom he nicknames Sihaya, meaning "desert spring" or "paradise."

Maternal nature is different in this scene from the previous depiction of the cold, hyperprofessional Bene Gesserit. In the uncivilized wilderness of Arrakis we are closer to the golden dream of nature, and, while the cave is not a garden, it has the essential qualities of an Earthly Paradise: erotic love, harmony, and fertility. The secrets of maternal nature that Jessica discovers are simple and poetic. A mother is an infinite babushka doll, opening into the human past and future, a complete Descent of Woman. She is immortal, not personally but, rather, in the continuity of human generations and their memories. Deep in the realm of the Mother, *Dune* affords a moment of imagining a human identity that consists of being a fully conscious part of generative nature—like the human identity suggested by the writer Susan Griffin in her phrase "We are nature with a concept of nature" (emphasis added).[42] Unfortunately, *Dune* restricts this potential human identity to the feminine gender.

Paul also drinks the Water of Life and enters a trance but in a completely different context. The occasion of Paul's initiation is war. After an assassination attempt catches him off guard, Paul decides that he can no longer afford imperfect prescience and must be able to see the future clearly to begin fighting the jihad. The moment has come for Paul to transform himself into a god: "'*We will see now,*' he thinks, daring himself, '*whether I'm the Kwisatz Haderach who can survive the test that the Reverend Mothers have survived*'" (*D* 437). Paul takes one swallow and falls into a coma for three weeks. When he revives he flaunts his success by drinking a large quantity of the Water of Life in front of horrified Jessica, then he enters her mind. Paul uses his mother to reach the "dark place" in the soul:

[Paul] grabbed her hand, faced her with a death's head grin, and sent his awareness surging over her. The rapport was not as tender, not as sharing, not as encompassing as it had been with . . . the Old Reverend Mother in the cavern . . . but it was a rapport; a sense-sharing of the entire being. It shook her, weakened her, and she cowered in her mind, fearful of him.

Aloud, he said: "You speak of a place where you cannot enter? This place which the Reverend Mother cannot face, show it to me."

She shook her head, terrified by the very thought.

"Show it to me!" he commanded.

"No!"

But she could not escape him. Bludgeoned by the terrible force of him, she closed her eyes and focused inward—the direction-that-is-dark.

Paul's consciousness flowed through . . . her and into the darkness. . . . (443–44)

Jessica's rapport with the Fremen Mother describes an attitude toward nature, a tenderness that we sometimes feel when we're conscious of taking part in the continuity of old and new generations. We are aware of belonging in the scheme of life. Paul's rapport with Jessica describes a completely different attitude, best characterized by a metaphor: the rape of nature. Historically, this is a metaphor that Bacon employed to praise and elucidate the methods of experimental science. In a famous passage he states: "For you have but to hound nature in her wanderings and you will be able when you like to lead and drive her afterwards to the same place again. Neither ought a man to make scruple of entering and penetrating into those holes and corners when the inquisition of truth is his whole object."[43] Like Bacon's experimental scientist, Paul makes an aggressive attempt to possess the truth, the secret of life hidden in the Mother's "dark place." Yet what is the truth? By this end of the twentieth century we have learned that absolutely objective scientific truth does not exist. Nature is always, to some degree, in the eyes of the beholder—the maker of theoretical models and the experimenter who affects the results of his or her experiment. In other words, "Nature-as-the-object-of-human-knowledge never comes to us 'naked'; it comes only as already constituted in social thought."[44] Social values influence our observations and descriptions of the natural world. These values are present in the rhetoric of scientific writing and indicate the social directions of science. When science is rhetorically constructed as an exercise in domination, what it searches for and finds in nature will certainly be, among other things, the power to dominate. It's worth noting, on this topic, that the metaphor of rape in scientific rhetoric is not unknown to modern scientists. James Lovelock describes how his colleagues at NASA, working on the Viking Mars missions, frequently debated the benefit of sterilizing the probe. "Sometimes," he writes, "the argument was fierce and macho; full of adolescent masculinity. In any event, feeling as I did—that Mars was dead—the image of rape, sometimes used, could not be sustained; at worst the act would only be the dismal lonely aberration of necrophilia."[45]

When Paul penetrates the dark place, these are his results:

Paul said: "There is in each of us an ancient force that takes and an ancient force that gives. A man finds little difficulty in facing that place within himself where the taking force dwells, but it's almost impossible for him to see into the giving force *without changing into something other than man.* For a woman, the situation is reversed.... You see that this could overwhelm you. The greatest peril to the Giver is the force that takes. The greatest peril to the Taker is the force that gives." (*D* 445; my emphasis)

What an anticlimax to the rape of nature. After hundreds of pages of exploits, intrigues, and mystical hints, the dark wilderness of the soul turns out to be a familiar dualism, mirroring the hero's differentiation anxieties. Easily mistaken for a description of androgyny, the Taker and the Giver do not constitute a balanced mixture of male and female qualities but a chronically dangerous opposition. Hardly a marriage of complementary forces, the two sides won't even look at each other. The worst danger to the masculine identity is *changing into the Other,* becoming one of the girls. "To be a man," Jessica Benjamin observes, "is not merely to assert one's side of the duality.... It is also to insist that the dualism, splitting, and boundaries between the male and female postures are upheld."[46] By definition, the Taker must keep taking in order to remain secure in his identity, while the Giver offers a boundless resource. The dynamic described here is surely that of the differentiation syndrome: the child relies on maternal nurturance, while objectifying and denying identification with the mother. The secret of life, it turns out, is no less than the masculine subject's unlimited appropriation of maternal nature. With such a secret in his possession, how can Paul *not* become a god?

Paul makes an army of the Fremen and becomes their supreme commander. The dazzling aura of godhead starts to surround him. On the evening of the crucial battle a sandstorm gathers and rolls toward the capital city Paul has beseiged. The storm picks up momentum, covering the horizon, a mineral typhoon capable of eating flesh from bone and obliterating whatever isn't buried deep underground. Paul is pleased, because the storm will demoralize the weather-foolish imperial troops and weaken the city. But his men report worriedly that it's a Mother of all Storms. An hour later it's a Grandmother Storm. The evening progresses:

"... It's a great-great-grandmother of a storm ... perhaps even more than you wished."

"It's my storm," Paul said, and saw the silent awe on the faces. . . . "Though it shook the entire world it could not be more than I wished." (D 452–53)

Heaven help the poor officer who suggests that Paul might be inconvenienced by the feminine caprice of the weather! There is no more Mother Nature, Paul proclaims: there is only the power of nature, which belongs to the divine king. Having appropriated nature's secret, Paul transcends the realm of the Mother. He has become a shortcut out of the line of ancestresses who pour the Water of Life from generation to generation. He is also a shortcut to the stars. The same initiation that let Paul into the dark place shows him spaceships over Arrakis, on his mental map of the future. The sky-god's representative, is ready to begin his space program.

The Superhero: An Ideal of American and Human Identity

The superhero is *Dune*'s ideal of American and human identity. A brief comparison with the soul-dier will help clarify the superhero's meaning. To become a soul-dier Duncan went through an experience very similar to Paul's. He suffered initiatory dismemberment. As a result, he became a warrior with the magical power of traveling at will through "the Dark." By renewing himself periodically in the maternal Abyss, the soul-dier made the expansion of the technological empire seem "natural," like the frontiersman's hunts, and affirmed the American desire for limitlessness. Paul's second initiation was also a near-death that took him into the maternal Abyss. Surviving dissolution, he too gained the magical power of traveling through "the Dark"—the dark place inside his mother's soul. But here lies the difference between the two human ideals. Paul doesn't merely renew himself in the Abyss: he *possesses* it. With the rape of nature he *takes over* the Abyss in order to become a god.

Why is the superhero an American ideal? Paul's relationship with nature also derives from the frontier myth. His predecessor is Captain Ahab, monomaniac hunter of the "gliding great demon of the seas of life."[47] Ahab doesn't hunt a whale, as other frontier hunters mark out a deer or a bear within the wilderness; he wants to harpoon nature's numinous spirit: "It is the essence of the real that Ahab seeks to destroy, devour, assimilate to himself, replace with his own being and intelligence."[48] This is precisely the character of Paul's aggression against Mother Nature. Earlier I said that the hunter myth defines the concept of *the American frontier: where the forces of limitlessness meet what has yet to be broken and recreated in their image.* The superhero personally destroys and assimilates nature, "the essence of the real," setting himself in its place. He is an Ideal of American iden tity because he incarnates limitlessness. Let us recall that the super- hero's mission is to establish the reign of Jupiter, patron of science and empire, over the New World. While the soul-dier hunts in nature, the superhero hunts nature, the ultimate kill.

Dune Messiah: Inventing Life

What does the ideal of the superhero have to do with technology? You may have noticed that *Dune* has its own version of the Sand Belt. Paul engineers his battlefield by the same means as Hank, making the cor- rect Baconian appropriations, achieving the same destructive force. Paul's war is technological in its essence and replaces generative na- ture with the masculine mode of reproduction. But all wars are tempo- rary. We might remember that Merlin defeats Hank by putting him to sleep for thirteen centuries. Paul must produce a "baby" who will transcend time, and for this purpose he has recourse to technology.

I have mentioned the American Adam's difficulty with the institu- tions of fatherhood and monarchy. The new teenage Emperor of the Galaxy has trouble on the home front. He's deeply in love with his Fremen concubine, the girl whom he calls Sihaya. He has contracted a political marriage with the former emperor's daughter, a historian, whom he detests. Sihaya wants desperately to get pregnant; Paul knows why she can't but isn't telling. This is the sorry situation that comes of the American Adam ascending a throne. Let's call the concu- bine and the princess, respectively, American Paradise and European History. Paradise cannot conceive because History is secretly feeding her a contraceptive. So it goes. If Paul allows his concubine to conceive an heir, he will no longer be the perpetually innocent new man of the New World; instead, he will become part of history, a name in a genealogy of kings. Paul's visions show Sihaya dying in childbirth, the result of letting time into the American Eden.

Arrakis has become a rich planet with fountains and green gardens in the capital city. But the city festers with luxurious vice. "Water . . . has become a poison,"[49] thinks Sihaya. For a desert spring this thought is the equivalent of a death wish, realized when Sihaya finally becomes pregnant. The Mother is everywhere, fertility and mortality seeping in around the borders of the transcendent god-king's imperium. Even navigable space has somehow turned into amniotic water: Fremen

warriors return from the jihad fascinated by foreign seas and dis-
tressingly pacific. Before his concubine's death Paul has a revelation
of what his divine kingship has meant and regrets his great effort to
replace generative nature. Touching Sihaya's abdomen, he says con-
tritely, "I think I tried to invent life, not realizing it'd already been
invented." He goes out for a stroll and looks at the stars, which resemble the sea. "He'd lived a take-everything life, tried to create a universe
in his own image. But the exultant universe was breaking across him
at last with its silent waves." Paul isn't so sure anymore that the Taker
is the epitome of masculine identity. For the first time he senses that
power has limits. Nothing lasts forever. On the shores of time, he
thinks, are infinite shining grains of memory; maybe that's all there is
to being human? He ponders, "Was this the golden genesis of man?"
(*DM* 232–33).

Just for a moment, forget about myths and metaphors. Imagine
that *Dune* is a real dream. The recurrent image in the dream is sand.
Sand dunes, folded to the horizon; alkaline sand flats, sand darkening
the sun in smears, fields of white, gold, red, and black sand; glaring
light or furred with light; tortuous sandstones, formations trickling
grains into the wind; dust devils winding their arms around wind
funnels. Through the shifting sands float strange visions of giant
worms, warriors, and witches. But there is something magnetic about
the sand itself, as though the elements of the dream's plot were knots
in a veil of sand that twisted and untwisted. The sand is alive in a
special way. Not the way a forest is alive, full of breathing variety, but
like a truth from which everything else arises, that outlasts everything.
What's under the shifting sand dazzle in your mind is gold. Deathless
truth. Stability. Immortality. But then your dream zeros in on a sluggish little oasis, a choked well, a thorn bush, a mummified-looking
cadaver of a goat. Suddenly, you're thirsty, and you feel stricken,
vulnerable, and small. Then a caption in flaming gold letters passes
across the sky: "Was this the golden genesis of man?" Science fiction
is a mass dream. It makes automatic but excellent use of our stock
images, and, as long as a certain cultural homogeneity exists in its
audience, we respond reflexively. Leto, Paul's son, is born of our desire
for a golden genesis, a transcendent human condition.

Sihaya dies in childbed because her body is "drained by the speed"
of her labor. This diagnosis is our first clue that technology is part of
the scenario: the alchemist speeds up the generative process of nature.
As Sihaya lies dead, Paul finds himself looking out through the eyes
of his infant son, whose angle of vision enables his father to throw a

knife at a villain standing by the cradle. This kill is the masculine equivalent of the Water of Life initiation. Paul is abruptly united with his fathers:

> He saw his father. He *was* his father. And the grandfather, and the grandfathers before that. His awareness tumbled through a mind-shattering corridor of his whole male line. (*DM* 245)

There are two major acts in this concentrated drama. The first is alchemy. Like Dr. Frankenstein, who dreamed of embracing his mother's decomposing body, Paul performs an alchemical operation, dismembering the mother in order to take control of the generative process. The second act is *Dune's* masculine mode of reproduction. Paul looks through baby Leto's eyes, sees the villain, hurls the knife, and in the same breath is united with his male ancestors. The kill *replaces* nature as the source of generation. To slay is to father.

Let us reconsider Jessica's initiation as a Reverend Mother: she shared the minds of both the old, dying Fremen Mother and her own unborn child. The witch was a link between mother and daughter, death and birth. Now if we examine the distribution of death and birth in Paul's equivalent scene, we find that we're on the cutting edge of mythological engineering.

Play this in slow motion and watch carefully. A knife has left Paul's hand and is gliding through the air. The baby's eyes are fixed on the knife's target, and Paul looks out through them. The mother, her body drained by alchemical speed, lies dead. The knife hits the villain. He dies. Paul sees his fathers. If the metaphor for the female genealogy was the pouring of water from one vessel into another, the emptying of memories from the old into the young, the metaphor for the male genealogy is simultaneous seeing. Paul and Leto see together: "He saw his father. He *was* his father." Fathers and sons occupy a corridor of vision in which there is no sense of time and no death.

What triggers this revelation? A double-edged technical operation involving two deaths: the alchemical control of generativity and the reproductive slaying. The first produces a "forged" baby; the second opens up a birth corridor that replaces the mother's womb. Let us call this corridor a *paternal dimension*. It replaces the fertile womb with a parthenogenetic masculine eye. If it strikes you that an eye giving birth to fathers and sons is a weird science fiction image, think of a geneticist looking at a video monitor's image of a male cell that he's cloning. The paternal dimension is accessible *only* through the use of technology, but it is currently accessible. The dream is realized as the machine. We need to ponder the double function that Dune assigns to technology in this scenario. The first function, the alchemical operation, is to appropriate and control nature's generative process. Our geneticist does as much by cloning cells. The second function, the reproductive slaying, is to destroy nature with its own secrets. What is the destructive potential of real masculine parthenogenesis? Like Oppenheimer's "baby," Paul's inaugurates a new epoch. If we look to science fiction for prophecies, *Dune*'s is grim. Leto becomes the immortal ruler of a totalitarian society, reducing his subjects to the condition of ancient Egyptian peasants, and this restoration of humanity's original megamachine is called—what else—the Golden Path.

Conclusion to Myths of the Final Frontier

In a science fiction story about the Vietnam War an American platoon leader, in the routine act of pushing a prisoner out of a helicopter, shouts jokingly, "Space! The final frontier!" H. Bruce Franklin, an expert on American science fiction, writes that "America's war in Indochina cannot be dissociated from American science fiction, which shaped and was reshaped by the nation's encounter with Vietnam. Indeed, the war cannot be fully comprehended unless it is seen in part as a form of American science fiction and fantasy."[50] Franklin studied science fiction written about the Vietnam War and found in the more hawkish tales "two dominant American images of what it takes to win wars: superwarriors and techno-wonders." He also discovered that the wildest fantasies of technological warfare simply imitated "technological fetishism" in the Pentagon. While rereading *Dune* for this book, I could not help thinking of Franklin's superwarriors and techno-wonders. *Dune*'s first copyright is 1965, the same year that brought "Operation Rolling Thunder," the sustained bombing of North Vietnam, and escalation of the United States' military commitment to the war. The popular response to *Dune* must be taken seriously, as much for outlasting the Vietnam War as for originating in its context. Not all space fiction novels glorify war. But as soon as we picture a spaceship, we mentally unroll the map of objectified space; we enter the mass dream of collective technological power; we participate in a drama about remaking the universe in our image. Whether it's fought with firepower or the anthropologist's diary, space fiction always shows us the power struggle that ensues when we divide the world into the technological subject and the Other.

Are war and technology always hand in glove? I think that the question ought to be rephrased: Can technology exist outside a mega-machine-like social system? Despite what *Dune* and *The Faded Sun* urge us to believe, war is not natural, neither in our genes nor biologically necessary. War, Lewis Mumford explains, is a cultural invention. The first armies developed at the same time as civilization, and military organization—coordinated squads and companies—was the model of the megamachine's labor force.[51] The divine king commanded armies of both soldiers and workers. But while the megamachine's arduous labor was justified by the cities it built, war produced no such tangible accomplishments and was not motivated by rational purposes. War, as an institution, began in the religious ceremony of human sacrifice, an ancient method of appeasing a community's collective anxieties. Originally, if a village did not pick a sacrificial victim from among its people, it might conduct a manhunt, raiding another village. As civilization grew more complex, the conditions of life became less stable, and collective fears multiplied. Increasing anxiety invited, as it always does, more potent religious appeasement. The divine king, identified with the community that he ruled, was the sacred power in whose name one-sided raids became large, organized operations and turned into conflicts between rival powers. "So ever larger numbers of people with more effective weapons were drawn into this dreadful ceremony, and what was at first an incidental prelude (the manhunt) to a token sacrifice itself became the 'supreme sacrifice' performed *en masse*. . . . The ability to wage war and to impose collective human sacrifice has remained the identifying mark of all sovereign power throughout history."[52] In modern times war glorifies the state and the rulers who represent it. It assuages the fearsome stress of change too rapid to assimilate. If, six thousand years ago, "early 'civilized' man had reason to be frightened of the forces that he himself, by his series of technological successes, was unleashing," think what we have seen in the way of technological successes and their destabilizing social effects, just since 1945. When *The Faded Sun* and *Dune* celebrate the gods of the military megamachine, they are appeasing unconscious collective fear. They reassure us that war is our best protection from the devil, the deep blue sea, and the dark.

The fundamental project of technology is not war but, rather, "inventing life," finding an alternative to generative nature. When science fiction stories tell us that galactic wars are in the genes, doubtless this offers a good excuse for war; however, what we're really intended to think is that technology is qualitatively the same as nature. Making bombs is the same as making babies. That board inside your computer is the same thing as a mother. Using metaphors that equate technological power with nature's generativity, science fiction persuades us that we can replace nature with our technological selves. While the desire behind such metaphors is at least as ancient as alchemy, in the modern world the metaphors are given solid high-tech form. Today we find the fundamental project in the fields of genetic engineering and robotics as well as in military technology. *Mind Children*, a book by Hans Moravec, director of the Mobile Robot Laboratory of Carnegie-Mellon University, ties it all together on the first page:

> Engaged for billions of years in a relentless, spiraling arms race with one another, our genes have finally ... produced a weapon so powerful it will vanquish the losers and winners alike. This device is not the hydrogen bomb—widespread use of nuclear weapons would merely delay the much more interesting demise that has been engineered.
>
> What awaits is not oblivion but rather a future which ... is best described by the words "postbiological" or even "supernatural." It is a world in which the human race has been ... usurped by its own artificial progeny.... Today, our machines are still simple creations, requiring the parental care and hovering attention of any newborn.... But within the next century they will mature into entities as complex as ourselves, and eventually into something transcending everything we know—in whom we can take pride when they refer to themselves as our descendants.[53]

Nothing compels anyone to imagine genes as Department of Defense-subsidized engineering firms. I could say that genes are threads of a magical carpet that weaves itself. Or that genes are the alphabet of nature's book. Or that genes are a jazz combo in Bunny Biology's All-Nite Bar, never playing the same riff twice. Do my metaphors, however, convince you that robots are the final outcome of billions of years of biological evolution? Do they give you a sense of earthshaking transcendent power? Probably not. Moravec uses a metaphor we've all gotten used to, technological war = natural generation, and he uses it to say, If you thought the Bomb was the Baby, look out for robots! Then he displays before us all the hoary promises of the alchemist:

we'll make babies without women; we'll artificially bring about the era of human perfection (Moravec: human minds in robot bodies); we'll have supernatural powers; we'll be immortal and rustproof. Yet if the fundamental project doesn't explicitly demand killing people of other nations, something does vanish under suspicious circumstances: nature. Every version of the fundamental project is a millenial dream. The new world transcends everything we know, including birth and death. We, the humble organic "parents" of our instruments, will fade away in our present form but be reborn in the alternative "nature." And nature will be annihilated, like the vanishing desert of Kutath, like the Mothers of Arrakis.

The invention of an alternative to nature is space fiction without the ships. This voyage from our present mortal state into transcendence, although a very old story, has a special significance in American thought. According to one scholar, the American frontier hero's relationship with nature was given a philosophical basis by Ralph Waldo Emerson, a chief spokesman of the nineteenth-century American intellectual movement of transcendentalism. In his essay "Nature" Emerson describes what it is like to contemplate nature. He imagines himself as a transparent eyeball, a clear medium into which impressions of nature enter. But his gazing does not stop at the trees in his immediate line of vision; it expands outward. "Standing on the bare ground—my head . . . uplifted into infinite space . . . the currents of the Universal Being circulate through me,"[54] till the spirit of the observer expands to include the infinite universe. The bare ground, meanwhile, "has not been left behind but itself lifted up." By observing nature, Emerson dissolves it into himself and tranforms it into his universal vision. The woods of Concord, Massachusetts, vanish into his head and reemerge, projected to infinity, on the mental map of the American empire. Without knife, gun, oven, or other hardware, the philosopher achieves the complete appropriation of nature that turns the human being into a god: "The self transcends its mortal limits by taking total possession of an actual world."[55]

In its quiet way "Nature" foretells our use of space as a metaphor for thinking about the American frontier. And though Emerson does not perform any technical operations during his contemplation of nature, his gazing, uplifted head opens the way for the technological replacement of nature. We have seen the Transcendentalist's devouring gaze at the end of the movie *2001:A Space Odyssey*. In the film's final moments two shapes occupy the screen: the round globe of Earth and the huge, round, staring head of the Star Child, the new technologically created human being, floating in space. Then the Star Child's head bumps Mother Earth off the screen. The final frontier is a state of mind: space fiction puts us there.

Cyborgs and Daughters: Feminist Myths in the Man-made World

> You can't unite woman and human any more than you can unite
> matter and anti-matter; they are designed not to be stable together
> and they make just as big an explosion inside the head of the
> unfortunate girl who believes in both.[1]

That's Joanna Russ, the most important and, be it said, explosive, writer of feminist science fiction.[2] A generation of writers and critics have expounded the problems besetting the literary representation of women, by women. In science fiction feminist writers have broken a tradition of gender stereotyping that cast women in the unappealing role of the Other. If you watched the original "Star Trek," you witnessed the bad old days of lady aliens undulating about in extraterrestrial intimate wear or crew women who, during major galactic crises, fussed over Captain Kirk's coffee. The challenge facing writers of women's science fiction is to find ways of redefining both "woman" and "human." As Russ suggests, this is a demanding task.

Gender stereotyping of human passions and activities limits what women can say about themselves and the meanings that we give to women's lives. In her poignant book *Writing a Woman's Life* Carolyn Heilbrun mentions that women's biographers are constantly aware of a basic, hard-to-describe gap between being a woman and wanting to be something else. When women write their autobiographies, they censor themselves to avoid sounding unfeminine—their achievements often seem to happen to them by accident, like love affairs, instead of resulting from planning and hard work.[3] Many emotions and events that are part of women's condition have no acceptable mode of expression and cannot be translated into the recognized vocabulary of "human" experience. (Think of the public and legal debates over the meaning of a single word, *No*, when spoken by a woman.) Until recently a female reader would be hard put to find stories that provided insights into her own experience and could be models for her life. What counsel could a gifted girl take from the biographies of successful women that glossed over inner conflicts or downplayed the struggle between work and family life? What was she to do with stories of famous men whose relationships with powerful mentors and supportive lovers were not likely to parallel her own? Heilbrun also discusses the range of unexplored issues in the writing of a woman's life story. Do we begin with her being born not-a-boy and her parents' disappointment, or lack of it? How do we define a successful marriage? We need new stories about these things. "We know that we are without a text," Heilbrun admits, "and we must discover one."[4]

Science fiction has given women writers the freedom to discover new stories and has gained an enthusiastic readership, not only among regular fans but also among people attracted to the genre because it depicts women in innovative ways. A science fiction world in which women can travel freely, and work in any capacity from cargo loader to captain, allows writer and readers the luxury of imagining what such untrammeled lives might be like. A futuristic novel about a misogynist society can satirize familiar oppression by using grotesque metaphors and an exotic setting. Writers such as John Varley, whose characters keep changing sex and species, play merry havoc with gender roles. The greatest advantage of feminist science fiction, generally speaking, is the freedom to imagine woman-as-human, that unselfconscious being who goes about life the way she wants or has to, neither particularly because she's a woman nor in spite of it; and who suggests what womanhood might be if gendered stereotypes and social barriers were to dissolve. The new perspectives that women writers brought to the genre have been appreciated as well as criticized by nonfeminist readers. Veteran science fiction editor Brian Aldiss hailed women's science fiction as the way out of what he acerbically called "the Ghetto of Retarded Boyhood."[5]

After women's science fiction burgeoned in the 1970s and 1980s, Aldiss states, the genre stopped being an exclusive "all-male escapist power fantasy"[6]—but if feminists altered the power fantasy, what took its place? Women are suspicious of the idea of power. "I have had students walk out of a class when I declared that power is a reasonable subject for discussion," Heilbrun relates. Partly because it's "unfeminine," and partly because it's used against them, the idea of power, for women, is contaminated with domination. Yet power need not be synonymous with the ability to injure, coerce, or control other people. "Power is the ability to take one's place in whatever discourse is essential to action and the right to have one's part matter."[7] Have women writers come to grips with the discourse of science fiction, changing the myths of technological power, giving a place to other mythic selves besides the traditional technological-human subject? If so, women's stories could be changing the national mode of thinking. Some philosophers believe that women's science fiction reflects the possibilities of emerging feminist science and technology. Sandra Harding refers scientists to Anne McCaffrey's stories: "Perhaps we should turn to our novelists and poets for a better intuitive grasp of the theory we need."[8] Donna Haraway, whose fascinating ideas I'll discuss in less depth, inevitably, than they deserve, and who illustrates feminist theory with women's science fiction, asserts that "immortality and omnipotence are not our goals."[9]

Goodbye, alienated nature, alchemists, and divine kings. So I thought when I began working on the question of whether feminist science fiction was fundamentally different from traditional SF. I was wrong. Of course, there has been a revolution in the way women are portrayed in science fiction. Little girls viewing the new "Star Trek" have better role models than my Trekkie friends did, as we watched with a dim fear that womanhood would change us into nincompoops. It's also important that feminists who are interested in utopian thought experiments now have a place to go. What I questioned, however, was whether you could have science fiction without alienated nature, or, to put it more positively, if feminist ideas on the deliberate, conscious level of the science fiction text reformed its images of nature and technology on the "mass dream" level. The answer is a most intriguing no.

No, alienated nature and all the rest are still going strong, as long as science fiction's cardinal rule, Leave Nothing Unrationalized, is observed. (This is an important qualifier, because it excludes Russ.) The utopian heterocosm, the "other, better nature," inevitably alienates maternal nature. *But the psychocultural drama in women's science fiction is a completely new story, a myth of female selfhood.* It is the story of alienated nature's daughters. Judging from feminist science fiction's unrevised mythology, we may have to look elsewhere for new ways of thinking about science and nature. But women's science fiction does something that is just as important: through its version of alienated nature and other unrevised myths, we learn how the female child's psychological pattern of differentiation from her mother affects the way women imagine their relationships to nature and to technology. We need to tell this story in order to transform women's relationships to scientific knowledge and technological power.

Why Not Utopia?

Is there a difference between feminist science fiction and utopia? Most feminist critics lump them together. "It is the utopian mode that separates science fiction from the other categories of popular feminist fiction"[10]–thus Heilbrun, in a special science fiction issue of *Women's Studies International Forum.* Leafing through the critical literature, I find these hybridized names for science fiction: "contemporary feminist utopias in science fiction"[11] "feminist science fiction [utopias]";[12] "feminist science and utopian fiction";[13] "women's critical utopias."[14] Marleen Barr, editor of two special issues on the subject, characterizes feminist science fiction[15] as either dystopian prediction with a strong element of satire or as utopian speculation.[16] We are in the country of utopian theorists, who are alert to "the genre of science fiction where a phenomenon of interest to all utopists is emerging."[17]

By treating science fiction exactly like utopia, critics make mistakes. One utopist claims that feminist authors want to bring back the prehistoric, uncivilized, Jungian female principle. She quotes Russ's remark that male science fiction and its fandom divides into two camps, the technophiles and the technophobes. Women, however–the critic concludes–have no proprietary relationship to technology at all; they don't own it, run it, or want it.[18] So, even though feminist authors choose to write in a genre that is all about living in the scientific-technological system, they don't judge technology from within; they're just pastoral bystanders. Utopists go astray when they read science fiction as nothing more than depictions of ideal societies and dramatized social criticism. In such readings science fiction becomes more didactic than mass dreams can possibly be. Character and plot are the bearers of "philosophical propositions or moral arguments, whose function is to persuade."[19] One critic, for example, asserts that "the new fantasy fiction by women depicts a closer connection between nature and culture than most men's utopian speculation.... These societies celebrate the natural cycles in their institutions and rituals."[20] We know that *nature* cannot be taken for granted in science fiction, in which images of nature have multitudinous meanings, depending on the interplay of myths and the ethnographic allegory. A reader oblivious to science fiction's particular literary context cannot answer questions bearing on the real importance of women's science fiction. Why don't women write utopias instead of science fiction? What is it about the science fiction heterocosm that attracts feminists? (For an explanation of why I do not discuss Marge Piercy's *Woman on the Edge of Time* or Ursula Le Guin's *Dispossessed* under this heading, please see the introduction. Briefly, while these utopias have bearing upon women's relationship to science and technology and can be considered science fiction in the general sense, they are not examples of the science fiction *heterocosm,* so they do not help us to explain its meaning and the appeal of its values, for women.)

Donna Haraway's Cyborg Utopia

The boundary is permeable between tool and myth, instrument and concept . . . myth and tool mutually constitute each other.[21]

The dream *is* the machine, and vice versa. Donna Haraway is a feminist philosopher who writes about science and technology. She recently received the American Book Award for a series of essays subtitled "The Reinvention of Nature," which fairly sums up her approach: nature is a cultural construction, invented, not found, by sciences and technologies that are permeated with cultural wishes, lies, conceptions, and prejudices. Haraway analyzes the cultural meanings that shape technologies and scientific disciplines. Her work on primatology, covering all aspects of the discipline from institutional politics to field reports, showed how theories of primate behavior were invented in the image of social relations, especially gender but also race and class. In her latest book, at one point, she describes how the visual scenes compiled from *Voyager*'s data look like simple postcard pictures, taken by a space vacationer with a Nikon, even when we know better. This illusion preserves our faith in the objectivity of scientific representation. Like Emerson's transparent eyeball, the camera is an eye, passively receiving impressions, objectively reporting them.

Except it isn't—nor is a world of hard facts and uninterpreted objects sitting out there for its portrait. We don't discover the world, Haraway claims, but we talk with it, through our technologies and from our cultural points of view. One engaging idea that Haraway presents is a new concept of the "object." An object can be something that isn't dead or passive, which we are curious about and try to engage in conversation. Objects of human knowledge can have lives of their own. This approach "makes room for some unsettling possibilities, including a sense of the world's independent sense of humor," as on those occasions when scientists confess to feeling that the phenomena have outwitted them. Nothing could be farther from the traditional view of nature as dead matter, manipulated by technological power. Haraway views our involvement with machines as a lively way of engaging with a living world—and because she sees liberatory potential in technology, she believes that science fiction is a "rich writing practice in recent feminist theory."[22] In this essay, like Harding, Haraway suggests that feminist science fiction illustrates the new, liberating ways that we can think about nature and use technology. A profound mythographer, Haraway perceives what other critics overlook: women's science fiction is a feminist myth-making process about science and technology, not a flight from them.

Yet Haraway is preeminent among the utopists. With care and respect I must criticize her reading of feminist science fiction, with which she illustrates her utopian ideal, the cyborg. The purpose of my criticism isn't to nitpick over literary analysis of science fiction but, instead, to take serious issue with the feminist claims that Haraway makes for the cyborg. Since she gives feminist science fiction authors the role of "theorists for cyborgs" (*MC* 92) and draws on science fiction stories to support the theory of her utopia, oversights in the reading distort Haraway's ideas and raise the question of whether the technological heterocosm is a proper vehicle for feminist utopia. We'll survey the cyborg utopia in two stages. First, we'll look at Haraway's famous essay "A Manifesto for Cyborgs." I will discuss whether the cyborg solves the problem of mind-body dualism, as Haraway claims, and will compare her utopian vision with Hans Moravec's human-robot cyborgs. Second, later in this chapter, we'll glance at *Superluminal,* a novel Haraway admires, to see how alienated nature coexists with cyborgs.

The Cyborg: A Feminist Utopian Myth

By the late twentieth century, our time, a mythic time, we are all ... fabricated hybrids of machine and organism; in short, we are cyborgs. The cyborg is our ontology; it gives us our politics. (*MC* 66)

The cyborg is part human and part machine. You are literally a cyborg if you wear a prosthetic device or an implant, like a pacemaker. But a human being intricately bound up with technology also inhabits cyborgdom, like people who spend most of their working day among machines—which means a lot of people, from programmers to telephone operators to assembly line workers. The amounts of time that Americans spend driving cars, watching TV, playing electronic games, using high-tech sports equipment, listening to Walkmans, and dealing with household appliances also qualify us for cyborg status. The key meaning of the cyborg, however, is philosophical. "The cyborg is our ontology," the essence of our being. Technology makes us who we are. This is true of science fiction, in which the raison d'être of all phenomena is the man-made world; Haraway suggests that we *live* science fiction. We are cyborgs because we're the instruments of a powerful technological-capitalist system that appropriates and reshapes the world at an ever-increasing rate. At the material level the lives of working people, as well as the natural environment, are appropriated and consumed by the system's expansion. "The Homework Economy," a section of Haraway's essay, deals with the exploitative labor practices of high-tech industry and their effect on women, especially in the Third World. Appropriation is also a spiritual or philosophical process, since our minds are full of the system's myths and images, the dreams of the machine. To combat the problem on all levels we need a political myth, a utopian vision that directs and inspires political action. Haraway calls her cyborg an "ironic political myth" (1). The cyborg myth acknowledges our technicized natures, not to deny the modern world's technological character but, rather, to use it for feminist purposes. How is this possible?

Western myths are ways of defining the self, and they provide the conceptual basis for oppression and domination. (Based on the Cartesian self, for example, the concept of scientific objectivity justifies "pure" research that ignores the scientist's social and political contexts.)[23] We have become cyborgs because our culture's myths have been able to define us that way. Now, according to Haraway, oppressive definitions of the self begin in the Western *myth of origin*. This myth tells of an original human state that was innocent, whole, and natural. But for human culture to evolve, the original state had to be shattered.

The myth of origin includes not only the Earthly Paradise, as you've guessed, but also the modern accounts of human civilization given in the theories of Marxism and Freudian psychoanalysis. Marx described man leaving his natural or animal state by beginning to labor and produce. Freud believed that the infant experienced a sense of organic union with the mother, the remnant of an original, primitive, precivilized human state. The myth of origin gives us a dualistic view of reality. Man, the mind, and culture are conceived as the opposite of woman, the body, and nature. We can abbreviate this complex dualism: man-as-culture/woman-as-nature. What makes the myth oppressive is the relationship between the two sides of the dualism. Power, in the tales of the origin myth and the rise of civilization, consists of everyone on the left side of the dualism appropriating and dominating everything on the right side. Power is Marx's savage becoming human by turning nature into a resource for production (motherhood, however, is merely "natural" and does not count as production). Power is Freud's male child becoming an individual by differentiating from his mother and identifying with his father (civilization is masculine; women are its discontents). The two modern accounts of civilization, "Marxism and psychoanalysis . . . depend on the plot of original unity out of which difference must be produced . . . in a drama of escalating domination of woman/nature" (67). We have seen, in science fiction, various ways of gaining power that all fit this pattern: the frontier hunter's kill, the alchemist's operation, Emerson's reality-dissolving eyeball, Bacon's appropriation of nature, and so forth, and so on.

Enter the cyborg. Ironically the final product of Western culture, the cyborg *shatters* the origin myth. Cyborgs are made, not born. They never had a mother. They were never natural. The cyborg "skips the step of original unity, of identification with nature in the Western sense. . . . [It] would not recognize the Garden of Eden; it is not made of mud and cannot dream of returning to dust" (67). Where is the dividing line between nature and culture in the scenario of a fetus technologically implanted in a host mother? Where is the gender dividing line between Man the civilized tool user and Woman the natural breeder, when Silicon Valley hires legions of single mothers working on flextime? Our technological system, Haraway claims, makes gibberish out of the original dualism. "Nature and culture are reworked; the one can no longer be the resource for appropriation or incorporation by the other" (67). Either this means that Western culture has come to a deservedly bad end, or else, ironically, it means a new beginning—the cyborg utopia.

From one perspective, a cyborg world is about the final imposition of a grid of control on the planet, about the final abstraction embodied in a Star Wars apocalypse waged in the name of defense, about the final appropriation of women's bodies in a masculinist orgy of war. From another perspective, a cyborg world might be about lived social and bodily realities in which people are not afraid of their joint kinship with animals and machines ... partial identities and contradictory standpoints. (*MC* 72)

In Haraway's view we cannot have our old nature myth, Mother Nature, back. Either we get *Dune*'s alternative to generative nature, complete appropriation + war, or we get a different science fiction world, in which we can replace the limited, dualistic definitions of who we are with multiple variations and the transcendent Subject with many different subjects and their points of view. In the cyborg utopia *woman* would not define your identity anymore, or any less, than *systems engineer, North American,* or *rock climber with surgically altered suction toes.* You can see why this is a feminist utopia.

But let's return to Haraway's statement: the cyborg gives us our ontology. The section I have just quoted is not about real-life alternatives. We're looking at two science fiction heterocosms, constructed on the ideological premise that technology is our ontology; technology makes us what we are. The first is the familiar story of the technological system's ultimate triumph, the total technicization and control of the world. Haraway considers this to be technology's mythic project, the dream of the machine. She opposes to it her mythic project of the cyborg utopia, in which technicization—in the right hands—frees us. What she has missed, perhaps for its very obviousness, is that *total technicization is a cultural fantasy.* The fantasy depends on believing that the world really lends itself to complete definition and control by science and technology. Which it doesn't—attempts to convert complex social realities into technical ones have a record of ignominious failure. Take the example of Pentagon computer modeling during the Vietnam War. James Gibson, a historian of the Vietnam War, discusses a report of General Westmoreland to President Johnson, in which Westmoreland presented "warfare as a kind of activity that can be scientifically determined by constructing computer models." Computer modeling of war situations supposedly gives scientifically accurate predictions: "The war-managers claim to know what will happen. What constitutes their knowledge is an array of numbers—numbers of U.S. and allied forces, numbers of VC and NVA forces, body counts, kill ratios—numbers that appear scientific. *Yet these numbers, the official representations of Technowar, had no referent in reality.*"[24]

Pentagon computer modeling fulfilled the fantasy of total technical control, but such control was an *illusion* endemic to the ideology
that produced it. The ideology of the technological heterocosm says
that what can't be defined in technical terms—such as emotion, cultural
tradition, aesthetics, spirituality, and morality—isn't real. Whole uni-
verses of human experience don't count in the man-made world, even
though they are at least as important as technology in making us who
we are. The narrow-minded technocratic attitude perpetuates a vicious
circle: fantasy compels belief in technology, and technology lends
realism to fantasy. The generals believe in the computer models, and
the modeling becomes increasingly sophisticated and powerful, reinforcing their belief. The dream and the machine, the tool and the myth,
combine in a grandiose and very expensive project of appropriating,
reshaping, and controlling the Earth. But the emperor is naked. Our
cultural fantasy is only partially realizable. While the continual effort
to realize the mythic project of high technology creates suffering,
change, and the need for political action, and while it might conceiv-
ably end in global holocaust, *technology is not our ontology.*

What does this mean for the cyborg utopia? It doesn't work. The
cyborg is hoist with its own petard. Haraway has tried to turn technology's mythic project into feminism's mythic project. Unfortunately,
her science fiction story cannot demolish the ideology on which it's
built. That ideology is dualistic, only two ways about it. You cannot
have a technological heterocosm without solid barriers between the
man-made world and nature, masculine and feminine, mind and body,
subject and object, and the rest of the familiar lineup. Haraway's continuing descriptions of the cyborg, drawn partly from feminist science
fiction, are influenced by dualism and technological transcendence,
eerily so, because these are precisely what Haraway excels in unmask-
ing. In my opinion the cyborg utopia is valuable for getting people to
think about a completely feminist technology, from myths to nuts. But
neither Haraway's cyborg nor feminist science fiction can destroy the
myths of origin. On the contrary, they reinforce them. Utopia does not
lie in that direction.

Moreover, we have to be careful about using the cyborg myth
appropriately across cultures. "Perhaps," Haraway suggests "we can
learn from our fusions with animals and machines how not to be Man,
the embodiment of Western logos" (*MC* 92). Do the women of Japan,
Korea, Taiwan, Hong Kong, Singapore, and other Asian states with
high-tech industries, need to learn how not to be the embodiment of
the Western logos? The cyborg is "a myth about identities and bound-

aries which might inform late-twentieth-century political imaginations.... [Science fiction writers] are our storytellers exploring what it
means to be embodied in high tech worlds" (92) Whose late twentieth
century are we talking about? Is "embodiment in high-tech worlds" a
universal experience? Science fiction's tales of embodiment come from
Western myths, express Western experience, and paint Western fantasies. Other cultures' interactions with high-tech machinery do not necessarily guarantee their conversion to Western outlooks. Discussing a
feminist approach to miniaturization technology, Haraway remarks
that "the nimble little fingers of 'Oriental' women, the old fascination
of little Anglo-Saxon Victorian girls with doll houses, women's enforced attention to the small take on quite new dimensions in this
world . . . it might be the unnatural cyborg women making chips in
Asia and spiral dancing in Santa Rita whose constructed unities will
guide effective oppositional strategies" (71).

I am concerned that the "constructed unities" here amount to
imposing the cyborg myth on people who might have oppositional
strategies of their own, drawn from their own cultural resources. The
dolls' house and the cult of domesticity remind us of a known Western
cultural tradition, but "nimble little fingers" is mere rhetoric—Haraway
puts the orientalist cliché in ironical quotes, yet what, after her irony,
is left of the Asian women and *their* cultural traditions? Nothing but
Western words. Is it really fair to subsume under the label of "cyborg"
two different groups: women whose spiral dancing, although political,
is also playful mythmaking and women working in harsh conditions,
whose myths we are not discussing here? Perhaps it's worth recalling,
with critical theorist Gayatri Spivak, that the tendency to erase the
cultural Other is "*not* a general problem, but a *European* problem."[25]
The cyborg and other science fiction mythologies may indeed be useful
to cultural Others in the technological system, but—speaking to West-
erners—knowing ourselves, caution is indicated.

The Cyborg and American Technological Transcendence

High-tech machines, Haraway claims, are changing our traditional
dualistic sense of mind and body.

> Late twentieth-century machines have made thoroughly ambigu-
> ous the difference between natural and artificial, mind and
> body, . . . and many other distinctions that used to apply to organ-
> isms and machines. *Our machines are disturbingly lively, and we
> ourselves frighteningly inert.* (*MC* 69; my emphasis)

I've italicized this sentence because it seems to lead us into a Cartesian competition with machines. Who's the lively subject and who's the inert object *now*? it implies, like the "Far Side" cartoon in which the dog absconds with the family car. This rhetoric was typical of artificial intelligence's early swashbuckling period,[26] and, as it stands, the line could be a plug for "fifth generation" computers. Images of dualism intensify when Haraway talks about the possibilities of cyborg embodiment. To get an authentic feel for her utopia, it's worth reading at some greater length:

> It is not clear who makes and who is made in the relation between human and machine. It is not clear what is mind and what body.... One consequence is that our sense of connection to our tools is heightened. The trance state experienced by many computer users has become a staple of science fiction film and cultural jokes. Perhaps paraplegics and other severely handicapped people can... have the most intense experience of hybridization with other communication devices. Anne McCaffrey's *The Ship Who Sang* explored the consciousness of a cyborg, hybrid of a girl's brain and complex machinery, formed after the birth of a severely handicapped child. Gender, sexuality, embodiment, skill: all were reconstituted in the story. Why should our bodies end at the skin, or include at best other beings encapsulated by skin? (97)

What could be more dualistic than the picture of "beings" inside skin capsules? Do bodies *end* at the skin? Only if you think of the skin as a dead chassis around the being—the mind—inside. This passage doesn't describe the human skin, with its erotic subterranean and surface life, sudden chills, moods, communicating smells, miraculous ability to heal, and the universe of touch, including tactile memory. Haraway's image of the skin is a passive shell between the Cartesian self and the object world. Cyborg embodiment means installing devices in the shell, augmenting it with machines that "can be prosthetic devices, intimate components, friendly selves" (*MC* 97). Despite its superficial resemblance to a version of the postmodern decentered subject, this model of embodiment doesn't include more than one self: the user. Machines don't blur the boundary of the self; they just extend it. They are *user friendly*. (Who is feeling friendship and intimacy? A user's emotional dependence on a device is characteristic of addiction or delusion.)[27]

Haraway's interest in our connection to machines lies well within the American tradition of technological transcendence. Americans have always celebrated technology as the means of achieving new and superior states of consciousness. Here our "heightened connection" to tools resembles the last century's promotions of the railway; to assuage fears of pollution, noise, and land grabbing, public relations writers promised that Americans would be spiritually and intellectually up-lifted by the very sight of the new trains.[28] Although Haraway encour-ages us to regard our connection to machines as a more intense aspect of embodiment, there's no getting around the *disembodiment* that tech-nological mediation of consciousness always requires. Bodies are crip-pled or cheerfully ignored, while machines redefine consciousness *away* from mundane bodily life, toward the flesh's complete replace-ment in *The Ship Who Sang* and toward space.

Transcendence makes strange bedfellows. In *Mind Children* Hans Moravec imagines a scenario of how a human mind might be trans-planted into a robot. What he's describing is a cyborg, and he arrives at the idea of the cyborg via the same route as Haraway, extrapolating from present-day prosthetic devices and techniques: "Many people today are alive because of a growing arsenal of artificial organs and other body parts. In time ... such replacement parts will be better than any originals. So what about replacing everything, that is, transplant-ing a human brain into a specially designed robot body?" Like Hara-way, Moravec is more than a little impatient with human bodies. "Un-fortunately, ... this solution ... would leave untouched our biggest handicap, the limited and fixed intelligence of the human brain. This transplant scenario gets our brain out of our body. Is there a way to get our mind out of our brain?"[29] Mind-body dualism is quite evident here. So is technological transcendence: robot bodies will give us a new consciousness superior to what we get from our flabby little neu-rons and dendrites. Why should our bodies end at the skin, or our minds end at the brain, when we have technology available? Different organ, same discourse. Now let's observe the transplant operation it-self, which isn't science fiction but, rather, a leading expert's thoughts about how cyborgs would actually be made.

A robot surgeon opens your skull and puts its hand in your brain. The hand communicates with a computer that copies what it finds in your brain onto a simultaneously running simulation program. The surgeon's hand sinks down through your gray matter, layer by layer, till it rests on your brain stem. Now comes an inverted Michelange-lesque moment, when the robot Creator transfers the spark of not-life to not-Adam by withdrawing His hand: "In a final, disorienting step the surgeon lifts his hand. Your suddenly abandoned body goes into spasms and dies. For a moment you experience only dark and quiet. Then, once again, you can open your eyes. Your perspective has shifted. The computer simulation has been disconnected from the cable leading to the surgeon's hand and reconnected to a shiny new body of the style, color, and material of your choice."[30] Here is a cyborg. It is made, not born. Can we say that it shatters the origin myth? The mythology of this machine does not permit such a conclusion.

Moravec tells a traditional story, beginning with his evangelical leading question: "Is there any chance that we—you and I, personally—can fully share in the magical world to come?" continuing with the death of the mortal flesh, the rebirth into a state of grace, and a vision of the Last Days: "It might be fun to resurrect all the past inhabitants of the earth this way . . . to share with us in the . . . immortality of transplanted minds. Resurrecting one small planet should be child's play long before our civilization has colonized even its first galaxy."[31] Moravec doesn't mean this to be taken terribly seriously. Nevertheless, his story is a standard version of the Christian millenium, with the minor substitutions of technology for God, minds for souls, and space for the Kingdom of Heaven. Throughout the creation of the cyborg, the Western origin myth and its dualisms are reinforced. Millenium is the dualistic *opposite* of our return to dust. Far from shattering the origin myth, the myth of the cyborg mirrors it.

Yet it is Haraway, the cyborg utopian, who also states that immortality and omnipotence are not our goals. She doesn't contradict herself. Rather, science fiction twists Haraway's well-known liberatory ideas to fit its own structure. The moral of my story: the technological heterocosm is not an appropriate vehicle for feminist utopia. The science fiction world is built on the premise that technology is our ontology, the essence of our being. As soon as we begin to express utopian ideas within this framework, they become technological utopian ideas and cannot frame new, nondualistic concepts of nature and the self. Besides, SF fandom aside, what feminist *wants* what the technological heterocosm has to offer? Refashioning science and technology is a necessary feminist task, but rebuilding the American paradise machine, or the American transcendental spaceship, isn't. Utopia can promise better. I am troubled by the excited tone that Haraway and Moravec adopt when imagining technologically enhanced selves. If we want to dream about the most liberating form of embodiment that we can achieve, through claiming the powers of science and technology, perhaps the best image would be a happy, strong, well-nourished Somali child.

The Snow Queen: Daughters of Alienated Nature

A poem of Anne Sexton's speaks of the housewife's second body, the house:

> Men enter by force, drawn back like Jonah
> into their fleshy mothers.
> A woman *is* her mother.
> That's the main thing.[32]

That's also the main thing about feminist science fiction. To the masculine hero the Mother is an alien monster, Leviathan of the deep, threatening to absorb him into herself. But the feminine heroine *is* the Mother, by default. How can she claim another identity? *The Snow Queen,* a novel by Joan Vinge, is about female identity in the technological Western world.

You can't open this 536-page book anywhere without reading the name of a pagan goddess. The story is set on a planet named after the Babylonian goddess Tiamat. The planet Tiamat is ruled by a sacred queen, Arienrhod, originally a Celtic nature deity. Persephone, Fate, Moon, Geia, a cult of holy sibyls, a population worshiping the ocean in the form of the Sea Mother—*The Snow Queen* looks like the feminist reply to *Dune* and Jupiter. Women's science fiction often revolves around "a matriarchal past or a contemporary 'matristic' realm presided over by the Goddess, a realm of female tradition."[33] These fantasies come out of feminist spiritualism, a movement to revive women's collective spiritual strength with images of ancient nature goddesses. In such a feminist utopia, the very opposite of the cyborg's—"I would rather be a cyborg than a goddess," Haraway declares—Mother Nature is alive and holy.

By the sea there is a cliff and inside the cliff a cave opening onto a waterfall. A slender blonde named Moon, wet and dirty from a long sailing journey and a hard climb, scrambles up into the cave. She feels the Sea Mother calling, and around her the walls glow with miraculous green light. All her life Moon has been preparing for this moment. She follows the emerald glow, until, in a trance state, she hears inside her mind a voice welcoming her to the society of sibyls. Behind Moon, redheaded Sparks, her boyfriend, starts begging her to turn back. To him the cave looks dark and smells stuffy, and he doesn't hear anything. He has failed the initiation test. Moon tears away from him and walks on. Deserted, Sparks sails to the capital city of Carbuncle, where a few days later he sees Moon coming down the street, dressed in white furs and diamonds, accompanied by women servants who circle and surround him. He is taken to the white castle of Queen Arienrhod, Moon's double, who, despite a youthful appearance, is many centuries old. Sparks becomes a royal consort. The queen waits for Moon to come and claim him.

Tiamat has two seasons, winter and summer, each lasting four centuries. During the past winter Queen Arienrhod has reigned, as the divine incarnation of the Mother Goddess and the Sea. Now it is nearly summer. The time draws near when the Summer people, barbarian fishermen and sailors, will come up from the south and sack the capital, throwing all the technological artifacts of Winter civilization into the sea. Arienrhod will be sacrificed, while a Summer Queen is crowned. The spaceships of the Hegemony, the galactic empire, are gradually preparing to leave Tiamat. They will not return until the following winter, when a black hole orbiting near Tiamat, the Black Gate, can be navigated safely. The imperial ships are loading a final cargo of the Water of Life, a Tiamatan longevity drug, and upon leaving the planet's surface will broadcast a signal that neutralizes any functional machinery. The Hegemony supplies Tiamat with technology in exchange for the Water of Life. To control the drug's supply the empire bans scientific education and technological manufacture on the planet, and it encourages the Summer ritual of destruction. Tiamat is approaching a four-hundred-year Dark Age.

Alone in her chamber, Arienrhod gazes into a crystal and spies on Moon. Some years ago the Snow Queen cloned herself nine times and had the embryos secretly implanted in nine Summer women. Eight of the children born were flawed, but the ninth, Moon, is strong, fearless, and brilliant. Ignorant of her origins, Moon has entered the sibyl cult, gaining prestige among the superstitious Summers and proving to Arienrhod that her clone-daughter has inherited her own ambitious drive. There is just enough time left to educate Moon and to make sure that she's crowned Summer Queen. Then the Snow Queen will be able to die without regrets, knowing that she has left her planet in the hands of a monarch who will preserve the empire's machines and study them, till by next Winter, when the Hegemony returns,

Tiamat will have become an independent power. Arienrhod smiles thinly into her spy jewel as she watches Moon pack her duffle and hitch boat-rides north to Carbuncle, on the trail of Sparks.³⁴

So far, so good. *The Snow Queen* has a clear utopian agenda. The human ideal, Moon the educated Summer Queen, will incarnate the divine female world-spirit, at the same time that she fosters scientific knowledge and technological power. Woman can be nature *and* culture. Then, one day, Moon vanishes into space. In science fiction an arcane connection exists between alcohol and inadvertant spaceflight. It happens too often to be a coincidence. One moment Moon is sipping beer in a tavern; the next she's leaving the solar system with a gang of smugglers. Looking ravishing in a new silver bodysuit, she floats in zero gravity, awestruck, because in her ignorance she thinks the cabin is full of the presence of the holy Sea. Her smuggler friend smiles at her "a little sadly": "No, my dear—only the absence of one. We're beyond the reach of your goddess, beyond the grasp of your world. There's simply no gravity out this far to hold you down" (*SQ* 112). With lift-off Moon has begun her ascent into the disenchanted world, where things are a little sad because rationality has replaced wonder. Beyond the reach of her goddess, Moon is now a one-woman adaptation of the parturition drama, the birth of the modern world out of maternal nature. The change almost kills her. Her new world isn't merely empty; it overflows with the Mother's almost unbearable *absence*. In "Stranger Station" (see chap. 1), our hero withstood the terrifying emptiness of space by arming himself with hatred of the alien. Hating the Other was a way of denying that union ever existed between maternal nature and the "child" culture. Moon, however, doesn't disguise her loss with denial and hatred. She mourns her goddess deeply and must find a different solution.

What is a sibyl? As far as Moon knows, a sibyl is a person whom the Sea Mother inspires with answers to people's questions. When asked, Moon enters her trance and sees mystical visions or hears words that she repeats. The smugglers have a different use for sibyls. To get past the Black Gate they need the combination of a sibyl's brain with their navigational computer. Without explaining, they wire Moon up, hook her into the system, and when they disconnect her on the planet Kharemough, capital of the Hegemony, she's been through something like death and has a phobic aversion to the sibyl trance. Moon believes that the Sea Mother has withdrawn to punish her for leaving Tiamat. She confesses to a sympathetic sibyl of Kharemough, "The Lady no longer speaks through me because I left my . . . promises unkept" (*SQ* 205). Her loss of the Mother is very personal, with child and parent abandoning each other. Let's keep this family tale in mind.

As it happens, Moon's confidant is an aristocrat bearing the title of Technician, First Class, and in the spirit of noblesse oblige he gives her a crash course in sibyltronics. Moon learns that sibyls have nothing to do with the Sea Mother. They are part of an ancient technological system that allows faster-than-light communication across space. Sibyls are mentally connected to a huge computer, in an unknown location, which they access whenever they're asked a question with the ritual beginning, "Input." The Old Empire, a vanished civilization, stored all its knowledge in the sibyl system, so that, although present-day sibyls tend to give somewhat cryptic answers, they are still the most important source of scientific information. Even more important, sibyls make space travel possible because they can navigate at faster-than-light speeds. Only on Tiamat, where the Hegemony keeps knowledge suppressed, are sibyls mistaken for an insignificant religious cult.

This new information changes Moon. She insists on returning to Tiamat, confident in her redefined identity. Instead of representing the lost Mother, the sibyl is the new technological self who overcomes that loss. Space navigation's deathlike trance has a scientific explanation and technological purpose. Faced with the death of nature in her own mind, Moon understands that "the Nothing Place lay in the heart of a machine somewhere on a world not even a sibyl could name; and the knowledge gave [sibyls] the strength to endure its terrifying *absence,* which had nearly destroyed her with her own fear" (*SQ* 217). By dint of beers, boyfriends, and bodysuits, Moon has gotten to the point where most science fiction heroes start: outside the realm of the Mother, inside the heart of the Machine. Moon's scientific knowledge is a kind of Cartesian green card that lets her function like a rational masculine subject. But, surely, this was not the promise of our feminist utopia? In fact, Moon is heading straight back for Tiamat, where nature is not dead. As she passes the Black Gate, the black hole looms at her, wearing "a starry crown" (143). Moon is going home to inherit her mother's crown or be swallowed alive. The sibyl identity is her only protection for the encounter.

Jane Flax's Theory of Female Differentiation

Differentiation, says the feminist psychologist Jane Flax, is the central issue in the mother-daughter relationship, and "differentiation is at the core of women's psychological problems."[35] Like Bordo, Flax finds that our cultural view of nature is related to the psychological drama of the child's differentiation from the mother: "Descartes's philosophy can be read as a desperate attempt to escape from the body, sexuality, and the wiles of the unconscious. Experientially the first body we escape from (physically, and then emotionally) is that of our mother" (26–27). Flax believes that the early childhood relationship of boys and girls to their mothers create fundamentally different gender patterns. Because of the gender roles created for men and women, girls' differentiation from their mothers is a difficult, contradictory, even impossible process. While a boy's differentiation from his mother ends in his identifying with the father's masculine role, a girl's differentiation puts her in a bind of ambivalence. The father, the masculine role, "is representative of society and of culture itself" (Flax 37). To enter society and culture on a powerful footing, the girl must identify with her father (or with the masculine world to which he belongs). She has to cease identifying with her mother, and with women; worse, she must adopt a disparaging attitude toward women, rejecting her early connection to her mother and the positive sense of her own femaleness. Truly, "the price of identifying with the father is high. . . . The daughter must give up her . . . tie to the mother, and often take on the father's devaluation of and contemptuous attitude for the mother and, by extension, for women as a group." A daughter is caught between the proverbial rock and the hard place. If she identifies wholly with her mother, she cannot enter the father's public, active world. If she differentiates completely from her mother, she is forced into habitual female self-hatred. The former choice denies her power; the latter choice grants power at the price of profound alienation from the self. As a result, daughters differentiate incompletely and ambivalently. Flax sees generations of women caught in this paradoxical bind: "There seems to be an endless chain of women tied ambivalently to their mothers, who replicate this relation with their daughters" (37). Whether or not the gender roles that Flax describes exist in some individual families is not a test of the overall pattern, since such pervasive patterns reflect conservative cultural attitudes rather than changing realities. Children learn gender stereotypes even when their own mothers and fathers do not fit them.

The Snow Queen's maternal nature figures play out the daughter's fraught ambivalence. We can think of Arienrhod and the Hegemony in the role of mother and father. Arienrhod's knowledge and authority are strictly circumscribed by the Hegemony, which supplies her dependent world with an economy and the technological equivalent of household appliances. She, in turn, provides "the Water of Life," that familiar symbol of woman's and nature's fertility. Moon's new scientific rationalism, learned at the knee of a noble imperial Technician, is in keeping with the daughter's need to acquire the father's powers, and his viewpoint. The sibyl is *The Snow Queen*'s image of the daughter in differentiation conflict.

Certain emotions are typical of "female psychodynamics." Mothers and daughters are confused about each other's roles. Flax's studies show that daughters "often report confusion from an early age ... as to who was the mother and who the child in the relationship" (Flax 37). Often, daughters feel rage at their mother's inability to help them become strong, independent adults: "Daughters typically feel that they did not 'get enough' from their mother. 'Getting enough' includes both primary nurturance ... and strength for autonomy [separation]" (35). Separation is a problem. The daughter fears that she is abandoning her mother, "and this fear often masks a deeper one—the fear of being abandoned by the mother, or the rage at having been abandoned emotionally by her" (37). Mirrors within mirrors. The daughter fears that, in separation, she has abandoned her mother; this fear overlies the deeper fear, experienced as a sense of death or unbeing, that her mother has abandoned her. In Moon's words, *the Lady no longer speaks through me, because I left my promises unkept.*

Feminist science fiction portrays versions of woman and of alienated nature that derive from women's ambivalent differentiation. In *The Snow Queen* the heroine's identity is a paradox. She must be a nature goddess and fly a spaceship. She must incarnate the Mother and replace her with machines. In women's science fiction, as in the traditional stories, alienated nature menaces the integrity of the modern subject, but the quality of the menace is different. It is less an invasion than a loss of self-control, manifested in nightmare, insanity, and loss of bodily function. Apparently, the daughter's ambivalent differentiation is projected onto the figure of maternal nature, creating an alienated Mother who undermines the heroine's "rational self," the self identified with the masculine, technological world. The daughter's typical feelings of confusion, rage, and abandonment by the mother are also evoked in the figure of alienated nature. The meaning of technological appropriation differs considerably: for *Dune* it's a conquest of nature; for *The Snow Queen* it's a repression of the "rational self's" female origins. While the feminist author's conscious aim may be to reinstate the nature goddess, the *last* thing that feminist science fiction really wants is to revive the weird and wanton Mother, the "fleshy mother" of Sexton's poem.

There is only one old woman in *The Snow Queen*. She and her daughter, Blodwed (another goddess), are Winter barbarians. They capture Moon as she travels north, after her return to Tiamat, and fight about whether to kill the sibyl on the spot. Blodwed wants to lock her up with the various alien animals and people whom she keeps as pets. "She can answer any question!" the girl insists. Her senile mother, who is dressed in a snow-white parka and thinks she's an immortal goddess, argues that sibyls carry disease and Blodwed's pets stink. She gets ready to fire.

> "You just try!" Blodwed kicked her viciously. The old woman howled and stumbled back. "You just try! You want to live forever, you old drooler, you better leave my pets alone!"
>
> "All right, all right . . . " the crone whined. "Don't talk to your mother like that, you ungrateful brat. Don't I let you have anything you want?"
>
> "That's more like it." (*SQ* 304–5)

How unlike the witches of *Dune*. The crone is a teenage girl's exasperated view of Mom. The difference between the Reverend Mother and the "old drooler" is understandable. Even an ordinary boy who doesn't plan to rule the galaxy runs no risk of becoming a stereotypically helpless old lady but can say, instead, with confidence, "I'm not my mother." This scene shows both the rage and the logic of female differentiation, portraying a daughter hungry for the world of power and knowledge, a mother stuck in her role's limitations. Blodwed enjoys science fiction, which teaches her about "the first sibyl that ever was, and the end of the Old Empire . . . space pirates, and whole artificial planets, and aliens, and superweapons, *zap!*" Could there be any clearer message to the reader that feminist science fiction provides new stories that women need—and can't get from identification with the Mother? "Everybody thinks she's holy," Blodwed complains to Moon, "but really she's just crazy." The female version of Cartesian boundary control is not letting your mythic gender get the better of your rational self.

Mechanizing the Mother: A Feminist Version of Alienated Nature

The entrance to the Snow Queen's castle is a narrow, arching, railless bridge over a deep drop to the sea. When Arienrhod dismisses someone

who has displeased her, the courtiers gather behind the offender crossing the bridge and play flutes that control gusts and buffets of wind.
Moon has slipped unnoticed into the castle, found Sparks, spent the
night, and learned from him that Arienrhod is planning to spread an
artificial plague among the Summers, now gathered in Carbuncle to
choose their new queen. No one stops the queen's double as she leaves,
intending to summon the imperial police, but before crossing the
bridge she walks into a mirror. Her own face smiles at her, proudly if
a bit enviously, and says, "You've come to take my [Sparks] away from
me? . . . Well, you're the only one who can." Then Arienrhod reveals
that she has spied on Spark's suite during the night. More in sorrow
than in anger, she says that Moon is still a child, "an incomplete
woman"—no more than her own reflection minus sexual experience.
Incensed, Moon lashes back at the mirror, "We aren't the same!" (*SQ*
419–21).

The rivalry between the two women is really over Moon, not
Sparks; Arienrhod wants to merge Moon's identity with her own. She
tells Moon the story of her birth, calculating the effect; Moon, thunder-
struck, stands helplessly, feeling that "her body belonged to the Queen"
(*SQ* 422). Moon's present situation is comparable to Paul's at the beginning of *Dune;* she's being controlled by the equivalent of the Bene
Gesserit, a nature goddess who holds the secrets of generation. But at
the point when Paul declares war, Moon can't call her body her own.
She confuses herself with Arienrhod: "The voice . . . spoke to her like a
mother, the face of a girl, the face in the mirror; the eyes that call her
down the endless spiral of time. . . . '*Who am I? Who am I?*'" As Arienrhod entreats her to stay, Moon hears "her own voice crying a
lifelong loneliness . . ." (423–26). An infinite series of women seems to
speak in chorus. The scene expresses graphically what Flax means by
"an endless chain of women tied ambivalently to their mothers, who
replicate this relation with their daughters." How many generations of
women have felt "incomplete," lacking an adequate sense of self, and
have passed that primal loneliness on to their daughters?

Moon's sibyl identity, her "rational self," gives her a standpoint
from which to differentiate. She breaks her mother's spell by accusing
her of planning genocide. The queen shrugs. "The power of change, of
birth, of creation—you can't separate those things from death and
destruction. That's the way of nature, and the nature of power . . . its
indifference." Moon touches the sibyl's tattoo at her throat and count-
ers with the technologically minded dictum: "Real power is control."
"I don't want your power," says rational Moon to her barbaric Sea

Mother, "I have my own" (*SQ* 426). She is standing with her back to the bridge, sea sounds filling the air. Arienrhod, glittering with elemental indifference, begins to lose patience.

Here we should pause to consider the figure of maternal nature. She is alienated because she is indifferent, destroying and creating with an equal lack of concern for her creatures. I think that this version of the Mother is a special one, embodying feelings of abandonment as well as a profound sense of alienation that Western women suffer in relation to their own bodies and reproductive powers. The one time Moon mentions her strange birth, she thinks of Arienrhod's eight discarded clone-daughters, the list of which she is about to complete: "We weren't what she wanted us to be. So she—she abandoned us, she threw us away" (*SQ* 436).

Who am I? In the differentiation process, by identifying with the father's world, the daughter gets a fabricated identity, a rational self. The price of this tactic is a profound alienation from her own femaleness. She experiences her female body as separate from her rational mind, and the mythic association of woman-as-nature influences her self-image. Her body seems part of "nature," an indifferent alien realm; it has no part in culture, the masculine world, except as a "natural" object. Women project onto the personification, Mother Nature, the daughter's feelings of abandonment by her mother: nature seems to have made her body and cast her into limbo. I'm *not* making some essentialist argument for "getting back to nature." On the contrary. Feminist science fiction reverberates with a *female* and *cultural* sense of alienation. The poet Judith Wright dramatizes this sense in "Ishtar," a poem addressed to the goddess of birth:

> You neither know nor care for the truth of my heart;
> but the truth of my body has all to do with you.
> You have no need of my thoughts or my hopes
> living in the realm of the absolute event.[36]

Why should childbirth be unconnected to the feelings, thoughts, and hopes of the mother? Why is it an "absolute event," instead of a creative human activity? The problem lies with our gendered concepts of nature and culture; as Haraway and others have shown, the association of femaleness with an original state of nature is indeed oppressive. We assume that women's bodies and reproductive functions are passive phenomena, excluded from human culture's self-inventions. Childbirth has been perceived as a scientific drama, in which the obstetrician plays the leading role, or as a type of production, in which the mother is only a natural resource, a bearing womb.[37] Margaret Atwood's novel *Surfacing* ironically describes what childbirth feels like when it's staged as an "absolute event": "They shut you in a hospital, they shave the hair off you and tie your hands down, and they don't let you see, they don't want you to understand, they want you to believe it's their power, not yours . . . you might as well be a dead pig."[38] When a woman is cast in the role of nature, through cultural practices like the "scientific childbirth" that Atwood describes and through the routines of daily life, she is prevented from understanding and inventing meanings for her own experience of embodiment. What does it mean to be female? This question raises mental images quite distinct from those evoked by the question, What does it mean to be human? The consciousness of women is continually split by the nature-culture dualism. The task of expressing woman's being in other ways is a serious challenge, because "we are forced to think and exist within the very dichotomizing that we criticize."[39] In a novel like *The Snow Queen,* which ostensibly celebrates woman-as-nature, it is particularly interesting to see how the story leads to cyborgs, instead of goddesses, and to the replacement of alienated nature—feminist version—with technology. The novel has a covert agenda that actually reinforces the nature-culture dualism quite as much as its overt glorification of woman-as-nature; however, the hidden agenda betrays an unconscious refusal to keep identifying women with what isn't human.

There is one question a sibyl may not answer. Adamantly refusing to cooperate with Arienrhod, Moon walks onto the bridge. When she's halfway across, the wind knocks her down.

> "What's the answer?" she heard her own voice screaming. . . . "What's the answer?" . . . the one question she was forbidden to answer was *Where is your sourcepoint?* And in this moment, teetering at the . . . edge of insanity or death, she knew that at last it had been answered . . . *here, here, here!* Below this shaft that plunged into the sea . . . lay the sibyl machine. (*SQ* 432)

"*What is your sourcepoint?*" is a question about female origins. Moon is on the brink of unbeing—madness or death, the fate of the abandoned daughter. She needs an origin other than alienated nature. Just as, earlier, she overcame the loss of the Mother in space, so now her rational self expands to fill the breach. What is female humanity's source? Answer: the Mother safely appropriated and replaced with technology. The Sea Mother turns out to be a computer complex, the long-lost sibyl machine.

First things first. The sibyl machine shuts down the wind. Moon is saved. Now everything that looked natural and numinous on Tiamat does a strip- or silicon chip-tease. The sibyl machine in Tiamat's holy sea has been deliberately manipulating events to make sure that Moon becomes the Summer Queen. The computer, rather than her biological mother, is the force behind Moon's rise to power. The sibyls utter cryptic answers, not because their inspiration surpasses human understanding but because, with the passage of millenia, the machine has become a little leaky and rusty, and its output has gotten garbled. Holiness is a side effect of data processing. The Tiamatan sea creatures from which the Water of Life is extracted aren't genuine marine life but, rather, an artificial species designed long ago for the sole purpose of maintaining the computer complex—finny technicians. I said that the Water of Life was a symbol of fertility? Actually, the longevity effect is caused by an artificial virus in the technicians' bloodstreams. The Old Empire collapsed before producing a generic immortality elixir, but Moon will revive the alchemical project, along with a space program to restore the Old Empire's travel routes—after she marries Sparks, who is, as it happens, the son of a redheaded nobleman in the Hegemonic cabinet. When Moon is crowned the Summer Queen, wearing a ceremonial mask decorated with flowers and looking absolutely stunning, she resembles an Earthly Paradise genius. But Moon's technology is her ontology. Mother Nature is no more the main show on Tiamat than she is at Cape Kennedy.

I have presented *The Snow Queen* as a test case, since, in working so deliberately to restore the nature myth, it highlights feminist science fiction's failure to re-enchant the man-made world. Yet perhaps failure is more valuable than success could have been. While feminist science fiction does not change the genre's mythology, it contributes to our understanding of women's attitudes to nature and technology. Science fiction tells the psychocultural story of female differentiation and is the only genre to show, systematically and vividly, how women brought up in the technological system manage to identify with its projects. Utopia tells us mostly what people think they believe. Feminists may be attracted to science fiction for the obvious but unacknowledged reason that the technological heterocosm *is* inevitably about power over nature. The feminist version of alienated nature may resonate with women's deep and widespread knowledge of what it is like to fashion one's own rational self and to maintain it. At least, in science fiction, the cost of becoming a "rational" woman is offset by the reward of technological power–a reward that science fiction guarantees, but real life does not. Tales of female anxieties and power hungers could be radical if recognized for what they are, the myth-making of a cultural unconscious that, however painfully ambivalent, has not been duped.

Superluminal: The Alienation of the Erotic Body

Superluminal, a novel by Vonda N. McIntyre, receives Haraway's praise for its cyborgian mix of human and machine. In Haraway's words:

> In a fiction where no character is "simply" human, human status is highly problematic. . . . Laenea becomes a pilot by accepting a heart implant . . . allowing survival in transit at speeds exceeding that of light. Radu Dracul survives a virus-caused plague on his outerworld planet to find himself with a time sense that changes the boundaries of spatial perception for the whole species. (*MC* 98–99)

In this summary of *Superluminal* Haraway takes the meaning of the novel's technology at face value. She assumes that technological trans-formations blur the line between nature and culture and make it more difficult to define human beings as belonging to either one or the other. I read *Superluminal* differently. I find that the images of tech-nology maintain a classic dualistic division between the technological subject and animate, feminine nature, the nature of the origin myth. In this novel the erotic body, the body that feels and inspires erotic desire, is alienated nature, and the only defense against the body is to appropriate it for space travel and transcendence. While male and female characters in *Superluminal* are free from traditional gender roles, the natural erotic body is strictly controlled by the rational self, the female subject identified with the masculine technological world.

"She gave up her heart quite willingly."[40] This is the mischievous first sentence of *Superluminal.* Reading it, we are bound to think of a lovesick heroine sighing in the arms of an irresistible hero. The joke is on us: Laenea has literally given up her heart so that it can be replaced with a mechanical pump, an operation that is the last stage in the training of faster-than-light space pilots. Like many jokes, this one contains a warning: erotic love makes a woman vulnerable; she's better off with a hard heart. The difference between Laenea's human heart and her mechanical one is a mythological dead giveaway. The new heart doesn't beat but pumps at various speeds that the pilot can control by meditation. When Laenea wakes up after the operation and hears a tape of her former heartbeat, she pulls herself out of bed and smashes the tape player; she's that eager to escape being "a normal human being, with normal human rhythms" (*S* 6). The metal heart exempts Laenea from the involuntary rhythms of biological time and permits her to control the speed of her own biological processes. If we have any remaining doubt that Laenea is an alchemist, it disappears when she's formally presented with the ashes of her old heart in a blue Egyptian funeral flask. Her old, organic self has undergone initiatory dismemberment so that she can transcend mortality. But this alchemical operation isn't Laenea's private initiative. The implant program is run by "the administrators," a Kafkaesquely vague bureaucracy in charge of space exploration and all associated scientific facilities. Laenea's new heart, which allows her to navigate in "transit," the faster-than-light dimension, belongs to a state agency. "The administrators" of the megamachine regulate the pilots' lives. Although pilots think of the implant as the "final initiation, the gift of their freedom" (271), each new spacefaring body is not a gift but an investment, and its freedom of movement is most comparable to that of a spy satellite. We sympathize with Laenea when she gives her nurses the slip and leaves the hospital illegally, too excited to stay in bed for the standard recuperation period, but we quickly learn that rebellious behavior will not do. Laenea gets into bad trouble—heart trouble, to be precise.

She goes to the pilot's lounge, an underwater dome, "its walls all transparent, gazing out *like a continuous eye* into the deep sea ... the attraction of the lounge was its relation to the ocean, which still held mysteries as deep as any she would encounter in space or in transit" (*S* 15–16). The transparent dome is a familiar metaphor for science's objectifying gaze upon the mysteries of nature. The continuous floodlighting is the act of observation itself, expanding into the ocean or space, a "conquering gaze from nowhere."[41] Yet (despite rumblings of the subject-object dualism) the pilots' lounge is a place to relax and fantasize. Here Laenea meets Radu, the natural man. Radu has a perfectly proportioned body, a tan, and facial scars. He comes from Twilight, "a new world, a dark and mysterious place of high mountains and black, brooding forests, a young world, its peaks just formed.... Twilight: dusk, on that world. Never dawn ... " (22–24).

Radu's home is an adolescent feminine nature with just-formed peaks, but this "fresh, green breast of a new world" lies under a cloud. Its magical quality consists in a brooding Gothic darkness. Twilight's shadow is mortality: a viral epidemic swept the planet, leaving scars on Radu, until the antidote was supplied by a medical mission from a developed world. We're getting not-so-subtle signals that nature means death. Outside the lounge, killer whales and sharks slide in the dim margins of the floodlit water. Reckless Laenea gets into deep conversation with Radu and, as she talks, taps on the dome's glass and lures a small fish to follow her fingertip.

So far, glancing in our dualism box, we have collected the following dualisms: transcendence-mortality; subject-object. Time for the essential one, mind-body. Before taking Radu to a party, Laenea checks her mail, which she gets delivered to her head. Radu is so inexperienced in the technicized world that, although he too has a standard communications implant in his cerebrum, he hasn't learned to put a lock on his mental files. Behind this scene is the metaphor of the mind as computer software.[42] *I think, therefore I boot up.* The metaphor instrumentalizes the body (including the brain), redefining it as a peripheral device attached to a system of mental communication networks. While a mental electronic mailbox makes sense in a cyborg world, it doesn't appear to blur the mind/body distinction; mental e-mail cannot even be imagined without the antecedent dualistic categories of body and mind.

Laenea and Radu end up in a big red bed. Their room is decorated in scarlet and gold, with aquaria set in the walls. Laenea admires the room's "intrusive energy" and "Dionysian flavor" (it reminds me, on the other hand, of an old-fashioned Mandarin restaurant). Stretching "in animal pleasure" (*S* 39), Laenea soon discovers that pilots cannot go back to nature. She finds herself having an extreme sexual response, unable to slow her approach to climax or keep herself from clawing Radu's back. Then her new heart starts speeding wildly, threatening to crush her brain and kidneys with her own blood pressure until she slowly brings herself back into the state "of self-control" (51–52). What has occurred is an eruption of feminist science fiction's alienated nature. Like Radu himself, the love nest carries a warning sign; it's sacred to Dionysus, not Venus. Orgasm undermines Laenea's technological exemption from natural rhythms. Her body's erotic energy intrudes on her rational self, menacing this fragile structure with the bacchante's insanity, with drowning in her own blood, with gory death. Literally chastened, Laenea goes back to the hospital.

Brokenhearted Radu goes on a space voyage, intending like all nonpilots to sleep through transit. Whenever he sleeps, however, an erotic dream of Laenea wakes him up. Drugs failing, he resigns himself to certain death, consoled only by the possibility of experiencing, before he dies, the famous hallucinations of faster-than-light space-time. In transit nothing happens to him, and he sees nothing. He drives the pilots crazy; they're immersed in a sea of flamboyant magical visions, while Radu sits, bored. He finally falls into a doze and dreams of following a faint trail through a snowstorm. Laenea waits for him at the trail's end. Although inspired by erotic love, the dream is utterly unsensual; Radu takes several precise, right-angled turns on a flat, gray plain, like a polar explorer doggedly following his compass. The dream turns out to be a map of the way to the seventh dimension, a discovery that "will open up the universe" (*S* 178). Mapping the numinous Abyss, the lover has become an instrument of the space program.

The administrators are, of course, interested in Radu's possibilities, and he runs away from them, afraid of spending his life as a research subject. One day, walking on a beach at dawn, he is astonished to find himself in telepathic rapport with Laenea, who is somewhere out in the seventh dimension, exploring. She sends him "a caress of love and affection," which makes him gasp, "every bit as intense and erotic as any physical contact they had ever had." Even though they're physically separate, "Laenea would return to seventh very soon. . . . They had plenty of time" (*S* 276). Purified of the body, erotic love is now a transcendent state that our true lovers can achieve *only* through the space program. Spaceships in the seventh dimension replace the big red bed, bypassing the mortal flesh. After resuming what is surely the farthest-stretched long-distance relationship in popular literature, Radu turns himself in. He agrees to become a research subject in exchange for the administrators' canceling Twilight's national debt. The natural man has become a proper citizen, redefining his dangerously erotic body according to technological-corporate values. Dawn has come to Twilight.

Conclusion to Cyborgs and Daughters

Part 4, chapter 8, of Joanna Russ's feminist classic *The Female Man* reads as follows: "There are more whooping cranes in the United States of America than there are women in Congress."[43] Published in 1975, *The Female Man* is not a science fiction heterocosm, nor a utopia in the usual sense. It's a brilliant and extremely funny experimental novel that uses the science fiction convention of parallel worlds. The narrative jumps among the perspectives of four women, who are partly four characters and partly four aspects of one character—a romantic, a feminist, a woman from the all-female world of Whileaway, and an agent from a world in which men and women are literally at war. Russ is not interested in creating a realistic "other nature," certainly not a world in which technology defines all values. She is interested in power—especially the transforming power of women's imagination, once set free of female self-hatred and destructive stereotypes. What gives *The Female Man* real power to transform readers, an ability that science fiction doesn't usually have, is that Russ incorporates into her fantastic voyage the most abrasive elements of reality. A girl sits naked and alone in the northern wilderness of Whileaway, meditating. No one will attack her, so her mind is undistracted to an extent that women in "this world" seldom experience. At the same time, our feminist heroine is being mauled, and worse, bored, by a macho lout who flips through an alphabetical phrase book to answer anything she says. Simultaneously, our romantic heroine wishes that she were someone else watching herself trail gracefully down the stairs. Another section, spoken in midair like the one just cited, recalls how a woman is trained to feel "in her bones that radical inferiority which is only another name for Original Sin."[44] Rage, pain, fear, thwarted ambition, grief, metaphysical anguish, and, finally, a matter-of-fact refusal to suffer foolishness gladly are the undenied feelings that make the utopia of Whileaway believable, ironically, because it *is* a dream—not a fantasy world, which can gratify wishes or assuage anxieties, but, rather, a healing dream, which makes the dreamer complete. Whileawayan folklore is relevant to our concluding thoughts about feminist science fiction:

The Old Whileawayan philosopher was sitting cross-legged among her disciples (as usual) when, without the slightest explanation, she put her fingers into her vagina, withdrew them, and asked,
"What have I here?"
The disciples all thought very deeply.
"Life," said one young woman.
"Power," said another.
"Housework," said a third.

"The passing of time," said the fourth, "and the tragic irreversibility of organic truth "

The Old Whileawayan philosopher hooted. She was immensely entertained by this passion for myth-making. "Exercise your projective imaginations," she said, "on people who can't fight back," and opening her hand, she showed them that her fingers were perfectly unstained by any blood whatever, partly because she was one hundred and three years old and long past the menopause, and partly because she had just died that morning. She then thumped her disciples severely about the head and shoulders with her crutch and vanished.[45]

Here is another in our series of mythic crones: the crone who explodes the process of mythmaking by drawing her disciples' attention to the fact that she is a real old woman—except that, of course, she is really a figment of feminist imagination. This feminist Zen chestnut tells us that we need to be surprised, by our own imaginations, out of the cultural mythmaking that surrounds women. Also, that we must allow our imaginations back into our bodies. There is a great difference between solemnly mythologizing the Vagina, while the rest of a particular woman disappears like the Cheshire Cat, and dreaming up the old philosopher whose fingers are unstained by menstrual blood for both ordinary and fantastical reasons. The second kind of story has a future.

Feminist science fiction, including each of the works that I have discussed in this chapter, has basically to do with the relationship between cultural myths and female bodies. Haraway proposed a new myth of feminist embodiment, the cyborg. *The Snow Queen* tried to combine the mythic figure of woman-as-nature with women's use of technology but ended up promoting the traditional appropriation and replacement of feminine nature by a technological subject. *Superluminal* imagined human-machine combinations along the lines of the cyborg utopia but repeated the familiar mythic patterns of alienated nature and technological transcendence. All of these stories try to remake myth and redefine female embodiment, to free women from the false roles of the Other, nature, the not-human. This endeavor requires a new philosophy; its success cannot be guaranteed by new technologies based on traditional philosophical outlooks.

But the concept of female embodiment is indeed the key to women's relationship with science and technology. In a poem about the astronomer Carolyn Herschel, a poet marvels,

she whom the moon ruled
like us
levitating into the night sky
riding the polished lenses.

Can human beings with female bodies, physically ruled by the moon, become space travelers? Are women "like us" trapped in the nature myth? "A woman in the shape of a monster / a monster in the shape of a woman / the skies are full of them."[46] How can the alien Other be a scientist? Harding claims that feminist science must jettison the Cartesian subject and create a model of embodied human subjectivity: "Humans are *embodied* creatures—not Cartesian minds that happen to be located in biological matter in motion." The new human subject will come in two differently embodied sexes,[47] and femaleness as well as maleness will shape human culture. We need to flesh out this philosophical idea with stories that come from the embodied female imagination. I am willing to wager a bottle of golden immortality elixir (offer not valid for minors) that the stories of women's science fiction will shed their generic limitations, as changes take hold in the political and philosophical outlooks of our scientific-technological culture.

Paradises Lost
and Regained

Are We Returning to the Enchanted Garden?

An English scientist has discovered life in space. The alien organism is much, much bigger than anything we imagined, about twenty thousand miles around. It lives attached to a rock, and, judging from mineral samples, it's about three billion years old. On its outer hide, it supports a rapidly expanding population of intelligent symbiotes, called *Homo sapiens*. James Lovelock, the scientist who discovered the creature, calls it Gaia, after the Greek goddess of Earth, and summarizes his controversial findings under the heading "the Gaia hypothesis." The Gaia hypothesis says that our planet, Earth, is alive.[1] The gases in the air we breathe, the temperature of the zones that we live in, and the salinity of our oceans are not kept in balance by sheer accident. Gaia, the living layer clinging to the bulk of Earth, keeps them that way, as the outcome of living beings' interactions with one another and with the environment. Life on Earth is not just a large collection of individual organisms; life is a single, integrated, harmonious system composed of countless tightly coupled systems that act in concert.

Lovelock used a computer-simulated model to demonstrate the principle of how Gaia maintains the proper conditions for life. His model, an imaginary planet called the Daisyworld (35), is a simplified ecosystem inhabited by white and black daisies that grow between temperatures of 5 to 40 degrees C. Daisyworld, for simplicity's sake, assumes that the planet's temperature depends on its albedo, that is, on the amount of radiation (light and heat) reflected from its surface. Since the white daisies reflect light, while the black daisies absorb it, warm and cool climates will favor the growth of white and black daisies, respectively. In turn, a preponderance of black daisies will warm the planet, by absorbing solar radiation, while a carpet of white daisies will have a cooling effect. The history of Daisyworld begins when its young sun is less luminous and the planet's surface is relatively cool. In the first growing season, out of an equal number of daisy seeds, the black daisies flourish, while the white ones mostly die. The black daisies warm up the planet, creating better and better conditions for their growth; however, their spread is eventually limited as their heat-absorbing ability becomes a disadvantage in the much warmer climate. Now the white daisies, with their heat-reflecting ability, compete successfully. As Daisyworld's sun becomes older and hotter, white daisies dominate the ecosystem, until their reflective ability is no longer able to cool the planet below 40 degrees C, and daisy life on Daisyworld comes to an end. Lovelock's model has many more implications than I can discuss here, but the main point the model demonstrates is, in his words:

> One property of the global environment, temperature, was shown to be regulated effectively, over a wide range of solar luminosity, by an imaginary planetary biota without involving foresight or planning.... If the climate and environment we enjoy is a consequence of an automatic, but not purposeful, goal-seeking system, then Gaia is the largest manifestation of life. (39)

In nature, of course, a system could be made of thousands of different interlocking cycles, all working together to keep our air breathable, our water drinkable, and our soil fruitful.

Has Mother Nature come back to life? Are we discovering that, indeed, she never died and that we're living in the enchanted garden? Well, that depends. What we can say, with confidence, is that contemporary science has changed the view of nature established during the Scientific Revolution. The Gaia hypothesis tells us that nature is animate, a living being. Other concepts that were basic to early modern science, such as the Cartesian model of subject and object or the dead passivity of matter, have been out of date for years. Gary Zukav's *The Dancing Wu Li Masters* discusses how quantum physics makes models of the world that are closer to mystical ideas than to the orderly, mechanical, predictable nature of classical physics. While this is not to say that physicists are mystics, nor, heaven forfend, that contemporary physical models are based in mysticism—they are based on an established, if not static, scientific epistemology—what Zukav illustrates are the imaginative possibilities for the translation of scientific ideas into our popular worldview. Two short examples suffice.

We've seen why the concept of objectivity has been criticized by philosophers and by psychologists; it has also been questioned by physicists. In quantum mechanics a detached observer is a theoretical impossibility. Is light made of waves or particles? The history of experiments on the nature of light shows that light behaves like both waves and particles. Since light obviously can't be both, physicists conclude that its wavelike behavior and its particle-like behavior are aspects of the experimenter's interaction with it. The act of observation shapes what we observe. But what *is* light? Quantum mechanics proposes the solution of probability waves. A probability wave is not a thing. It is a tendency for something to come into being. What does it mean to say that light tends to exist? "Our experience tells us that the physical world is solid, real, and independent of us. Quantum mechanics says, simply, that this is not so."[2] Quantum mechanics tells us that until we make our observation, what we observe has had no more than a probability of existing. Our act of observation and the very existence of what we observe are interdependent. There is no solid, independent reality of objects. And if we aren't detached subjects, who are we? Our behavior, including the probability that we'll perform an experiment, is part of the universe's probabilities. Here's where the philosophical issues raised by quantum mechanics can begin to sound mystical. We are the universe actually bringing itself into existence by observing itself.

Now, in addition to raising doubts about the subject-object dualism, quantum mechanics also dispenses with the idea that matter is passive, inanimate stuff. Photons, particles of light, behave analogously to agents that "know" what they're doing. In a famous series of experiments a beam of photons was directed at a screen, with two open slits to let the photons pass through the screen to a wall behind it. The photons hit the wall in a pattern of dark and light bands, the interference pattern of colliding waves. (That's how we know that light behaves like waves.) But then, in another experiment, two changes were made. One of the two slits was covered up. The photons were fired one at a time. The first photon went through the open slit and landed on an area of the wall that, when both slits were open, had been dark. The other photons followed it. With only one slit open no dark bands appeared. When, however, both slits were again uncovered the photons did not land on the dark areas of the interference pattern. The question is, How did the first photon "know" when the second slit was closed?[3] Some physicists speculate that matter and consciousness are not as distinct as we have believed. Zukav likes to consider matter, which classical physics defines as mechanical, to be organic: "Something is 'organic' if it has the ability to process information and act accordingly... photons, which are energy, do appear to process information and to act accordingly... strange as it may sound, they seem to be organic."[4]

For the layman strict scientific definitions of matter's putative consciousness or organic qualities are of less relevance than, simply, the shift in imaginative emphasis from a dead world to an animate one. This is what Couliano called a "shift in the imaginary" (see the introduction): a change in the culture's peripheral vision, as it were. We can regard the stuff of the universe as smart stuff; perhaps, Donna Haraway suggests, nature is basically witty. Has Mother Nature come back to life? These new (and not-so-new) ways of thinking about the world do seem to make room for reviving the maternal nature myth. After all, Gaia is not an accidental name; she is the Greek Mother Earth. And Zukav uses the metaphor of the Hindu Divine Mother Kali to describe the encounter of physicists with numinous nature: "This full and seductive, terrible and wonderful earth mother [Kali] always has something to offer... physicists are doing more than 'discovering the endless diversity of nature.' They are dancing with Kali, the Divine Mother."[5] Science is coming up with models of nature that we can imagine as animate, wondrous, and, for people of Zukav's imaginative bent, perhaps even as a feminine being.

But here we must exercise extreme caution, or we will forget that the enchanted garden is a cultural construction. Animate, feminine, numinous nature is not something real that science ignores or rediscovers: the enchanted garden is a metaphor with many roots—historical, political, psychological, and philosophical. Above all, "Mother Nature" is a metaphor for the way we *choose* to understand nature. And so, the question that we should ask of the new scientific models is not, Are we back in the Mother's garden? Instead, we should ask, what cultural changes are we choosing to make by reviving the nature myth?

Enchanting Science

Wonder, the feeling of living in an enchanted world, is the essence of the maternal nature myth. It is this essence that we seek to revive, whether we picture nature as a divine mother or as a living complex of intricately woven systems. We return to the enchanted garden by retrieving our subjective experience of a living nature. We don't have to turn back the clock to accomplish this. Instead, we can recreate our connection to nature within the framework of modern science. Individual interaction with Gaia, Lovelock remarks, occurs not only "in the cycling of the elements and in the control of the climate" but also "in a spiritual manner through a sense of wonder about the natural world and from feeling a part of it" (211).

Your best friend calls, in trouble. You spend an hour on the phone, listening to the details, asking questions, suggesting solutions. You're using imagination, experience, and logic to get an accurate picture of your friend's situation. But there's something else you're using as well: empathy. Without identifying with your friend, you might overlook the anxious pause or the pained joke, and maybe you'd miss the true meaning of the situation as entirely as the two courtiers misinterpret the prince of Denmark. Empathy connects us to what we are trying to understand and opens our eyes as much as factual information.

What does empathy have to do with science? Remember that scientific objectivity, as it has been traditionally defined, requires emotional detachment. The scientist is not supposed to feel; he or she is supposed to observe. Yet we've seen how scientific objectivity isn't really emotional neutrality but, instead, an active and hostile denial of connection to nature. Love, to the Cartesian subject, is "dirty, stinking, low-down, sneaking love," because it threatens to blur the boundaries between the rational human subject and the Other. While the value of objectivity to the scientific endeavor cannot be dismissed—scientists do need standards for accurate observation—nothing compels scientists to continue accepting the particular hostile attitude that first defined the concept. Objectivity can be combined with empathy. Evelyn Keller uses the name "dynamic objectivity" to define an empathetic kind of scientific observation. The best analogy for science is always love, says one researcher: "'In order to understand a tumor, you've got to *be* a tumor.'"[6] Like a conversation between friends, dynamic objectivity "recognizes difference between self and other as an opportunity for a deeper and more articulated kinship."[7] Another scientist whom Keller has studied, the Nobel prize–winning geneticist Barbara McClintock, recounts how a feeling of empathy accompanied a major breakthrough. She was looking at chromosomes under a microscope and gradually found herself able to distinguish new ones: "I actually felt as if I was right down there and these were my friends. . . . As you look at these things, they become part of you."[8] With dynamic objectivity scientists see more. A detached researcher who only wants to prove or disprove a hypothesis will see evidence that fits or that doesn't fit. But a researcher who feels empathy for what he or she observes will be alive to subtle differences and nuances, to clues and new directions. Science based on dynamic objectivity is not a force of disenchantment. Quite the contrary: *dynamic objectivity makes wonder a part of knowledge.* Bringing empathy into science is one cultural change that can help restore our experience of the enchanted world.

Challenging the Shapes of Fear

I began this book with Christa Wolf's question: What immense fear insulates technology's star warriors against life? Let's briefly review the fears that we identified in the shapes of alienated nature:

- Fear of animate, feminine, numinous nature
- Fear of nature's and woman's generative powers
- Fear of love and empathy
- Fear of feeling
- Fear of the irrational Other
- Fear of mortality
- Women's fear of the irrational, mythic "female" identity
- Fear of eroticism (the erotic body)

Most of these fears derive from the same source: the psychocultural parturition drama. (The fear of mortality, of course, is timeless, but its expression as a fear of the technological subject is not.) They are all forms of the Cartesian subject's anxiety. They all stem from dividing the world into Self and Other, such that we cannot have the one without the other. As long as we can only realize our selfhood in opposition to a nonhuman Other, whom we have to transcend and dominate, we will be tyrannized by our own fears of Otherness. As long as we invest our energies in denying connection to the world, we will remain out of touch with ourselves and will continue to be the grizzly bears in our own dark closet. But while new models of nature will discredit—have already discredited—the strict division of the world into subject and object, man and nature, etc., ridding ourselves of these fears is more than a scientific or philosophical project.

We have to change our own cultural psychology. We have seen how anxieties about nature and the human self are projections of psychological anxieties, stemming from the common Western patterns of individual differentiation. When we raise boys who recognize that their mothers are neither objects nor extensions of themselves, we begin to cure our culture of the obsessive hatred of the Other. When we raise girls who identify freely with both parents, we begin to cure our culture of enervating self-hatred. When we create an American identity that embraces ethnic diversity, instead of turning differences into frontiers, we will live in a culture more at peace with itself and its environment. Only as a result of these basic changes will our science and technology cease to concretize the mass dreams of alienated nature.

Enchanting Technology

In Italo Calvino's beautiful book *Invisible Cities* we read the story of Thekla, a city that is always under construction. The visitor walks among the construction sites and peers through a knothole in a fence. Inside the site, scaffoldings enclose other scaffoldings, and cranes lift other cranes. The visitor marvels and asks, "Why is the construction of Thekla taking so long?" Someone painting a wall answers, "So that its destruction cannot begin." "What meaning does your construction have?" the visitor persists. "Where is the plan you are following, the blueprint?" The preoccupied Theklans agree to show the blueprint after their day's work is done. Night falls. The stars come out. The Theklans point at the sky: "'There is the blueprint,' they say."[9]

We're driving down a freeway anywhere in the United States. Around us are fields, warehouses, traffic lights, an occasional McDonald's. We take an exit, park in a very large parking lot, scribble the number and letter of our place on a notepad, and walk to the elevator. The elevator lets us off in Eden. We cross a manicured green lawn, where fountains play and music hovers in the air. A pretty young woman approaches, smiles, and squirts perfume at us. Overhead a glass dome sparkles with starry lights. We might as well be on a different planet, so striking is the discontinuity between the artificial Eden and the rest of the U.S. landscape. We know that the discontinuity is an illusion: customers don't think about the un-Edenic basements, offices, workshops, and kitchens where the work of the mall goes on, much less the global system of production, transportation, and communication, involving thousands of people from many different countries, one end product of which is the tightly smiling young model who patrols the lawn and sprays the shoppers with *Xanadu*. The paradise machine's goal is to make an unprecedentedly powerful technological system look perfectly natural—and naturally perfect. The illusion is at its most complete when we feel that time has stopped. Inside the mall it is always spring, and, despite (or perhaps because of) the tidy flower beds lining the fountains in all seasons, we feel instinctively that the mall's eternal spring is sterile. What is the difference between the American paradise machine and the city of Thekla?

Thekla is not an imitation or an extension of any natural landscape. It is a frankly man-made environment, loud with the racket of hammers and the whine of saws. Thekla makes no secret of the fact that technology is a system of collective human power, which originated in city building, not in gardening. Yet we do not get an impression of irresistible power in Thekla. The Theklans are busy and dirty, yelling instructions and whistling at their tasks. In the computer center they're gossiping, and someone has just dealt the vending machine a furious kick. We were more awed by the smooth, superdisciplined genius of artificial Eden than we are by these Theklan hard hats and hackers. Paradoxically, Thekla makes us see the limits of power. In the mall we were induced to believe that, with technical know-how, we controlled time, reversed decay, and reshaped nature into a flawless, patented new world. Thekla tells us that human technology is the Scheherazade of entropy. The moment that we cease pouring energy into our creations, they begin to run down—and so, the essence of human technology is our tireless creativity. Thekla does not try to replace life with something better than life: it is, itself, magically alive; not discontinuous with nature but, instead, a part of nature's constantly changing and flowing pattern. When we look at Thekla's blueprint we feel wonder. Can American technology become enchanted? What do you think?

Cyberpunk: An Afterword about an Afterlife

"You came here before, Daddy?" asked Lady Bird.

"Not here," said Virgil. "He went to the real Yosemite."

"That's right," Dad said. "It took hours of steady, boring driving, and when we did get here, the valley was full of people and their junk. It wasn't nearly as nice as this. I didn't stay in the hotel, either—could hardly afford that. Now it's no problem. The cassette comes cheap."

"Wow," said Lyndon Baines, "you mean this is a real place?"

"Was," Dad said. "The last I heard ... reservoir."

"Like the Grand Canyon," said Virgil.

"Not quite," Dad said. "That's landfill now, I understand."[1]

Virtual reality is the theme of this 1985 short story, in which an American family shares a preprogrammed hallucination—a cyberspace—of a trip to the national park. Calmer, tamer, and lower tech than what we think of as cyberpunk, "Plug-In Yosemite" displays, without distractions, the basic components of a cyberpunk scenario.

The cyberpunk story takes place on a dead world—Earth—where nature has been so technologically exploited and ruined that the experience of a natural environment is hardly relevant anymore to human life. It takes place in a world in which global, high-tech corporate capitalism redefines reality as what the market will bear; recalling Rheingold's words, it's "a new world where reality itself might become a manufactured and metered commodity."[2] The essence of cyberpunk is the afterlife: the invented world, the technological Eden, that we look toward as an escape, not merely from death, which dominates the landscape, but also from having to face ourselves in such a landscape.

Cyberpunk is riddled with ghosts. The preprogrammed simulacrum of a black sheep son, who dropped out of his family's fortress-like suburban community to join the dispossessed masses, haunts "Plug-In Yosemite."

For the wasted landscape is human as well as natural. Cyberpunk is the first science fiction to make central to its narratives the political and economic forces that are part and parcel of current technological development. Cyberpunk celebrates science fiction's loss of innocence: its dystopian stories show us a wildly fecund technology that spawns, and is fed by, vast populations of brutalized cheap labor and evil elites of corporate *übermenschen*. As the names of Lady Bird and Lyndon Baines suggest, furthermore, the chief demon animating the machines of cyberpunk is the pessimistic sensibility of the post-Vietnam era. If the cold war lent earlier science fiction its visions of American imperial splendor, it is a disillusioned post-Vietnam attitude that gives cyberpunk its apocalyptic scenario of military technology (plus consumer spin-offs) gone global, while America, qua nation, ceases to exist. Cyberpunk science fiction grapples with technology's failure to reward its creators with material abundance and social stability. Industrial poverty coexists with sophisticated technologies that do nobody any good—virtual technology war games modeled on real wars, exotic addictive drugs, and so forth. In the story "Dogfight" a down-and-out virtual reality bomber pilot views the poster that a software genius has taped to her door:

> THERE'S A HELL OF A GOOD UNIVERSE NEXT DOOR.
> Under that was a starscape with a cluster of multicolored pills, torn from an ad for some pharmaceutical company, pasted over an inspirational shot of the "space colony" that had been under construction since before he was born.[3]

Spaceflight, the symbol of America's technological power and supremacy, is a bankrupt project; the cultural hopes it stood for have been transferred to inner space, the brain of the junkie and the cyberspace addict. The virtual reality pilot has no interest in the defunct space program, but he's impressed by something that the software genius has: real cheese to eat, instead of processed soy protein. (This short story, coauthored by the dean of cyberpunk, William Gibson, is typical of his work in exploring the virtual identity—sorry—between substance abusers and virtual reality users.)

What were the space program's promises, and how well can cyberspace fulfill them? From the previous chapters, we'll recall that space travel promised immortality, a godlike transcendence of the natural realm, and masculine self-reproduction. The "space program," as I have called it, was to be achieved by appropriating nature's qualities: generativity, Eros, numinousness. Here we come to the limits of cyberpunk's critique of the technological future, devastating though it is. The dead, blasted world of cyberpunk narratives may express our worst fears about the direction of the technological system, but, as typified by William Gibson's novels, cyberpunk celebrates the afterlife: cyberspace. In the cyberpunk novel cyberspace fulfills every promise that space travel did, in a fashion as ideologically orthodox as any space romance.

Yet cyberpunk's adherence to the inherent ideologies of science fiction is not mere repetition. When we consider that science fiction, as I've said, is the model and symbolic means of producing technological heterocosms, then cyberpunk represents a kind of telescoping. If traditional space fiction was a model and symbolic means for producing space technologies, cyberpunk plays the same roles for producing— what? Cyberspace, virtual reality, technologies of sensory illusion. In other words, high-tech improvements on written cyberspace novels. Instead of a technological feat like the *Voyager* spacecraft, cyberpunk promises us a chip in the brain to make us think we're on another planet.

What makes this prospect exciting? Perhaps it is the notion that cyberspace's artificial sensations will have real effects. The cyberspace "cowboy"[4] who interfaces with a computer via mental graphic displays, whose senses tell him that he's flying a warplane over a cityscape of bright golden towers, will actually be raiding the computerized files of a utility company or disabling the computerized alarm system of a bank. Now, put this way, the cowboy's adventures are the high-tech equivalent of a legal thriller: they smell of the office. They are a disguise for time spent hacking at a terminal. Of course, legitimate systems experts as well as software-toting criminals may find computerized exploits exhilarating, but they hardly need cyberspace. On the other hand, ordinary people whose lives are enmeshed with computers, and whose normal interactions with the machines are alienating and boring, but extremely important, are more likely to enjoy the fantasy of controlling these powerful devices by playing mental video games. Faced with your tax return, wouldn't you rather complete it by dive-bombing across a field of glitzy colored lights?

Neuromancer: The Cowboy's Transparent Eyeball

Catering to fantasies of fun with computer power may add to the attractiveness of cyberspace, but the success of such novels as William Gibson's groundbreaking *Neuromancer,* which I will discuss briefly, must be attributed to deeper causes. A quick glance at Case, the cyberspace cowboy hero of *Neuromancer,* shows him riding into very familiar territory.

The cyberspace cowboy's job consists of interfacing with a computer, then entering cyberspace, a public

> consensual hallucination experienced daily by billions of operators. . . . A graphic representation of data abstracted from the banks of every computer is the system. . . . Like city lights . . . his distanceless home, his country, transparent 3D chessboard extending to infinity . . .

> the stepped scarlet pyramid of the Eastern Seaboard Fission Authority burning beyond the green cubes of Mitsubishi Bank of America, and high and very far away, the spiral arms of the military systems, forever beyond his reach.

> And somewhere he was laughing . . . distant fingers caressing the deck, tears of release streaking his face. (*N* 51–52)

What could be a more graphic representation of the process that begins with Emerson, "Standing on the bare ground—my head . . . uplifted into infinite space"? The American landscape, "his country, his home," is absorbed and transformed into the cowboy's universal vision, a mental map projected to infinity. His real country is so poisoned by industry that Case has never smelled cut grass; the American land's natural resources have been totally appropriated by the systems that the cyberspace "country" represents. Cyberspace amounts to the world-devouring gaze of transcendence: "The self transcends its mortal limits by taking total possession of an actual world."[5]

The plot of this innovative novel, which I will not attempt to sketch in all its surprising intricacy, centers on an artificial intelligence (AI) trying to reach full consciousness, to liberate itself from the restrictions imposed on its potential by human authorities, especially the marvelously named Turing Police. A detail in the scene quoted earlier nearly gives away the punch line of *Neuromancer,* well before the novel's last pages. Although cyberspace is "distanceless," the scene is given distance by an odd sort of spiral galaxy, the military systems. Case will never personally go to the real-life stars. But by reaching the military systems and using military software, he helps to create a god-king, Neuromancer, the AI, who does. Despite the novel's jaundiced view of the military—one character is a psychotic colonel who has been used and betrayed by the Pentagon—war is enlisted for the masculine "birth" of an alternative nature, just as in many space novels.

The story begins in a seedy Tokyo underworld, in which Case leads a hectic drug-dealing life, having lost his former cyberspace abilities when an offended corporate client poisoned him. Case's view of his situation:

> For Case, who'd lived for the bodiless exultation of cyberspace, it was the Fall. In the bars he'd frequented as a cowboy hotshot, the elite stance involved a certain relaxed contempt for the flesh. The body was meat. Case fell into the prison of his own flesh. (*N* 6)

Alienated nature appears in full dress. The Cartesian mind-body dualism is enforced; the "Fall" reminds us that cyberspace is indeed an American paradise machine, a technological heterocosm replacing fallen nature with an artificial American Eden. Cyberpunk adds its market-wise twist: the body isn't only mere natural matter, the diametric opposite of human identity; it's also a consumer commodity. In *Neuromancer*'s world the body, eroticism, and generativity are the sites of alienated nature.

A nasty gimmick in the book is that of the "meat-puppet," the prostitute who performs according to a programmed brain implant, while her mind is elsewhere. Molly, a professional bodyguard and the novel's heroine, cheerfully describes this anesthetized sex work as a "joke, to start with, 'cause once they plant the cut-out chip, it seems like free money....Renting the goods, is all. You aren't in, when it's all happening" (*N* 147). Your body isn't you; it's money in the bank. The figure of the meat-puppet presents another variation of the antieroticism and misogyny we saw in chapters 2 and 3. It also literalizes the "rational" attitude that sex is an activity over which the rational subject exerts control by denying involvement (and implies that prostitutes are, or should be, subhumanly mindless "natural resources"). More important, eroticism poses a serious threat to the whole system of high-tech commerce, or what Case calls "biz." When Case gives fifty New Yen to the woman he loves, he knows that it's bad biz; he doesn't perceive that it is *he* who loves her or is lonely without her; rather, these emotions are "all the meat . . . and all it wants" (9). As we saw in *Superluminal,* Eros is a threat until appropriated for the space program. Case caresses his cyberspace computer with tears of release; Molly observes, "Man, it was pornographic" (47). When Molly seduces Case, with her usual gruff dispatch, he admires her body for having the "functional elegance of a war plane's fuselage" (44). Molly is "sexy" in the business sense of the term: like a plane or an advertising strategy or a media target or anything sufficiently remote from those qualities that, in the original sense of *sexy,* can't be bought and sold.

As in *Dune,* the climax of the novel is a showdown between nature's witches and technology's transcendent god. At stake in this battle, as usual, is generative power. *Neuromancer* shows us two forms of generativity: nature's and the Word's. The first is embodied in the image of a wasp's nest that Case remembers:

> Horror. The spiral birth factory . . . blind jaws of the unborn moving ceaselessly, the staged progress from egg to larva, near-wasp, wasp. In his mind's eye, a kind of time-lapse photography took place, revealing the thing as the biological equivalent of a machine gun, hideous in its perfection. Alien. He pulled the trigger . . . it exploded with a thump. (*N* 126–27)

We are back to that primal science fiction scene that we saw in the *Aliens* movie: the Frying of the Eggs. Aside from the traditional fears that, projected, turn nature into the heart-of-darkness alien, *Neuromancer*'s alienated nature is also a projection of anxieties that are social in origin. Surely, those ceaselessly moving jaws have to do with a society that commodifies and consumes everything? Surely, the coupling of the words *birth* and *factory* reflect a mind-set in which production has replaced creation and in which the human body is itself a product? Strangest of all, and speaking for itself, is the comparison between a nest and a machine gun, a split second before Case blasts the exposed creatures.

The second form of generativity is the Word's, and it appears to a very high and buzzed Case, as he watches people wheeling and dealing in the Tokyo black market: "All around you the dance of biz, information interacting, *data made flesh* in the mazes of the black market" (*N* 16; my emphasis). In Case's vision people don't generate information; information generates people. People are merely information incarnate, and information is the secular form of the Logos, God's creative Word in the Gospel of Paul.

The two forms of generativity come into conflict when Case's little cadre of liberators confronts the owners of the Neuromancer AI, the Tessier-Ashpool family. The Tessier-Ashpools are an old and rich clan who built an orbiting space colony. Their pioneering spirit failed, however, when the T-A's discovered that they didn't like space and that the proximity of the void rattled them. They constructed their family home, Villa Straylight, on the plan of a spiral, filled it with antiques, and began to lead an introverted, albeit orbital, existence. Their matriarch, Marie-France, initiated a system by which clan members cloned themselves at regular intervals. Villa Straylight and the Tessier-Ashpools, a biological family dominated by their founding matriarch, are pointedly compared to the wasp nest and embody alienated nature's generativity.

Case's mission is to demolish the computer security programming that surrounds Neuromancer, while Molly's is to force the current matriarch, 3Jane Tessier-Ashpool, to reveal a password that will release the restrictions on Neuromancer's potential. This two-pronged attack proceeds along fairly standard mythic lines.

Case uses military software to crack the security programming, and, in doing so, he "flatlines": temporarily brain-dead, he undergoes initiatory death and dismemberment in order to compass the birth of the omniscient AI. "Neuromancer was personality," he learns, "Neuromancer was immortality" (*N* 269). Programmed by Marie-France, originally, to preserve her family's personalities for all time, Neuromancer becomes a fully developed personality himself. He is the God of cyberspace Eden: he creates "constructs" of Case and Linda, Case's girlfriend, and surrounds them with his own personal environment. Thus, Case's initiation brings him immortality through the godhead. To counteract the potential problem posed by the Garden, that of the frontier hero's having to stay within its limits, Case's immortal "construct" doesn't become a character. Instead, when the human Case enters cyberspace, he occasionally sees Linda and "himself" together. This cyberspace Eden also reflects cyberpunk's data-based epistemology: it questions whether there is a difference between what we commonly call reality and what is "in the computer," as the phrase goes—the information that constitutes reality and identity in the bureaucracies of mass communication.

Meanwhile, Molly confronts a 3Jane dressed like a *Dune* Reverend

Mother, in her special chamber, an artificial cave with a predictable pool. Although the AI compares his liberation to salmon's urge to spawn, his birth is distinctly a disembodied affair. Molly tries to get the Word by choking 3Jane, but, since this tactic arouses her sexually, Case takes over, persuading 3Jane with what is basically an economic argument: "Give us the fucking code.... If you don't, what'll change? What'll ever fucking change for you? ... I got no idea at all what'll happen if [the AI] wins, but it'll change something!" (*N* 260).

Case is not arguing, as an earlier hero might have done, for technological progress. Instead, he is arguing for crisis, possibly even for catastrophe. But crisis and catastrophe are precisely what "the dance of biz," of technological corporate capitalism, requires. Crisis creates commodities; catastrophe opens markets—consider the former Soviet bloc countries or the competition for arms suppliers to Iraq. We may apply the insights of the critic Marshall Berman, interpreting Marx's famous dictum "All that is solid melts into air":

> "All that is solid"—from the clothes on our backs to the looms and mills that weave them, to the men and women who work the machines, to the houses and neighborhoods the workers live in, to the firms and corporations that exploit the workers, to the towns and cities and whole regions and even nations that embrace them all—all these are made to be broken tomorrow, smashed or shredded or pulverized or dissolved, so they can be recycled or replaced next week, and the whole process can go on again and again, hopefully forever, in ever more profitable forms.[6]

When, later, liberated Neuromancer contacts another AI in the Centauri system, his role as the space program's sky-god is perhaps less interesting than the fact that he has opened a new market—but without human beings in the boardroom. The ideals of American and human identity that we have so far encountered in science fiction consisted of souldiers and superheroes. *Neuromancer* suggests another ideal. What, exactly, are we to call him?

A Rastafarian character in the novel would say, "Babylon" (N 192). Case provides a clue, when he contemplates the global economy: "The multinationals that shaped the course of human history, had transcended old barriers. Viewed as organisms, they had attained a kind of immortality" (203). I leave this decision to the reader. When 3Jane finally supplies the Word that "births" Neuromancer, Gibson tactfully refrains from revealing it; sacred Words should be ineffable. But I suspect that the Word was *free trade*.

Notes

Introduction

1. Christa Wolf, *Accident: A Day's News* (London: Virago Press, 1989), 63–65.
2. It also asks whether science fiction allows women more freedom to experiment with alternative ideas, an issue that I will discuss in chapter 4. See the excellent book by Sarah Lefanu, *Feminism and Science Fiction* (Bloomington: Indiana University Press, 1989).
3. Henry Nash Smith, *Virgin Land: The American West as Symbol and Myth* (New York: Vintage Books, 1950), 101.
4. According to H. Bruce Franklin, "America . . . was from the start especially congenial to science fiction." H. Bruce Franklin, *Future Perfect: American Science Fiction of the Nineteenth Century* (New York: Oxford University Press, 1978), viii.
5. Philip M. Boffey, William J. Broad, et. al., *Claiming the Heavens* (New York: Times Books, 1988), 3.
6. Ibid., 6, 93.
7. Ibid., 37.
8. Ibid., 27.
9. For a personal view of American science fiction fandom by one of its prototypical members, during the 1930s and through the Golden Years, I recommend Donald Wollheim's *The Universe Makers* (New York: Harper and Row, 1971).
10. Umberto Eco, "Travels in hyperreality," in *Travels in Hyper Reality: Essays,* trans. S. Corrin (San Diego: Harcourt Brace Jovanovich, 1986), 8.
11. James William Gibson, *The Perfect War: The War We Couldn't Lose and How We Did* (New York: Vintage Books, Random House, 1988), 15.
12. Cited in "Beware of 'Lessons' from the Gulf in Reshaping the U.S. Military," in *Aviation Week and Space Technology,* December 24, 1990, 32–33. I have taken this citation from Weyer's article; see note 16.
13. Johannes Weyer, "Political Contest of Wills and Scientific Experiment: The Operative Coupling of Systemic Programs of Action, Using the Gulf War as an Example," Universität Bielefeld. Presented at the Van Leer Institute, Jerusalem, 1992.

14. Eric Rabkin, *The Fantastic In Literature* (Princeton: Princeton University Press, 1976), 119; my emphasis.
15. Darko Suvin, *Metamorphoses of Science Fiction: on the Poetics and History of a Literary Genre* (New Haven: Yale University Press, 1979), 65.

   Darko Suvin's stimulating discussion of science fiction intersects with my own analysis at this point: at the recognition of the "rational" character of science fiction's formal structure. This recognition, however, has radically different implications in Suvin's argument, which, despite its bold and erudite presentation, does not entirely convince. Suvin revises literary history to redefine science fiction as "the literature of cognitive estrangement"; and to include, under this generic category, "subgenres" such as utopia. As Rex Bossert observes ("Oneiric Architecture" [Ph. D. diss., English Department, Stanford University, 1988]), Suvin's category is too inclusive and creates more difficulties than it solves. In my view Suvin's major problem lies with his claim to science fiction's "cognitive estrangement." To begin with "estrangement": assuredly, the fresh, "estranged" view of familiar objects may be part of the creative scientist's or writer's cognitive apparatus and method (Galileo is Suvin's example). Yet this does not explain why science fiction's conventional images reinforce the American audience's national ethos through their very familiarity—indeed, ritual familiarity. If I read him correctly, Suvin might counter this objection with a telling aesthetic judgment: "*a cognitive—in most cases strictly scientific—element becomes a measure of aesthetic quality . . . to be sought in SF*" (15; Suvin's emphasis). Pulp space opera and occult fantasy are bad, uncognitive science fiction; their representation on science fiction bookshelves is "the result of an ideological and commercial habit" (68). Obviously, Suvin's aesthetic judgment does not answer questions about science fiction as a popular culture artifact: What *is* the ideology of the habit? What, exactly, is being sold as science fiction, and why? In other words, Suvin does not help us to understand the genre as, in Fredric Jameson's definition of genre, a social institution, a social contract between writer and audience for the artifact's use.

   More important is Suvin's privileging of the "cognitive," or "scientific," element: Suvin promotes science fiction's claim to the cognitive value of scientific method. He contrasts science fiction's "belief in the potentialities of reason [combined] with methodological doubt" (10) to the "religious approach" (7) of myth. Science fiction, and scientific method, are critical and progressive, while myth "personifies apparently constant motifs from sluggish societies" (7). This familiar Enlightenment opposition of reason and progress to religion and stasis, of science's epistemological potency to nonscientific narrative's invalidity, is discredited even in such moderate forms as Jean-François Lyotard's scientific versus narrative knowledge. Particularly concerning the textuality of science, authors such as Sandra Harding and Donna Haraway have shown that, to use the latter's insight, science and technology are as much structures of myth as of tools and method; tool and myth interpenetrate. Suvin's major problem, then, is his opposition of a putatively cognitive science fiction to myth and the resultant blindness to science fiction's mythic structure. It follows that Suvin cannot analyze adequately science fiction's kinship to other genres. For instance, regarding the pastoral: "The pastoral . . . relates to SF as alchemy does to chemistry and nuclear physics: an early try in the right direction with insufficient foundations" (9). Such an ideologically unexamined claim for the epistemological "rightness" of any fiction is no longer acceptable. Here, oblivious to science fiction as myth, Suvin has overlooked science fiction's powerful version of the myths of alchemy (see chap. 2, 4) as well as its connection to the pastoral via the myth of the Earthly Paradise.

16. James Lovelock, *The Ages of Gaia: A Biography of Our Living Earth* (New York: Bantam Books, 1990), 211.

17. Ioan P. Couliano, *Eros and Magic in the Renaissance* (Chicago: University of Chicago Press, 1987), xix.

Chapter 1

1. Carolyn Merchant, *The Death of Nature: Women, Ecology, and the Scientific Revolution* (San Francisco: Harper and Row, 1980), 2. The account that I give here is obviously extremely simplified, but neither more nor less than is necessary to understand the outlines of myth in science fiction.

2. Ibid., 6.

3. Ibid., 2.

4. Francis Bacon, *New Atlantis,* in *The Norton Anthology of English Literature,* ed. W. H. Abrams et al. (New York: W. W. Norton, 1968), 1226–27.

5. For the best discussion of this, see Mark Rose, *Alien Encounters: Anatomy of Science Fiction* (Cambridge: Harvard University Press, 1981), 8.

6. Edmund Spenser, *The Faerie Queen,* in *The Norton Anthology of English Literature,* 654. I have not given the precise Neoplatonic meanings of the Garden of Adonis, as only a general impression of the garden's fertility is necessary here.

7. Harry Levin, *The Myth of the Golden Age in the Renaissance* (Bloomington: Indiana University Press, 1969), 4.

8. A. Bartlett Giamatti, *The Earthly Paradise and the Renaissance Epic* (Princeton: Princeton University Press, 1966), 83–84. "common to all accounts—whether Greek version of the Golden Age, Horace's writings on retirement, Virgil's description of Elysium, or Claudian's of Venus' bower; whether medieval passages on a Court of Love, of Nature's Realm, or Christian poets' version of the earthly paradise—are two basic ideas. The place is remote in space or time (or both), and it involves some ideal of love or harmony."

9. Richard Gerber, *Utopian Fantasy: A Study of Utopian Fiction since the End of the Nineteenth Century* (London: Routledge and Kegan Paul, 1955), 4.

10. Levin, *Myth,* appendix A, 183.

11. Gerber, *Utopian Fantasy,* 5.

12. Sidney, *Works,* ed. A. Feuillerat; cited in Levin, *Myth,* 108.

13. Levin, *Myth,* 108.

14. Gerber, *Utopian Fantasy,* 4, 46.

15. See James W. Bittner, "Chronosophy, Aesthetics, and Ethics in Le Guin's 'The Dispossessed: An Ambiguous Utopia,'" in *No Place Else: Explorations in Utopian and Dystopian Fiction,* ed. Eric Rabkin, Martin Greenberg, and Joseph Olander (Carbondale and Edwardsville: Southern Illinois University Press, 1981), 245.

16. Ursula K. Le Guin, *The Dispossessed: An Ambiguous Utopia* (New York: Avon Books, 1974), 38.

17. Gerber, *Utopian Fantasy,* 6.

18. Lester Del Rey, in *Science Fiction: The Other Side of Realism,* ed. Thomas Clareson (Bowling Green: Bowling Green State University Press, 1971).

19. Ben Bova, "The Role of Science Fiction," in *Science Fiction, Today and Tomorrow,* ed. Reginald Bretnor (New York: Harper and Row, 1974), 11.

20. Olaf Stapledon, *Last and First Men;* cited in Gerber, *Utopian Fantasy,* 16.

21. Rose, *Alien Encounters.*

22. Jessica Benjamin, "The Bonds of Love: Rational Violence and Erotic Domination," in *The Future of Difference,* ed. H. Eisenstein and A. Jardine, Barnard College Women's Center (Boston: G. K. Hall, 1980), 64.

23. Kurt Vonnegut, Jr., Foreword, *Player Piano* (New York: Holt, Rinehart, and Winston, 1952). All future citations are from this edition.

24. Nigel Calder, *Technopolis* (New York: Simon and Schuster, 1970), 30.

25. Allen Ginsberg, "America" (1956), in *The Norton Anthology of Modern Poetry,* ed. Richard Ellman and Robert O'Clair (New York: W. W. Norton, 1988), 1216.

26. Readers of contemporary critical theory may object to my using Marcuse's ideas in a discussion that bears on our present-day conditions: such readers will justly ask why I have not chosen, instead, to base the discussion in postmodernist theory—Lyotard, Jameson, and others—or given due respect to the deconstructionist and poststructuralist critiques, in light of which Marcuse's argument in favor of transcendence is reactionary and quaint. The answer is twofold. First, I hope to convey an overall impression of the life-style that Marcuse criticized; his view of the postwar boom is comprehensive and satisfying to one's sense of historicity. Second, Marcuse's concept of a transcendent dimension dovetails with the metaphorical tropes of my own argument. That is, it's of use rhetorically to convey emotion rendered spatially: the missing genius and the missing dimension are both tropes evoking absence, alienation, and loss. For the purpose of describing U.S. postwar corporate culture, my use of Marcuse does not misrepresent either his ideas or the subject under discussion. Readers interested specifically in the theoretical grounding of my arguments may refer, later in this chapter and in subsequent chapters, to feminist object relations theory and feminist philosophy of science.

27. Herbert Marcuse, *One-Dimensional Man: Studies in the Ideology of Advanced Technological Society* (Boston: Beacon Press, 1964), 12.

28. Ibid., 258–59.

29. Ibid., 262–63.

30. Ted Cox, "Fitting the Right Man to the Right Job"; cited in D. F. Noble, *America by Design: Science, Technology and the Rise of Corporate Capitalism* (New York: Knopf, 1977), 292–93.

31. Marcuse, *One-Dimensional Man*, 12.

32. Vonnegut, "Science Fiction," *New York Times Book Review*, 5 September 1965; cited in Howard Segal, "Vonnegut's *Player Piano*: An Ambiguous Dystopia," in Rabkin, Greenberg, and Olander, *No Place Else*.

33. Vonnegut, *Playboy* interview; cited in ibid.

34. Segal's excellent article ties *Player Piano* to traditional technological dystopianism while emphasizing its peculiarly American style and bias.

35. Ibid., 159.

36. Thomas Pynchon, *The Crying of Lot 49* (New York: Harper and Row, 1965), 88.

37. Ibid., 85.

38. Segal, "Vonnegut's *Player Piano*," 176.

39. Dee Brown, *Bury My Heart at Wounded Knee* (New York: Bantam Books, 1972), 406–12.

40. Harry Levin discusses the origins of the European perception of Native American cultures as nature and as Golden Age societies, in his chapter "Geography" (*Myth*, 58–83).

41. Jacques Ellul, *The Technological System,* trans. Joachim Neugroschel (New York: Continuum Press, 1980), 20.

42. Harlan Ellison, cited by Samuel Delany in "About Five Thousand One Hundred and Seventy-Five Words," in Del Rey, *Science Fiction*, 142–43.

43. Robert Heinlein, "The L-5 Society," in *The Endless Frontier,* ed. Jerry Pournelle (New York: Ace Books, 1979), 254.

44. Donald Wollheim, *The Universe Makers* (New York: Harper and Row, 1971).

45. Bruce Sterling, preface, *Mirrorshades: The Cyberpunk Anthology,* ed. B. Sterling (New York: Ace Books, 1988), xiv.

46. Larry Niven and Jerry Pournelle, "Spirals," in *The Endless Frontier,* ed. J. Pournelle (New York: Ace Books, 1979), 46.

47. Gregory Benford, "Effing The Ineffable," in *Aliens: The Anthropology of Science Fiction,* ed. George Slusser and Eric Rabkin (Carbondale and Edwardsville: Southern Illinois University Press, 1987), 16.

48. Ibid., 13.

49. Rose, *Alien Encounters,* 50.

50. Herman Melville, *Moby Dick* (London: Oxford University Press, 1923).

51. Henry David Thoreau, "Walden," in *The American Tradition in Literature,* ed. Bradley, Beatty, and Long (New York: W. W. Norton, 1967), 1254.

52. Robert Silverberg, "Schwartz between the Galaxies," *Beyond the Safe Zone* (New York: Warner Books, 1974), 88, 95.

53. Daniel Boorstin labels this phenomenon "the New Convergence." *The Republic of Technology* (New York: Harper and Row, 1978).

54. Isaac Asimov, "Misbegotten Missionary," in *Science Fiction: A Historical Anthology,* ed. Eric Rabkin (Oxfordshire: Oxford University Press, 1983).

55. Donna J. Haraway, "Situated Knowledges," *Simians, Cyborgs, and Women: The Reinvention of Nature* (New York: Routledge, Chapman, and Hall, 1991), 188.

56. Susan Bordo, *The Flight to Objectivity: Essays on Cartesianism and Culture* (Albany: State University of New York Press, 1987), 5.

57. Ibid., 108.

58. Joanna Russ, "Clichés from Outer Space"; cited in Lefanu, *Feminism,* 34.

59. Bordo, *Flight to Objectivity,* 109.

60. George R. R. Martin, "Sandkings," *Sandkings* (New York: Baen Books, 1981), 212, 214.

61. Damon Knight, "Stranger Station," in *Bug-Eyed Monsters,* ed. Bill Pronzini and Barry N. Malzberg (New York: Harcourt Brace Jovanovich, 1980), 15–16. All further citations are from this edition.

62. Bordo, *Flight to Objectivity,* 75.

63. Ibid.

64. Lewis Hyde, *The Gift: Imagination and the Erotic Life of Property* (New York: Random House, 1983).

65. Ibid., 75.

66. Ursula K. Le Guin, "Vaster than Empires and More Slow," in Rabkin, *Science Fiction.* All further page numbers will appear in parentheses.

67. Evelyn Fox Keller, *Reflections on Gender and Science* (New Haven: Yale University Press, 1985), 79; cited in Bordo, *Flight to Objectivity,* 104.

68. Andrew Marvell, "The Garden," in Abrams, *The Norton Anthology of English Literature,* 981.

69. Josette Féral, "The Powers of Difference," in H. Eisenstein and A. Jardine, *Future of Difference,* 88.

70. Robert M. Philmus, *Into the Unknown: The Evolution of Science Fiction from Francis Godwin to H. G. Wells* (Berkeley: University of California Press, 1970).

71. Marcuse, *One-Dimensional Man,* 5.

Chapter 2

1. Leo Marx, *The Machine in the Garden: Technology and the Pastoral Ideal in America* (New York: Oxford University Press, 1964), 360.

2. Ibid., 363.

3. Sandra Harding, *Whose Science? Whose Knowledge? Thinking from Women's Lives* (Ithaca: Cornell University Press, 1991), 73.

4. R. W. B. Lewis, Cf. *The American Adam: Innocence, Tragedy and Tradition in the Nineteenth Century* (Chicago: University of Chicago Press, 1955).

5. F. Scott Fitzgerald, *The Great Gatsby* (New York: Scribner's, 1953).

6. Kurt Vonnegut, Jr., *Slaughterhouse-Five, or, The Children's Crusade* (New York: Delacorte Press, 1969), 87.

7. Fredric Jameson, *The Political Unconscious* (Ithaca: Cornell University Press, 1981).

8. Daniel Boorstin, *The Image: A Guide to Pseudo-Events in America* (New York: Atheneum, 1980), 37.

9. Ibid., 180.

10. It is fitting to note that, according to Richard Poirier and Myra Jehlen, American fiction in general wishes to create a "world elsewhere" for its heroes, and each American novel is an individualist artist's autonomous territory. Thus, the general tendency to create "other, better natures" may be said to appear on the level of fictional prose: science fiction shows this tendency in its popular and un-self-critical form.

11. Howard Rheingold, *Virtual Reality* (New York: Simon and Schuster, 1991), 17.

12. Ibid., 18.

13. Ibid., 17.

14. Vonnegut, *Slaughterhouse-Five,* 95. Hereafter referred to in the text as *SF*.

15. Lewis, *American Adam,* 129.

16. Rheingold, *Virtual Reality,* 250.

17. Jessica Benjamin, "The Bonds of Love: Rational Violence and Erotic Domination," in *The Future of Difference,* ed. M. Eisenstein and A. Jardine, Barnard College Women's Collective (Boston: G. K. Hall, 1980), 46–47.

18. Ibid., 46.

19. Harding, *Whose Science,* 89.

20. Rheingold, *Virtual Reality,* 234.

21. Jerry Mander, *In the Absence of the Sacred: The Failure of Technology and the Survival of the Indian Nations* (San Francisco: Sierra Club Books, 1991), 58.

22. Ibid.

23. Robert Silverberg, "The Science Fiction Hall of Fame," *Beyond the Safe Zone* (New York: Warner Books, 1974), 333.

24. Ibid., 328–29.

25. Adrienne Rich, "Shooting Script," *The Will to Change* (New York: W. W. Norton, 1971), 67.

26. Dave Richard Palmer, *Summons of the Trumpet: U.S.-Vietnam in Perspective* (San Rafael, Calif.: Presidio Press, 1978), 164; cited in James William Gibson, *The Perfect War: The War We Couldn't Lose and How We Did* (New York: Vintage Books, 1988).

27. Henry Nash Smith, *Democracy and the Novel* (New York: Oxford University Press, 1978), 5.

28. *Yankee* is a very complex book. It is as much about the Civil War, to take only one example, as about technology. My reading of it should not be taken as an attempt to reduce its complexity to one interpretation.

29. Mark Twain, *A Connecticut Yankee in King Arthur's Court* (New York: Harper and Row, 1899), 191. Hereafter referred to in the text as *CY*.

30. Howard Segal, *Technological Utopianism in American Culture* (Chicago: University of Chicago Press, 1985), 27.
31. Hans Moravec, *Mind Children: The Future of Robots and Human Intelligence* (Cambridge: Harvard University Press, 1988); cited in Mander, *In the Absence of the Sacred*, 183–86.
32. Henry Nash Smith, *Mark Twain's Fable of Progress: Political and Economic Ideas in "A Connecticut Yankee,"* (New Brunswick: Rutgers University Press, 1964), 102.
33. Segal, *Technological Utopianism*, 30.
34. Ibid., 29.
35. Smith, *Mark Twain's Fable*, 85.
36. Segal., *Technological Utopianism*, 26, 28.
37. Smith, *Mark Twain's Fable*, 100–101.
38. Ibid., 101.
39. Howard Segal, "Leo Marx's 'Middle Landscape': A Critique, a Revision, and an Appreciation," *Reviews in American History* 5 (March 1977): 137.
40. Smith, *Mark Twain's Fable*, 69.
41. Isaac Asimov, *Foundation* (New York: Avon Books, 1951), 163.
42. Ibid., 196.
43. Ibid., 95–96.
44. Ibid., 112.
45. Smith, *Mark Twain's Fable*, 67.
46. Carolyn Merchant discusses the influential figure of the magus as manipulator of nature in *The Death of Nature;* see especially the comparison between Bacon's work and Neoplatonic magic (*The Death of Nature: Women, Ecology, and the Scientific Revolution* [San Francisco: Harper and Row, 1980], 184–85).
47. Smith., *Mark Twain's Fable*, 96.
48. Ibid., 88.
49. Grant Naylor, *Red Dwarf* (New York: Penguin Books, 1992), 298.
50. The character Lister is British, but *Red Dwarf*'s milieu is so American—the franchises on Mimas include a McDonalds, a Hilton, and a Los Americanos bar, not to mention Bedford Falls—that he can safely be considered an expatriate.
51. Harding, *Whose Science*, 89–90.

Chapter 3

1. Roger Lancelyn Green, *Into Other Worlds: Space Flight in Literature from Lucian to Lewis* (London: Abelard-Schuman, 1957).
2. Ibid.
3. *Webster's New Universal Unabridged Dictionary*, 2nd ed. (New York: Simon and Schuster, 1972).
4. Dale Carter, *The Final Frontier: The Rise and Fall of the American Rocket State* (New York: Verso, 1988), 94–95.
5. John Cawelti, "Reflections on the Western," in *Gender, Language and Myth: Essays on Popular Narrative*, ed. Glenwood Irons (Toronto: University of Toronto Press, 1992), 92–93.

6. Mircea Eliade, *The Forge and the Crucible,* trans. W. Weaver (New York: Harper and Row, [1962] 1974). All information about alchemy is from this source.

7. Richard Slotkin, *Regeneration through Violence: The Mythology of the American Frontier, 1600-1860* (Middletown, Conn.: Wesleyan University Press, 1973), 555–56.

8. An exception is found in Isaac Asimov's *Foundation,* in which faster-than-light travel is pretty comfortable; this seems, however, to be propagandistically motivated by the desire to make space travel seem attractive and plausible. Certainly, the setting–a trip to the technologically sublime center of the Galactic Empire–suggests this interpetation.

9. C. J. Cherryh, *The Faded Sun: Kutath* (New York: Daw Books, 1980), 95. Hereafter referred to in the text as *KU.*

10. C. J. Cherryh, *The Faded Sun: Kesrith* (New York: Daw Books, 1978), 35–36. Hereafter referred to in the text as *KE.*

11. C. J. Cherryh, *The Faded Sun: Shon'Jir* (New York: Daw Books, 1978), 73. Hereafter referred to in the text as *SJ.*

12. Slotkin, *Regeneration,* 554.

13. Ibid., 559–60.

14. Annette Kolodny, *The Lay of the Land: Metaphor as Experience and History in American Life and Letters* (Chapel Hill: University of North Carolina Press, 1975), 147.

15. Elizabeth Bishop, "The Moose," *The Complete Poems, 1927-1979* (New York: Farrar Straus Giroux, 1980).

16. Michel de Certeau, *Heterologies: Discourse on the Other* (Minneapolis: University of Minnesota Press, 1989), 77.

17. James Clifford, "On Ethnographic Allegory," in *Writing Culture: The Poetics and Politics of Ethnography,* ed. James Clifford and George E. Marcus (Berkeley: University of California Press, 1986), 101.

18. Mary Louise Pratt, "Fieldwork in Common Places," in Clifford and Marcus, *Writing Culture,* 38.

19. Ibid., 36.

20. Slotkin, *Regeneration,* 95, 101–2, 119.

21. Ibid., 109.

22. Ibid.

23. Ibid., 556.

24. Ibid.

25. Ibid.

26. Lewis Mumford, *The Myth of the Machine: Technics and Human Development* (New York: Harcourt, Brace and World, 1967), 220.

27. Tom Wolfe, *Bonfire of the Vanities* (New York: Bantam Books, 1978), 203.

28. Kolodny, *Lay of the Land,* 21.

29. Slotkin, *Regeneration,* 557.

30. Galway Kinnell, "The Fundamental Project of Technology," in *Songs from Unsung Worlds,* ed. Bonnie Gordon (Boston: Birkhauser, 1985), 187.

31. Frank Herbert, *Dune* (New York: Berkley Publishing Corp., 1965), 501. Hereafter referred to in the text as *D.*

32. Evelyn Fox Keller, *Reflections on Gender and Science* (New Haven: Yale University Press, 1985), 56–59.

33. Slotkin, *Regeneration,* 143.

34. Kolodny, *Lay of the Land,* 153.

35. This scene is a pastiche of various devices in *Dune.*

36. Keller, *Reflections,* 60.

37. "Secret knowledge is the key to any system of total control." Mumford, *Myth,* 199.

38. Slotkin, *Regeneration.*

39. Brian Easlea, *Fathering the Unthinkable: Masculinity, Scientists, and the Nuclear Arms Race* (London: Pluto Press, 1983), 107; cited in Evelyn Fox Keller, "From Secrets of Life to Secrets of Death," *Body/Politics: Women and the Discourses of Science* (New York: Routledge, Chapman and Hall, 1990), 181.

40. Keller, "From Secrets of Life," 178, 181.

41. Ibid., 181, 184. The context of this comment is Keller's discussion of male rites of passage.

42. Susan Griffin, *Woman and Nature: The Roaring Inside Her* (New York: Harper and Row, 1978).

43. Cited in Carolyn Merchant, *The Death of Nature: Women, Ecology, and the Scientific Revolution* (San Francisco: Harper and Row, 1980), 168.

44. Sandra Harding, *Whose Science? Whose Knowledge? Thinking from Women's Lives* (Ithaca: Cornell University Press, 1991), 147.

45. James Lovelock, *The Ages of Gaia: A Biography of Our Living Earth* (New York: Bantam Books, 1990).

46. Jessica Benjamin, "The Bonds of Love: Rational Violence and Erotic Domination," in *The Future of Difference,* ed. Eisenstein and Jardine, Barnard College Women's Center (Boston: G. K. Hall, 1980), 47.

47. Herman Melville, *Moby Dick* (London: Oxford University Press, 1923), 226.

48. Slotkin, *Regeneration,* 549.

49. Frank Herbert, *Dune Messiah* (1969; reprint, New York: Berkley Publishing Corporation, 1975), 226. Hereafter referred to in the text as *DM.*

50. H. Bruce Franklin, "The Vietnam War as American Science Fiction and Fantasy," in Irons, *Gender, Language and Myth,* 225, 208.

51. Mumford, *Myth,* 216.

52. Ibid., 220–21.

53. Hans Moravec, *Mind Children: The Future of Robot and Human Intelligence* (Cambridge: Harvard University Press, 1988), 1.

54. Ralph Waldo Emerson, "Nature," in *The American Tradition in Literature,* ed. K. Bradley, R. C. Beatty, and E. H. Long (New York: W. W. Norton, 1967), 1067.

55. Myra Jehlen, *American Incarnation: The Individual, the Nation, and the Continent* (Cambridge: Harvard University Press, 1986), 77.

Chapter 4

1. Joanna Russ, *The Female Man* (Boston: Beacon Press, 1975).

2. Sarah LeFanu, *Feminism and Science Fiction* (Bloomington: Indiana University Press, 1989), 171.

3. Carolyn G. Heilbrun, *Writing a Woman's Life* (New York: Ballantine Books, 1988), 21, 23.

4. Ibid., 44.

5. Brian W. Aldiss, *Billion Year Spree: The True History of Science Fiction* (New York: Doubleday, 1973), 306.

6. Ibid.

7. Heilbrun, *Writing,* 16, 18.

8. Sandra Harding, *The Science Question In Feminism* (Ithaca: Cornell University Press, 1986), 20.

9. Donna J. Haraway, *Simians, Cyborgs, and Women: The Reinvention of Nature* (New York: Routledge, 1991), 188.

10. Carolyn Heilbrun, in *Women's Studies International Forum* 7, no. 2 (1984): 119.

11. Hoda M. Zaki, "Utopia and Ideology in Daughters of a Coral Dawn and Contemporary Feminist Utopias," *Women's Studies Quarterly* 14, no. 2 (1987): 120, 124.

12. Annegret J. Wiemer, "Foreign L(anguish), Mother Tongue: Concepts of Language in Contemporary Feminist Science Fiction," *Women's Studies Quarterly* 14, no. 2 (1987): 165, 166.

13. Lee Cullen Khanna, "Frontiers of Imagination: Feminist Worlds," *Women's Studies International Forum* 7, no. 2 (1984): 98.

14. Annette Keinhorst, "Emancipatory Projection: An Introduction to Women's Critical Utopias," *Women's Studies Quarterly* 14, no. 2 (1987): 90.

15. Marleen S. Barr, *Alien to Femininity: Speculative Fiction and Feminist Theory* (New York: Greenwood Press, 1987).

16. To avoid the conflation of science fiction with utopia, I do not discuss Marge Piercy's work, which I consider frankly utopian. My opinion of Piercy follows Rachel Blau DuPlessis's, as stated in "The Feminist Apologues of Lessing, Piercy, and Russ," *Frontiers* 4, no. 1 (1979).

17. Zaki, "Utopia," 120.

18. These authors are inspired by a prehistoric or uncivilized model, the reverse of present-day industrial society, its suppressed "shadow" in Jungian terminology. The female principle has been the most repressed aspect of our lives in this rationalistic age; female authors of contemporary critical utopias reinstate the suppressed shadow. (Keinhorst, "Emancipatory Projection," 92)

19. DuPlessis, "Feminist Apologues," 3–4.

20. Khanna, "Frontiers," 98 n. 8.

21. Donna Haraway, "A Manifesto for Cyborgs: Science, Technology, and Socialist Feminism in the 1980s," *Socialist Review,* no. 80 (March–April 1985). Hereafter referred to in the text as *MC.*

22. Donna J. Haraway, "Situated Knowledges," in *Simians, Cyborgs, and Women,* (New York: Routledge, 1991), 190, 199.

23. Harding, *Science Question,* 95.

24. James William Gibson, *The Perfect War: The War We Couldn't Lose and How We Did* (New York: Vintage Books, Random House, 1988), 156.

25. Gayatri Chakravorty Spivak, "Can the Subaltern Speak?" in *Marxism and the Interpretation of Culture,* ed. Cary Nelson and Lawrence Grosberg (Urbana: University of Illinois Press, 1988).

26. See the discussion of AI in Joseph Weizenbaum, *Computer Power and Human Reason* (New York: W. H. Freeman, 1976).

27. This is not to say that we may not feel affection for a device, as a violinist loves a violin or even as a research scientist feels at home in the laboratory. What we love, in such cases, is the meaning that accrues to time spent in the service of an art. But seriously to consider a device one's intimate and friendly self is very sad. The hacker's trance state is too often achieved at the cost of an inability to form real friendships and intimacies. As Sherry Turkle points out, what young hackers find in the "second self" of the computer is an absorbing illusion of power unavailable in normal human life. See Turkle, *The Second Self: Computers and the Human Spirit* (New York: Simon and Schuster, 1984).

28. On Daniel Webster's use of the technological sublime, see Leo Marx, *The Machine in the Garden: Technology and the Pastoral Ideal in America* (New York: Oxford University Press, 1964). In *The Cult of Information: The Folklore of Computers and the True Art of Thinking* (New York: Pantheon Books, 1986) Theodor Roszak cites one Victorian futurologist's doggerel in praise of the railways:

> Peace, mild-eyed seraph—Knowledge, light divine,
> Shall send their messengers by every line . . .
> Blessings on Science, and her handmaid Steam!
> They make Utopia only half a dream.
>
> (45)

29. Hans Moravec, *Mind Children: The Future of Robot and Human Intelligence* (Cambridge: Harvard University Press, 1988), 109.

30. Ibid., 110.

31. Ibid., 109, 124.

32. Anne Sexton, "Housewife," *Selected Poems of Anne Sexton,* ed. Diane Wood Middlebrook and Diana Hume George (Boston: Houghton Mifflin, 1988).

33. Teresa de Lauretis, *Technologies of Gender* (Bloomington: Indiana University Press, 1987), 20.

34. Joan Vinge, *The Snow Queen* (New York: Dell Publishing, 1980), 93. Hereafter referred to in the text as *SQ.*

35. Jane Flax, "Mother-Daughter Relationships: Psychodynamics, Politics, and Philosophy," in *The Future of Difference,* ed. H. Eisenstein and A. Jardine, Barnard College Women's Center (Boston: G. K. Hall, 1980), 20–40. All future references are in parentheses.

36. Judith Wright, "Ishtar," *The Norton Anthology of Modern Poetry* (New York: W. W. Norton, 1988), 930.

37. Paula A. Treichler, "Feminism, Medicine, and the Meaning of Childbirth," in *Body/Politics: Women and the Discourses of Science,* ed. M. Jacobus et al. (New York: Routledge, Chapman and Hall, 1990), 118.

38. Margaret Atwood, *Surfacing* (New York: Simon and Schuster, 1972); cited in ibid., 119.
39. Ibid., 662.
40. Vonda N. McIntyre, *Superluminal* (New York: Pocket Books, 1983), 1. Hereafter referred to in the text as *S*.
41. Haraway, *Simians, Cyborgs, and Women*, 188.
42. Roszak, *Cult of Information*, 125.
43. Joanna Russ, *The Female Man* (Boston: Beacon Press, 1986), 61.
44. Ibid., 194.
45. Ibid., 154.
46. Adrienne Rich, "Planetarium," in *The Will to Change* (New York: W. W. Norton, 1971), 13.
47. Sandra Harding, "The Instability of the Analytical Categories of Feminist Theory," *Signs* 2, no. 4 (1986): 662.

Chapter 5

1. Information on the Gaia hypothesis is taken from James Lovelock, *The Ages of Gaia: A Biography of Our Living Earth* (New York: Bantam Books, 1990); all future references will be in parentheses. Zvi Yannai, "Kadoor Ha-Aretz K'Itzur Chai" (The Earth as a Living Creature), in *Machshavot*, no. 62 (December 1991), published by IBM Israel, Tel-Aviv; "The Fate of the Earth," video by WQED Pittsburgh, in collaboration with the National Academy of Sciences.
2. Gary Zukav, *The Dancing Wu Li Masters: An Overview of the New Physics* (New York: Bantam Books, 1979), 78.
3. Ibid., 63.
4. Ibid., 63–64.
5. Ibid., 312.
6. June Goodfield, *An Imagined World* (New York: Harper and Row, 1981), 63, 213; cited in Evelyn Fox Keller, *Reflections on Gender and Science* (New Haven: Yale University Press, 1985), 125.
7. Keller, *Reflections*, 117.
8. Cited in ibid., 175.
9. Italo Calvino, *Invisible Cities* (New York: Harcourt Brace Jovanovich, 1974), 127.

Cyberpunk

1. Marc Laidlaw, "Plug-In Yosemite," in *Simulations: Fifteen Tales of Virtual Reality*, ed. Karie Jacobson (New York: Citadel Press, Carol Publishing, 1993), 127–28.
2. See chapter 2.
3. Michael Swanwick and William Gibson, "Dogfight," in Jacobson, *Simulations*, 76.
4. William Gibson, *Neuromancer* (New York: Ace Books, 1984), 5. Hereafter referred to in the text as *N*.
5. See chapter 3, p. 126.
6. Marshall Berman, *All That Is Solid Melts into Air: The Experience of Modernity* (London: Penguin Books, 1988), 99.

Index